A STATE OF DISUNION

Also by Calton Younger:

NO FLIGHT FROM THE CAGE (*Muller, 1956*)

LESS THAN ANGEL (*W. H. Allen, 1960*)

IRELAND'S CIVIL WAR (*Muller, 1968*)

Calton Younger

A STATE OF DISUNION

Arthur Griffith
Michael Collins
James Craig
Eamon de Valera

FREDERICK MULLER LTD.

First published in Great Britain by
Frederick Muller Ltd., 110 Fleet Street, London, E.C.4

Printed in Great Britain by
Ebenezer Baylis & Son Ltd
The Trinity Press, Worcester, and London
Bound by G. & J. Kitcat Ltd., London
SBN: 584 10275 5

Contents

Illustrations

Preface

As men make history so men also are the stuff of history. Arthur Griffith, Michael Collins, James Craig and Eamon de Valera were all dedicated men born at a crucial moment in Ireland's history, the further shaping of which devolved largely upon them. Of incommensurably disparate character, each possessed that peculiar amalgam of human qualities which marks out the leader. They inherited and were moulded by a strange and tortuous history. Men of their time and of their environment, they were inevitably to become men of conflict.

It can be said that each achieved most of what he set out to do: Arthur Griffith, a man of peace, founded an obscure political party the name of which, Sinn Fein, was to become a household word associated with a physical force movement, but it was essentially the instrument of a political philosophy on which the fight for Irish freedom was based; Michael Collins dominated the armed revolution which altered the whole British Imperial structure and won independence for the Twenty-six counties, while James Craig led the resistance of the Protestant minority to the nationalist ambition, succeeded in creating an enclave which stubbornly clung to its British origins and built it into a state within a state. The most remarkable of the four, Eamon de Valera, by sheer personal magnetism and a relentless awareness of human rights and dignity, fused the whole independence move-ment and, later, emerged from a political wilderness to lead the people of the Twenty-six counties towards the Republic of which he is still President.

These studies are intended to show how four men used the pieces of the historical jigsaw they inherited and, together with

others who had a part in assembling the picture, through contra-
temps and compromise produced a pattern some of which
remains with pieces fitting snugly and some a tragic hotchpotch
of misplaced pieces which must be reassembled.

Griffith, Collins and de Valera were all practising Catholics,
though through the revolutionary era often at odds with the
Hierachy, and Craig was a firm Protestant, but not one of them
was a religious zealot. Collins, it is true, was extremely agitated
by the killings of numerous Catholics in the North in 1922
and became embroiled in clandestine counter-measures in breach
of the Treaty he had recently signed; Craig boasted of his
Protestant State for a Protestant people; and de Valera used
Catholic precepts as the inspiration of his Constitution of 1937,
and under it recognised the special position of the Catholic
Church in Ireland. But he also recognised the rights of adherents
of other churches and asked only for their loyalty to the Irish
nation; Craig was happy to appoint Catholics to prominent
places, provided they were loyal to the British connection, and
from early in his career opposed education on sectarian lines. In
short, these leaders were not motivated by religious prejudice but
were concerned primarily with political principles and patterns.

"We could have enriched our politics with our Christianity;
but far too often we have debased our Christianity with our
politics."

In these words Captain Terence O'Neill cut through to the
bone of truth. They were words spoken with infinite sadness in his
prime ministerial farewell on television to the people of Northern
Ireland. Since that night of April 29th 1969 Terence O'Neill has
stepped back into the shadows. Given time, he might have
introduced into the Six Counties of Northern Ireland what he
called the "enduring standards" of justice, equality and generosity.
But for nearly fifty years there had been injustice, discrimination
and prejudice which had hardened like glue. These were vices
manifested instinctively by a majority in a truncated province
which feared absorption by the rest of the country to which
historically it belonged. And O'Neill knew that "any leader who

wants to follow a course of change can only go so far. For change is an uncomfortable thing to many people, and inevitably one builds up a barrier of resentment and resistance which can make further progress impossible."

O'Neill's most significant attempt to change the granite-hard pattern of a Protestant-dominated province, suspicious of the Catholic Republic beyond the border, was to establish communication with the South. But his meetings with Sean Lemass, Taoiseach (Prime Minister) of the Republic, arranged with much secrecy in early 1965, antagonised the hard-liners of his own Unionist Party who henceforward watched with sharp hostility for any further sign of weakness. Steadfastly, O'Neill set about changing the harsh social and political climate of Northern Ireland and, as happens almost invariably when oppressive conditions are relaxed, those who have lived in hopeless acceptance of them lift their heads like long-becalmed sailors sensing the air stir and the canvas tauten.

So the Northern Ireland Civil Rights Association came into being and, on August 24th 1968, organised the first protest march, from Coalisland to Dungannon in County Tyrone, a peaceful demonstration which infuriated the Protestants despite their own predilection for processions and banners and bands, for any concerted action by the Catholics to improve their lot spelled danger. A second march, planned for October 5th in Derry, was banned by William Craig (Home Affairs Minister), a move which provoked sullen Catholics to militancy and encouraged the delighted Protestants to close their ranks. The march went defiantly on and ended in a horrifying confrontation with the police which demonstrated all too clearly that the police were committed almost fanatically to the upholding of Protestant supremacy. That night the streets were full of the fury of Protestants and Catholics unleashing against each other the pent up hatred of years.

And yet, as O'Neill knew, the issue was not essentially a religious one. Even in times of venomous conflict, Catholics and Protestants stand back with icy respect to allow their adversaries to make their Sunday morning peace with God in their own way, and except for the egregious Ian Paisley and his followers few Protestants in Northern Ireland today believe the Pope has political designs on their land. Nevertheless, O'Neill's percipient utterance rings anachronistically in the twentieth century, especially to most British people, whose political pattern has developed on class rather than religious lines. In some European countries religion is still a political dynamic and in Ireland it is entwined through the political structure like ivy through an oak tree's branches. One cannot be detached from the other.

The antipathy between Protestant and Catholic is not inspired by theological or doctrinal differences but is a potent residue of the religious conflict which persisted in England from the Reformation until James II was ousted in favour of William of Orange. It is an unreasoning hostility which has much in common with anti-Semitism and colour prejudice, rooted in history, smacking of superstition, aggravated by ethnic differences and economic and social circumstances.

Unemployment and lack of housing have been powerful factors in Northern Ireland's explosion into violence for it is when men contend for work and somewhere for their families to live that they gang up protectively with their own kind against those who are in some way different from them. Race and religion become emotive forces—and in Ireland the temperaments of the two communities are as spikily different as their creeds.

It would be fallacious to believe—as from outside it is easy to believe—that there is an implacable frontier dividing one community from the other. If this were so there would be no hope of peace but only of suppression by one side or the other. What must not be forgotten is that the vast majority of the people, Catholic and Protestant, have wanted only to live in peace.

Protestant moderates have lived complacently, rather than wickedly, indifferent to injustice to fellow citizens, while Catholic moderates have simply accepted the situation hoping that one day it would change. The trouble with moderates is that they refuse to be involved; they criticise, they grumble but they acquiesce. It is usually extremists who initiate change and the transition can be traumatic. But revolution is never complete until the moderates are won over. If Northern Ireland is not to become a battlefield, the moderates must be mobilised and must work out a solution so palpably just that extremists who pursue violence will be isolated. There is not much time, for indignation and growing bitterness on both sides polarise moderate opinion towards the two extremes; the widening gap could become invincible.

Any solution must hurt some sections of the people and there are times when it would seem the only solution is to change human nature. But that is to deny the fundamental good in man and to decry the Christian ethic to which both sections so fervently adhere.

Constant eruptions of running sores signal an unhealthy body and it serves little purpose to treat the sores without seeking the causative malady. The chronic sickness of Ireland is Partition and it is to the removal of the border that one must look for a cure, whether by sudden surgery or the patient application of unguents. It is no use the Unionist Government of Northern Ireland shrilling piously that democracy is being undermined by a recalcitrant minority. Democracy means more than eternal domination by the larger section of the community; it means the fair representation of all minority groups and no discrimination. In Northern Ireland the Protestant-Unionists have sought by specious means to ensure that their supremacy through every skein of the life of the State remains absolute. They forget that they were themselves an intransigent minority, that their Six County State came into existence only because a British Government, bent on preserving their own political hides, disregarded the wishes of the majority in the whole of Ireland.

Nor should present day British Governments follow obstinately in the wayward steps of their predecessors, pompously insisting that the Six Counties are and ever will be an indistinguishable part of the United Kingdom. The truth is they belong with the rest of the nation of Ireland. Whether or not it is practicable to reconstitute Ireland as one entity is a different matter, but at least the truth should be acknowledged.

During the Second World War Britain was ready to buy Eire's entry into the war, and with it the use of her ports, by

offering to issue a declaration accepting the principle of a united
Ireland and undertaking that the union should at an early date
become an accomplished fact from which there would be no
turning back. A joint body to work out the constitutional
details was to be set up. It was a desperate ploy which de Valera,
though tempted, rejected, aware that Northern Ireland would not
agree to it.

Britain cannot *force* the Six Counties into a united Ireland, but
if the British Government were prepared in June 1940 to recognise
the principle and work to that end, there is no logical reason why
they should not do so now. Either the principle is right or it is
wrong; it is not right with a price tag and wrong without one. A
united Ireland may not be feasible for years to come but I believe
the British Government should work to end Partition in the course
of time. They should declare now their acceptance of the principle
of a united Ireland and pledge to repeal the Government of Ireland
Act of 1920, under which the Northern Ireland Parliament was
constituted, by a definite date, perhaps ten or even twenty years
hence. This might well open the way to the ultimate solution: at
the very least it will show plainly that the Irish people are expected
to work out a *modus vivendi* for themselves and it will give a
new generation the opportunity to establish *rapport*. Unhappily,
the children in the Six Counties are being deliberately educated in
hatred and used in violence and unless this process is soon reversed
there can be no hope of a solution except from violence. Such a
declaration should be made, not to buy off the IRA, not as an
act of appeasement, but because it is right.

From the moment that Partition was suggested during the
agonised debates following the introduction of the Home Rule
Bill of 1912, the British Government took the wrong road.
Hustled along it by the militant dissidents of the North, un-
protesting for the sake of their own political skins, they hoped it
would somehow lead to a peaceful destination. In both the 1920
Government of Ireland Act and in the Treaty of 1921 provision
was made for a united Ireland. But in the 1920 measure the country
was partitioned and the proposed Council of Ireland which
could one day lead to reunification was an empty gesture; and

although the Treaty established a British dominion comprising all thirty-two counties, it included a clause which allowed the Northern minority to opt out.

It must be emphasised that the Protestant-Unionists were not asked to yield their link with Britain. They resisted Gladstone's two Home Rule Bills and that of the Asquith Government with hysterical cries of "Home Rule is Rome rule", but none of those Bills envisaged more than a glorified County Council government At the time, the aspirations of the majority would have been satisfied and Ireland might well have progressed peaceably to dominion status, and perhaps, in her own time, to a republic, though it is likely that in a contented dominion the voice of republicanism would have been small. It was British policy which drove the moderates into the republican camp, British policy which today is still driving moderates into alliance with the extremists.

It is true that the Irish signatories to the Treaty accepted the "opting-out" clause well knowing that the Six Counties would take advantage of it, but Griffith and Collins were over-persuaded by Lloyd George's irresponsible half-promise that a Boundary Commission would revise the border so drastically that the rump of the Six Counties could not survive as an economic unit. The outcome of the Treaty was civil war in the South, by which time the Crown was held in such opprobrium—with reason, as Lloyd George admitted to his Cabinet—that the failure of the plenipotentiaries to win a republic transcended resentment of the mutilation of Ireland. Not Ireland alone but even the ancient province of Ulster had been torn apart. For although the Protestant-Unionists cherished Ulster, they parted with Donegal, Monaghan and Cavan at their own request because the balance between Catholic and Protestant populations was too fine for comfort. Wherever the border was to be drawn they were determined that it should remain sacrosanct.

That border was scrutinised by a Boundary Commission whose findings neither side relished and so the governments of the Irish Free State, Northern Ireland and Great Britain, in December 1925, signed a tripartite agreement by which the boundary was to remain unaltered. Reluctantly, and against the will of most of the people of Southern Ireland, the leaders of the day abandoned their claim to the Six Counties. In any consideration of the future of Northern Ireland this should not be overlooked. Nevertheless, the agreement compounded a situation which was neither just nor realistic. The evil of Partition is not only that it contains one third of the population within a border they neither recognise nor want, but that it puts the majority on the defensive; almost instinctively they employ every device to ensure that the minority are never in a position to challenge the *status quo*.

One has only to look at Europe to realise that reluctant minorities are, almost as a matter of course, suppressed by the majority to whom they have been attached simply because of the hazard that they will defect. This situation exists in Ireland, and would arise again if the Protestants of the Six Counties were coerced into a united Ireland. That would be no solution and it is unlikely that the leaders of the Republic would wish for it, whatever the views of the IRA.

In Northern Ireland the urge to protect majority supremacy filtered down from the closed minds of Orange Lodge diehards and the more fanatical opponents of the Catholic faith to ordinary working people who, not surprisingly, took advantage of the isolation of a large section of the community to ensure that they were not left behind in the race for too few houses and too few jobs. Full employment and adequate housing would have lessened appreciably the animosity between Catholic and Protestant.

Until the eruption of violence in 1968 and 1969 that animosity was more latent than real. In many neighbourhoods Catholics and Protestants lived together in reasonable harmony and in areas where deprivation and poverty were general that in itself was common ground. For many Catholics the benefits of the Welfare State (which ameliorate though they do not eliminate poverty) and the security of homes and jobs for those who had them transcended the dream of reunification but they always hoped that time would bring an end to discrimination. Now they have lost any faith they ever had in the Stormont Government.

In the South, too, reunification was a lodestar, a comforting light on the horizon, a dream to be realised one day. Practically, the absorption of the Six Counties into the Republic would have been an embarrassment and, although the emotional pull becomes ever stronger, even now instant reunification would create more troubles than it would solve. If the elimination of the border is to be a panacea for the perennial malaise of Ireland, it is something which requires time and much careful planning. But is this the answer? The State of Northern Ireland has existed for half a century. It was founded on the shifting sands of injustice, but it is a fact. Moreover, the Protestants are not newcomers, their antecedents go back to the seventeenth century and earlier. How far are we justified in demanding that errors of the past be rectified, that the consequences of ancient episodes of aggression be reversed? Is the answer really to implement reforms and aim for a stable community, all sections of which have equal opportunity, politically, socially, and economically within the orbit of the United Kingdom? I believe it is too late for that now. The time to offer equal opportunity is long past. Today the situation is almost exactly that of 1921 and even the utterances of the politicians of all three governments involved have the platitudinous crackle of an old gramophone record.

It is probable that if a solution is not reached by negotiation in which all concerned eschew recrimination, put partisanship aside and consider only the future good of all the people of Ireland, it will be produced from the exhaustion of tragic and long drawn out internecine battle. Unhappily, reforms in Ireland have seldom been achieved by negotiation without a bloody prelude. Blatant denial of human rights has been persisted in by generation after generation of hidebound politicians who, in the end, have yielded to violence. The lesson, clear though it is, seems never to be learned. Violence and the fear of more violence somersaulted the Stormont Government, spurred by a belatedly awakening British Government, into offering a package of reforms which should never have been necessary. Little wonder that the Catholics are sceptical of Stormont's determination to implement those reforms and discard the Protestant-Unionist philosophy of privileged supremacy.

Stormont's insistence on law and order has appeared to mean only that the Catholics should keep their place and, unwittingly but inevitably, the British army has become their instrument. In the beginning the army protected the Catholics from Protestant mobs, earning the plaudits of the Catholics, the abuse of the Protestants. Inexorably, the balance has swung the other way. As the Catholics steeled themselves to shake off the Unionist harness altogether, the Protestant mobs were enabled to stay home and let the army do their fighting for them.

So the battle now is the traditional one between Great Britain and the Irish Nationalists. As in the Irish War of Independence of 1919–21, it is a war of propaganda and nerves as much as it is of physical clashes. The headlines and the politicians talk only of the IRA which has become as emotive as the other, more universally employed propaganda word, "terrorist". What is too often over-looked is that the IRA is no longer the handful of extremists who from 1956 to 1962 conducted a bloody campaign along the border and finally desisted when they realised their activities were dis-crediting their cause both in the Six Counties and in the Republic. Although the "Official" IRA was ineffectual in the early Civil Rights campaign in Northern Ireland and is still, in the main, a left-wing political movement bent on establishing a workers' republic, its militant offshoot, the "Provisionals" has become the spearhead of the Nationalist movement, drawing into its ranks men and women of erstwhile moderate views who see no other way of settling their grievances. It is for this reason that the Government of the Republic is reluctant to take action against the IRA although it is still an illegal organisation. To the people of the Republic it seems that Britain has the same answer to trouble in Ireland as she always had—military force—and traditional hatred of the British Government and their armed forces, though not of the British people, never far below the surface, is resurgent.

Despite IRA propaganda, ever one of their sharpest weapons, the British army have behaved with admirable restraint. But in the end armies carry out the policies of governments and, so long as the British and Northern Irish governments insist upon military containment as a first priority, the British army will find themselves becoming ever more deeply involved in a deadly game of tit for tat. Even if successful, they will seem to the Irish Nationalists merely to have re-established the occupation of Ireland and any terms offered, however just, however generous, will seem to have been imposed by force of arms.

Insistence on "law and order", in other words a return to the *status quo*, led to the policy of internment. In the circumstances, internment became virtually a necessity, but these circumstances would never have arisen if a political solution had been striven for from the outset. This is easy to say and one has only to look at the parallel pattern of some of the more bitterly contested industrial disputes of recent years to realise that, unfortunate though it may be, settlements seem to be reached only after both sides have been hurt, when the same settlement ought to have been reached before trouble developed.

Internment is a war measure and its application was tantamount to recognition of a state of war. Since then the British Prime Minister has confirmed that Britain is at war with the IRA. The methods of the IRA are pitiless and horrible, as the tactics of urban guerrillas must be if they are to be effective. In an age of explosive nationalism they are all too familiar. But one has to ask whether the killing of innocent civilians by gelignite bombs planted in public houses by remorseless men is any different in kind from the destruction of Dresden by RAF bombers or the obliteration of Hiroshima by an atomic bomb. The only conclusion, so obvious as to be trite, is that war on any scale is intolerable.

Whatever short-term solution may be adopted to silence the guns in Northern Ireland will be ineffective unless the long term solution is agreed. That pre-supposes the readiness of three governments to forget face-saving formulae and get down to working things out, which is not without the bounds of possibility. An agreement is more remote but the choice is a simple one: it may be achieved in time to avert complete anarchy or it can be tragically postponed until anarchy supervenes and it becomes a matter of total reconstruction.

Concession on all sides is demanded. The Protestant-Unionists

must recognise that the sanctity of the border and their domination of the Six Counties unto eternity can no longer be sustained.
Great Britain must assert the rights of the majority of the people
of all Ireland to move towards their own destiny and bring to an
end the miserable arrangement of a divided Ireland which she
entered into, not with any conviction of its justice but simply
because she took refuge in compromise rather than resist the
vociferous and threatening minority of the day. And the Republic
of Ireland must step down from her "holier than thou" pedestal,
recognise that she has not always made reunion an inviting
prospect and suggest how she might incorporate the Protestant
community of Northern Ireland as free and equal citizens, with a
real understanding of their difficulties and some regard for their
long-standing attachment to the United Kingdom and the
Commonwealth.

The proclamation of the Republic of Ireland and the severance
of official links with the British Commonwealth, to which the
Unionists are determined to adhere though they become the last
survivor clinging to a floating spar from a sunken ship, was
almost to acknowledge that the border was a permanency. The
nearer Eire came to realising the cherished ideal of a republic, the
further receded the prospect of ending Partition. It must be
conceded at once that the prospect had always been remote—the
well-entrenched Stormont Parliament had no intention of going
out of business or subordinating itself to the Dail; but Dublin's
break with the Commonwealth undoubtedly made the mechanics
of reunion in the future, however distant, more difficult.

De Valera's proposal in 1921 was for an Irish Republic externally
associated with the British Commonwealth. He devised the
formula for the sole reason of enabling the Six Counties to become
once more part of the Irish nation while preserving their sentimental attachment to the United Kingdom and the Commonwealth. In the 1930s de Valera realised his externally associated
republic but thought it prudent to maintain the façade of a
dominion, a totally ambiguous position which, reluctantly, the
Commonwealth accepted. In 1949 the Costello Government came
out into the open and put through the Republic of Ireland Act.

But the strange, ambivalent relationship between Ireland and the United Kingdom still exists. The fortunes of Ireland seem inextricably bound up with those of the United Kingdom and the material links between the two countries are more significant by far than the symbolic ties of the old dominions. Reciprocal citizenship is of more consequence than the traditional, but largely theoretical, fealty to a distant monarch is whose name each Commonwealth country maintains bastions of immigration laws.

If a framework for a single Irish nation is to be devised, it is worth going back fifty years to look for it, and if it can be found then to see whether it can be adapted to the world of today.

I have put it that Great Britain should declare openly and irrevocably that she accepts the principle of reunification and that she would expect to repeal the 1920 Act within a given period. To the Protestant-Unionists this would seem to be a callous abandonment of responsibility. In the light of promises made to them by British governments since the days of Lloyd George, promises which at times have proved brittle, such a reaction would be as understandable as it would be predictable. One quality to which the Protestant-Unionists of Northern Ireland point with justifiable pride is their loyalty to Great Britain. They would have reason to feel bitterly hurt.

But those same people have failed over a long period to realise their responsibility towards the minority within their State, failed so lamentably that any promise of a new deal would be totally unconvincing. However it is done, the present system must be scrapped and a new beginning made. One can admire the adroitness and the persistence which won the Protestant-Unionists their Six County State against all logic and all justice, and had they established a model political system it would have been reasonable now to forget the equivocal origins and accept it for what it had become.

If the onus of establishing a new *modus operandi* within ten or twenty years rested on the leaders of Northern Ireland, I am convinced that, however unlikely it may seem now, they would succeed, and that they would realise there was no alternative to a

united Ireland. Without a massive subsidy from the British
Treasury the Six Counties would in any case disappear into an
economic abyss. Britain should not withdraw that subsidy entirely
but should be willing to help a reunited Ireland onto secure
economic terrain. It would be worth it to Britain if it resulted in a
stable and friendly country on her doorstep.

Northern Ireland should retain her own Parliament but the
powers which at present reside with Westminster should be transferred to an all-Ireland Parliament, a pattern which Southern
Irish leaders since 1921 have regarded as workable. But I would
advocate that the once-proud Province of Ulster be reconstituted,
that Donegal, Monaghan and Cavan be joined again to the Six
Counties. This would alter drastically the balance of political power
in Northern Ireland and would, I believe, lead to the breakdown of
the present party structure. One would envisage, for example, a
more powerful Labour Party as Protestant workmen, who now
vote Unionist simply to maintain Protestant-Unionist supremacy
against the Catholic-Nationalists, would transfer their allegiance
to where it more naturally belongs. The vote of prejudice would
become a vote of purpose.

It would be possible for the new Ulster Parliament to have the
same relationship with the Dail as Stormont now has with
Westminster and to send representatives to the Dail. But there is
much to be said for a system on the Australian model, for setting
up a new Federal Parliament to which both the Ulster Parliament
and the Dail would be subordinate. Legislating on matters of
national concern only, defence, trade and customs, transport and
communications, employment and the like, such a Federal
Parliament could meet alternately in Dublin and Belfast, or the
solution of Australia and Canada to provincial rivalries could be
adopted and a new capital established in an area designated as
Federal Territory, preferably near the present border, at Dundalk
perhaps.

All of this demands greater sacrifices from the Protestant-
Unionists and it is meet to remember and to understand that
they have an emotional and historical tie with Great Britain and
the Commonwealth every bit as strong as the Nationalist ideal, and

religious convictions as staunch as those of the Catholic faith. The Nationalists, too, must make concessions.

There was a time when de Valera's proposal of an externally associated republic seemed incongruous, even to his own colleagues, but today India demonstrates that a fiercely independent republic can exist within the Commonwealth system. The Commonwealth is now a very different political structure from that of the 1920s, Ireland herself having played an important part in its evolution, and it does not seem too much to ask that a reunified Ireland should be a member. On the other hand, the Commonwealth is already otiose and Great Britain's entry into the European Economic Community can only accelerate its decline. It would probably be more realistic to consider a link with the United Kingdom, a not too formal federation perhaps, which, as Welsh and Scottish nationalism develop, might evolve naturally enough into a group of four states. As the European Community moves towards political integration, such a federation might merge with the larger or remain as a constituent block of states with mutual interests. Some form of interim government would have to be devised. Direct rule from Westminster would be one possibility, a condominium another, but I would favour an elected legislative body, with representatives from all nine counties of Ulster, and a small ombudscouncil of distinguished men from Northern Ireland, the Republic and Great Britain.

Many changes are likely to occur in the next decade which may lead to a more propitious climate for a final solution to the Irish problem. Not the least of them may emanate from Rome. A more liberal Catholic Church in Ireland would mean a less militant brand of Protestantism. Catholicism pervades the whole structure of the Republic of Ireland in a way which still creates apprehension in the Protestant people of the Six Counties and Article 44 of the Constitution "recognises the special position of the Holy Catholic Apostolic and Roman Church as the guardian of the Faith professed by the great majority of the Citizens", but it also recognises —the same word is used—the rights of those who profess another faith. In the Irish Free State, become the Republic, there has been no serious discrimination against Protestants, but the Constitution does embody the moral law of the Catholic Church, the Hierarchy have exercised a profound though lessening influence in government, and education has been largely controlled by the Church with grant-aid from the State. Overall, the influence of the Church has been benign, although in matters such as censorship their hand has been more than a trifle heavy, and there are obvious controversial areas such as the constitutional denial of divorce where reform is needed. Certainly, as it stands, the Constitution of the Republic offers the Protestants of the Six Counties little inducement to transfer their allegiance to an all-Ireland Parliament.

It may be that in time the people of the Republic will modify their Constitution by referendum to exclude precepts of moral law which are the province of the Church rather than the State and especially those to which adherents of other churches, or of no church, do not subscribe. If such a referendum took place in a united Ireland one quarter of the electorate would be Protestant and there are already a great many Catholics who favour liberalisation.

But the question need not arise if a Federal Parliament were established whose powers were limited to matters of national concern, for the two provincial governments would legislate on domestic issues, including the prickly subject of education, to suit their own electorates. In other words, Ulster should keep divorce and contraceptives if they want and the rest of Ireland foreswear them still.

The situation in Northern Ireland is so volatile that I have refrained from speculating on short-term possibilities. Internment was an obvious wartime expedient and, for all their propaganda, is probably accepted as such by the IRA. Even so, imprisonment without trial is repugnant and it was very likely also a mistaken policy. The crux of the matter is that the British army were kept in Northern Ireland, and allowed to become ever more deeply embroiled, once it became clear that they had been compelled, by circumstances as much as by political intent, to take sides. What was needed at that point was an impartial peace-keeping force.

The help of friendly, uncommitted nations such as Canada and

New Zealand, rather than the United Nations, should have been requested jointly by the three governments concerned. The first historic meeting between Mr. Heath, Mr. Lynch and Mr. Faulkner presented the opportunity. Because of their remote Crown connection, troops from New Zealand and Canada would have been received without enthusiasm by some doctrinaire Irish people, but no one could reasonably hold that those countries are anything but disinterested parties and as intermediaries they would have represented a compromise between the view at one extreme that the problem is the occupation of part of Ireland by a foreign power and, at the other, that it is a domestic issue within the United Kingdom. In truth it is neither. On the practical plane, that the troops were English-speaking would have been an inestimable advantage.

The withdrawal of British troops and their replacement by a peace-keeping force of this kind—and with it the end of internment—could yet become a possibility if the British Government would concede the principle of a united Ireland and declare its intention to help realise it. I believe this would satisfy the Government of the Republic, who realise the impracticability of immediately absorbing the Six Counties, and the aspirations of most Irish Nationalists. One must be less sure of the IRA but, recognising that they are not murderous thugs but dedicated political idealists, one can at least feel hopeful. And the Protestant-Unionists? Will they be for ever irreconcilable? Much would be asked of them but much offered too. As well as an autonomous provincial government, they would have a profound influence in the affairs of a united Ireland. They would also have a great deal to contribute to it.

All who put their chosen way of worshipping God before God himself might well consider these words of Alexander Pope's:

> *Respecting Man, whatever wrong we call,*
> *May, must be right, as relative to all.*
> *In human works, tho' labour'd on with pain,*
> *A thousand movements scarce one purpose gain:*
> *In God's, one single can its end produce,*

Yet serves to second too some other use;
So Man, who here seems principal alone,
Perhaps acts second to some sphere unknown,
Touches some wheel, or verges on some goal;
'Tis but a part we see, and not a whole.

ARTHUR
GRIFFITH

I

WORDS PLAYED as large a part as guns in the Irish revolution of 1916–1921 and words were the weapons of Arthur Griffith. His father and his grandfather were printers, handling the words of other men; and in 1886, at the age of fifteen, Arthur Griffith was himself apprenticed to a small family firm of printers in Dublin. Long before that he had begun to read voraciously and had tried out his own pen. He gulped words because he thirsted for knowledge and he explored their use because he had ideas he wanted to express. But he had as well an ear for music, and soon he began to understand, and to become expert in, the music of language.

Most intelligent Irish lads of his time pursued learning insatiably and developed an aptitude for language. The Irish are an articulate people. They have a way with words, but they don't take their gift for granted. They practise. Griffith was rather more gifted than most of his contemporaries but there was little to suggest in those days that he would become perhaps Ireland's greatest political thinker.

He and his fellow apprentices would meet after work to talk about books and Irish history, to argue and to dream about redressing Ireland's wrongs. Groups of boys formed "Fireside Clubs" and rented cheap rooms where they could read to each other by candlelight and there were numerous more formal literary clubs and debating societies.

By the time he was seventeen, Arthur Griffith was running a debating society, which later merged with another to become the Leinster Literary Society, and it was there that he met William Rooney, a year younger than himself, in whom he perceived rare

qualities. The two became close friends. Griffith always rated
Rooney more highly than he did himself and, had Rooney not
died in his early manhood, it is likely that Griffith would have
been content to bolster Rooney's leadership and to remain in the
background. For Griffith was a diffident youth and became a man
who was, though never aloof, always barricaded behind his own
modesty.

He was nineteen when Charles Stewart Parnell, named as co-
respondent by the long-complaisant husband of his mistress,
Kitty O'Shea, fell in 1890 from grace and from power. Parnell's
leadership of the Irish Parliamentary Party had contained the
promise of a restored Ireland, though he had already lost the
respect of men like Davitt and Dillon and had for some time left
the hard work to others. Hopes of Home Rule rested with him.
His disgrace split the Party and caused a bitter schism in a people
whose admiration for him and faith in him were strained or
broken by his affront to their Catholic faith. Even so, one of his
biographers maintains: "Had the impetus for an anti-Parnell
drive not come from the Liberal party of England, the Irish people
would have stood by Parnell and the Church would have been
impotent to force a desertion from him."[1] Griffith remained
loyal to Parnell and tried to rally support for him, but within a
year Parnell was dead.

Shortly after Parnell's death, the Leinster Literary Society
reformed as the Celtic Literary Society with William Rooney as
president. Griffith, now a copy reader on the *Irish Independent*,
seemed more than ever convinced that his friend was destined in
time to become the new leader of Ireland. In his excellent biography of Arthur Griffith, Padraic Colum underlines an anomaly
in Griffith's thinking. He did not believe that the country should
pin all its hopes on one man and accept a political system or
philosophy created by that man and yet, as Colum puts it, "more
than any other man he believed in the avatar". He attributed
messianic qualities to Parnell, to Rooney, later to Eamon de
Valera.

The two young men, Griffith and Rooney, began to meet
people such as Maud Gonne, William Butler Yeats, James

Connolly and Douglas Hyde, all members of a dazzling generation who were to achieve for Ireland the freedom which venerated
generations of rebels and writers, politicians and fighters had failed
to do. Their success stemmed from the fusion of the physical
force movement and the adherents of political action whose
efforts in the past were not synchronised but alternated one with
the other. The catalyst was the literary resurgence of which
the Fireside Clubs, the literary and debating societies and even the
eager groups of polemical apprentices were precursors, and
the Gaelic League, founded in 1893 by Douglas Hyde, Eoin
MacNeill and Father Eugene O'Growney, was the culmination.

For several years Griffith thrived in this exciting milieu,
carefully backing out of the limelight whenever he could but
contributing so much to the Nationalist movement that inevitably he stood out. His ideas were maturing. Young people
were disillusioned with the Parliamentary Party which, after
Parnell, splintered into several groups hostile to each other.
Gladstone's Home Rule Bill of 1893, which he had piloted with
infinite patience through the House of Commons, was thrown
out by the House of Lords, and Griffith became convinced that
Ireland's freedom would never be gained at Westminster.

In Dublin Griffith's chunky figure and awkward gait (he had a
slight deformity in both feet) were a familiar sight and in the
many organisations to which he belonged he was well liked. Fair-
headed, he had a homely face with bright, solemn eyes behind
thick spectacles. To some he seemed withdrawn, sombre,
colourless, but those who knew him well discovered the magnetism of the man. All were aware of his rock-like honesty, an
invincible integrity which, a quarter of a century later, Lloyd
George was to use as a weapon for his own ends.

Griffith's friends were surprised when in 1897, at the age of
twenty-six, he suddenly cut his ties in Dublin and sailed for South
Africa. At the time his lungs were suspect and employment in the
printing trade was somewhat precarious.

For two years he lived in the Transvaal, since 1884 the South
African Republic, and here Griffith watched the creeping advance
of British colonialism, which he detested. In 1836 the Boers had

trekked north, away from their unhappy settlements in the Cape Colony: by the Sand River Convention of 1852 the independence of the Transvaal had been recognised; but, in 1877, the British annexed the State. After a policy of what has been called "loitering unwisdom", an expression which could equally well be applied to Britain's Irish policy, the Boers rebelled and in 1881 their independence was again recognised, though Britain insisted upon suzerainty until 1884 and retained certain rights even after that.

Gold, discovered in 1886, attracted hordes of cosmopolitan prospectors, the majority of them British. These *Uitlanders* threatened to outnumber the Boers and, to protect themselves, the Boers taxed them fiercely and denied them any political rights. A rebellion was brewing up but the Uitlanders could not agree among themselves, with the result that when Dr Jameson rode at the head of 600 horsemen to support the revolt he found no revolt to support. Rhodes, who was behind the raid, was less concerned for the Uitlanders than he was apprehensive of President Kruger's policy, which seemed designed to thwart his expansionist schemes.

Griffith met both Rhodes and Kruger, detested one and profoundly admired the other. It is inconceivable that an Irish Nationalist of the time could have been other than sympathetic to the Boer cause, but Griffith took the trouble to study the political trends and tried to form an objective judgment.

During his sojourn in the South African Republic he did a variety of jobs, including for a time the editorship of a publication called *Courant* which, being in English, was read largely by the British element. His point of view did not please them and the paper soon died. Both in Pretoria and in Johannesburg, where he worked in the mines, he entered the life of the local Irish community. With John MacBride, whom he was one day to introduce to Maud Gonne and who was to be executed after the Easter Rising of 1916, Griffith worked to ensure that the Irish took the side of the Boers. He was very short with any who showed signs of what he regarded as misbegotten loyalty to Britain. An Irish Society was formed which was hostile to the British and pro-British Uitlanders and from which, when the inevitable conflict broke out, sprang an Irish force under MacBride which fought on the side of the Boers.

Griffith corresponded frequently with Rooney who kept him informed of the plans to celebrate the centenary of the rebellion by the United Irishmen in 1798. A little humanity, a little justice on England's part would have prevented that rebellion, the intentions of which were put by Wolfe Tone, its leader, in these words: "To subvert the tyranny of our execrable government, to break off the connection with England, the never failing source of all our political evils, and to assert the independence of my country—these were my objects. To unite the whole people of Ireland, to abolish the memory of its past dissensions, and to substitute the common name of Irishmen in place of denominations of protestants, catholics and dissenters—these were my means." The aims of Arthur Griffith and his friends a hundred years later were precisely the same. "Loitering unwisdom" there had been indeed.

On the same day that Dublin celebrated the centenary of '98 Irishmen paraded the streets of Johannesburg and the occasion took on a wider significance as those Uitlanders of all nationalities who did not belong to the British camp seized the opportunity to demonstrate their loyalty to their Boer hosts. It was a triumph for Arthur Griffith, who soon afterwards returned to Dublin. In 1899, the Boer War broke out and the powerful though ill-prepared British forces found themselves up against an entirely new mode of warfare. Small, mobile bands of men, making the best use of their own familiar countryside, eschewed pitched battles and carried out short, sharp, unexpected assaults which baffled their enemies. (Twenty years later, the Irish were to adapt the Boer methods to their own landscape and win their independence.) Among the participants in that African colonial struggle were four men destined to play a variety of rôles in the Irish troubles: Winston Churchill, James Craig, Erskine Childers and John MacBride. The young Lloyd George risked his political career, and perhaps his life, in violent protest against the British campaign.

It was a more experienced, more mature Arthur Griffith who

returned to renascent Ireland. The Gaelic League flourished, re-kindling a love of the Irish language and Irish culture and, although the void left by Parnell was yet to be filled, and dissension stultified the Irish Parliamentary Party, there had been a movement forward towards self-government. Grand juries, the largely land-owning Protestant bodies which for more than two centuries had controlled local government, gave way by an Act of 1898 to elected County and District Councils, and this took local government out of the hands of the Ascendancy. It was hardly compensation for the destruction of Gladstone's Home Rule Bill but it did give the Irish some say in their own affairs.

Since Gladstone had come to power a virtual spate of legislation had ameliorated the lot of the Irish. In 1869 the Protestant Church was disestablished, and the Land Acts of 1870 and 1881 removed some of the injustices suffered by the tenant farmers. Gladstone was a friend to Ireland but it needed more than his benevolence to get these measures through Parliament. Davitt's Land League and the persistence of Parnell had much to do with it.

Arthur Griffith recognised the achievements of Irish leaders, but he did not agree that the Irish should be required to chip away with a jemmy at the door to Irish independence, when the key to that door had been wrongfully removed and should have been restored on request. Like O'Connell before him, Griffith sought the repeal of the Act of Union of 1800. This was the key to the door. Griffith argued that the Renunciation Act of 1783 established the Constitution of Ireland's Parliament and that the right to revoke it had never existed. Irish statesmen, however dedicated to Ireland's cause, had no place on the benches of Westminster; they belonged in their own Parliament.

With William Rooney, Griffith founded a weekly journal, *The United Irishman*. They had no money and at first wrote the whole paper themselves, Griffith setting the type. A polarity existed between the two young men which enhanced the endeavours of them both. "There is no doubt," Padraic Colum writes, "that in William Rooney, Griffith knew a spirit that expanded his own." *The United Irishman* soon attracted a variety of contributors, among them Yeats, whose great gifts Griffith was one of the first to perceive, and although its circulation was small it was read by those who most counted, those to whom the Nationalist cause was dear. It had strong ties with the Gaelic League, providing a cross fertilisation of cultural and political ideas, hardier seeds from which a strong plant of independence could be cultivated.

Griffith still happily played lieutenant to Rooney in their many activities—lecturing, debating, demonstrating, speaking at public meetings—but the ardent, energetic Rooney broke little new ground, was content to write and speak in the tradition of Thomas Davis. It was the slower, more solid Griffith whose mind was working creatively towards a new political future. Maud Gonne, Michael Davitt, the ageing Fenian John O'Leary, and James Connolly, whose political thinking was even more radical than Griffith's, knew him well and respected the breadth and depth of his mind, and the quirky sense of humour which lay, unsuspected by most, behind the square, bespectacled face.

In November 1900 Arthur Griffith's ideas crystallised in a new organisation. Formed from a number of national societies, Cumann na nGaedheal was ostensibly an educational body, but beneath that integument was a political core. John O'Leary was its commanding president. It was recognised at once as an organisation of potentially great influence which offered the Nationalist movement a homogeneity lacking since the fragmentation of the Parliamentary Party. This latter, however, was pulling itself together under John Redmond and was to have fifteen or so years more of profitable life before, irrecoverably impotent, it was finally overwhelmed by the country's vote for Sinn Fein, into which Cumann na nGaedheal was to develop.

William Rooney, not yet thirty, died in 1901. Stoically, Arthur Griffith put aside his grief and shouldered the burden of Rooney's work. It was now perhaps that Griffith, whose very personality had been augmented by Rooney's, allowed his own powers full rein. It may be that Rooney had bequeathed to him that essence of himself which Griffith had found necessary. He knew that he must now be the leader of the movement he planned.

2

Some inkling of his intentions he gave in an address to the Cumann na nGaedheal convention in 1902. In *The United Irishman* he had been critical of the Irish Parliamentary Party, not so much because it had failed, but because he would not concede that Westminster was the place for representatives of the Irish people. They argued that they must seek Ireland's freedom by peaceful means, by parliamentary activity at Westminster; the only alternative was insurrection and violence. Griffith's aim was "the restoration of Ireland to the status of sovereign state". The struggle for freedom should take place in Ireland he contended; the British Parliament had no right to legislate for Ireland and the Irish Parliamentary Party were wrong to lend themselves to such proceedings whether they voted for or against the measures. Their duty was "to remain at home to help in promoting Ireland's interest and to aid in guarding its national rights".

A student of Central European politics, Griffith sought a solution to the Irish problems on the lines of that engineered by the Hungarian statesman Deák to restore the sovereign status of Hungary. With Russian aid Austria had crushed the Hungarian revolt in 1848-9 and the short-lived republic under Kossuth. After ten years of centralised government, largely dominated by Germans, Austria suffered defeat in the Italian war and her empire creaked alarmingly. From 1860 to 1867 Austria tried to keep her miscellaneous states together, first by a form of federalism and then by parliamentary centralisation, but Hungary refused to send representatives to Vienna and in 1865 was invited by the Emperor Francis Joseph to submit her own proposals. In the following year the Austrian army was crushed at Sandowa by the Prussians and Deák was not slow to take advantage of this "softening up". A moderate, like Griffith after him, he did not seek to secede but was determined upon the political liberty of his country. With Beust, the Austrian Chancellor, he made an agreement which resulted in the Dual Monarchy of 1867. The final settlement was made, not between the Austrian and Hungarian Governments, but separately by each with the House of Hapsburg. Each country had sovereign independence but recognised the same king. There was no imperial parliament but certain affairs of mutual concern were discussed by delegations of sixty members from each country, which then deliberated and voted apart, communicating with each other only in writing.

Strangely, this rather cumbersome arrangement worked, largely because there was power parity between the Magyars and the Germans, the two dominant races within the Empire. "You look after your barbarians and we will look after ours," the Hungarian Andrassy told Beust. Sadly, the proud Magyars, who were so insistent upon their own right to self-government, showed little forbearance towards the Slav minorities under their sway.

The dual monarchy concept was not altogether new to Ireland. When Arthur Griffith described himself as a "King, Lords and Commons" man, he meant the King, Lords and Commons of Ireland and he was remembering Henry Grattan's Constitution of 1782, the Constitution which Griffith held still to be valid.

The Resurrection of Hungary caught Griffith's imagination and he wrote of it under that title, publishing the work first in serial form in *The United Irishman* and then as a pamphlet. Padraic Colum believes it is possible "to see the lineaments of Arthur Griffith in the person projected as the hero of *The Resurrection of Hungary*",[2] although their circumstances were poles apart. Certainly Griffith admired Deák profoundly, though he was too modest to imagine himself in a similar rôle. Had Rooney lived, Griffith would have handed the brief to him, playing the solicitor to Rooney's persuasive barrister.

Griffith dreamed of setting up the complete sovereign state, with legislature, executive and judiciary. Ireland should not simply have some kind of Home Rule grafted on to it by legislation at Westminster, assuming that even that was still a possibility, whether or not Irish parliamentarians influenced the course of events. Ireland's independence had to be won in Ireland. Deák had refused to allow Hungarian delegates to sit in the Parliament at Vienna and he had won. This, for Griffith, was the salient factor in the resurrection of Hungary. In another decade the refusal of elected Irish representatives to take their seats at Westminster was to be, as Griffith intended it should be, the basis for the re-establishment of an Irish Parliament. It was recognised as such by the electorate who gladly abetted the process of building sovereignty from within the country. For the moment and to a small minority, it was an exciting new twist in the long independence drama.

The Land Settlement Act of 1903 finally ended the bitter land war, but the removal of a longstanding injustice by those who have imposed it aggravates rather than slakes the thirst for change. Land reform had been wrenched from the British Government by forceful agitation, by the use of the boycott weapon and by a certain amount of violence. The lesson was plain enough and the aspirations of the Irish to govern themselves received fresh impetus.

Delving into Irish tradition and Irish history, the poets and playwrights filled Irish hearts with forgotten pride and the Gaelic League attracted to it many young men and women who were not politically aware but who, from an understanding of their cultural heritage, were to take the next step and seek the right setting for it. One such was Eamon de Valera in whom Arthur Griffith was to find the leader he had lost with Rooney's death.

Griffith did not lose touch with the literary revival but, in a way, it lost touch with him. Many of its protagonists seemed concerned with art for art's sake and he did not bother with them. His eyes were set on a distant goal and he had time only for those who would tramp unfalteringly towards the horizon with him. He was no Messiah; he had no personal magnetism; only those very close to him glimpsed his vision. Maud Gonne, who had thrilled audiences as Yeats's Cathleen ni Houlihan and had seemed to personify the spirit of Ireland, had married in Paris Griffith's friend from Transvaal days, John MacBride, and her going had deprived Griffith of his principal link with the intellectuals.

He became engaged himself, in 1904, to Maud Sheehan whom he had known since the days of the Leinster Literary Society ten years before. She had then been fifteen, an attractive child interested in music. They had to wait until 1910 to marry, for Arthur Griffith, already keeping his mother on his meagre earnings, was in no position to take a wife.

In 1905 Sinn Fein, a name which one day was to have connotations far removed from Griffith's own concepts, was formed. Sinn Fein, "Ourselves alone", was a singularly appropriate title for the policy he was advocating, a policy which had excited Tom Kettle, a gifted young member of the Parliamentary Party who was to die in France in World War I, to describe it as "certainly the largest idea contributed to Irish politics for a generation". But it was a policy which many to whom Deák was unknown, and Hungary remote, found a trifle baffling and there was a disappointingly small audience at the first convention of the National Council of Sinn Fein. It was, after all, a new name, though Griffith and *The United Irishman* were well enough known, and it was but one of several strands of the independence movement which were being ravelled or unravelled at the time. Most Nationalist Irish people still put their faith in the Irish Parliamentary Party and their aspirations went no further than Home Rule, the fiat to control domestic affairs only. The militants had insurrection in mind, the rebirth of the nation through a blood sacrifice, and the secret Irish Republican Brotherhood, centred on Tom Clarke's little tobacconist's shop in Parnell Street, was gathering new strength.

Griffith's address went beyond the concept of a sovereign state. He showed how he wanted it to work. Education, agriculture, a measure of protection instead of inclusion in Britain's free trade system, co-operation between farmers and manufacturers, these were the points he dealt with.

Before he was ready for it, Griffith's Sinn Fein concept was put to the test. Instead of another Home Rule Bill, which Irish Nationalists expected from the Liberals, who took office in 1905 and won a heady victory in the 1906 election, a watered-down measure called the Irish Councils Bill was introduced at Westminster in May 1907, and thrown out. Two members of the Irish Parliamentary Party resigned and one, Charles Dolan, contested the 1908 by-election at North Leitrim, which his own resignation had induced, promising that if he were elected he would not present himself at Westminster. The Irish electorate were not yet ready for this and Dolan was defeated. Although he

received sufficient votes to give Griffith new heart, the achievement, such as it was, was not inspiring and Sinn Fein seemed to
become just another independence movement in a rut. Griffith's
concept of a dual monarchy on the Hungarian model, his
advocacy of an economic policy derived from the German
protectionist economist, Friedrich List, whose ideas were already
seventy years old, all seemed rather far away and dreamy.

But Arthur Griffith plodded on his highly principled path,
always the supreme publicist, a man with a big idea which
interested but never fired the emotions. In *The United Irishman*, in
Sinn Fein—short-lived as a daily but running as a weekly—
Griffith steadfastly put the Nationalist cause. He scraped a bare
living from *Sinn Fein* and occasionally received a little money
from the sympathetic American-Irish. Lucrative offers to work as
a journalist he turned down, believing in his mission.

For some years his Sinn Fein party made little progress; other
more exciting movements diverted adherents. After their 1906
election success, the Liberals had an overall majority at Westminster. The support of the Irish Parliamentary Party was not
required and, except for the ill-fated Irish Councils Bill, the
Liberal pledge to give Ireland some form of self-government was
forgotten. But this condition soon altered. In 1909, the House of
Lords, which had already exasperated the Liberals, were provoked
by Lloyd George to reject the Budget. A huge crisis blew up and
was not resolved until the Parliament Act of 1911 restricted the
powers of the Lords. It took two general elections and the threat
to create a new block of peers to do it but at the end of the upheaval two factors favoured the Irish: the Liberals, with a
diminished majority, now needed their votes to remain in
power and could be made to buy them; and the Lords could only
twice reject a Bill. It was in the Upper House that the most
virulent opposition to Irish Home Rule was centred.

2

To THE rehabilitated Irish Parliamentary Party the majority of Irish Nationalists now looked for relief from British rule, but other strong forces had been gathering. The Irish Republican Brotherhood was again a going concern and had attracted into its secret ranks young men of staunch calibre, among them Padraic Pearse, a dark, brooding, dedicated young man, poet and visionary, with a magnetic personality and the chemistry of a martyr. Arthur Griffith left the IRB in 1910 because he needed independence to pursue his own policy.

Convinced that any Home Rule measure passed by the British Parliament would be as insipid as bread and milk, the IRB had set their sights on a republic and were prepared for an insurrection to win it. Griffith was against insurrection, but cautiously sympathetic to the idea of a republic. He was not tied to his Hungarian solution but advocated it because he believed that it offered the only hope of inducing the loyalist Protestants of the North to accept an all-Irish parliament. Even when there was an outcry from the North against the Home Rule Bill of 1912, he remained optimistic. Given time the Sinn Fein concept would prevail.

The IRB were not prepared to wait nearly so long as Griffith and even more impatient was James Connolly, who returned from America in 1910 after a seven-year absence. Connolly's objective was a socialist republic. Like Griffith, he was a redoubtable polemicist. Griffith saw in Connolly's ideas the seeds of class warfare and under his own name he published what Colum describes as a manifesto in which he denied "that Capital and Labour are in their nature antagonistic". He asserted that they were "essential and complementary to each other". He was not against Capitalism but the abuse of Capitalism. Sinn Fein would not tolerate injustice and oppression, neither would it be associated with class warfare. In 1913, Connolly and the mesmeric James Larkin began a campaign to get a better deal for the workers. The British Government had already faced in England industrial unrest and the baffling protest tactics of the suffragettes; party feeling ran so high on several issues that friends became implacable enemies and Conservative families would have nothing to do with those of Liberal persuasion. As W. S. Gilbert put it:

> That every boy and every gal
> That's born into the world alive
> Is either a little Liberal
> Or else a little Conservative.

It seemed to be an age of rebelliousness and fanaticism. Over all loomed the darkening threat of Germany; Haldane set about reorganising the British Army and Fisher the Navy. Ireland was just one more problem, but a vexatious one, and British parliamentary tempers were ruffled by agitation in the dominions and in America for Home Rule for Ireland.

In Dublin, workers' meetings were smashed by the police and, following the long drawn out transport strike of 1913-14, a Citizen Army was formed at the instigation of Captain J. R. White, V.C., a former British Army officer. With this well-drilled little force Connolly was quite ready to begin an insurrection. When the time came, he was persuaded to join forces with the Irish Volunteers formed in November 1913. The rival concern, the Ulster Volunteers, had burst into life with a flourish of drums a little earlier.

Sir Edward Carson had become leader of the Unionist group in the Commons in 1910. As soon as the scent of Home Rule was picked up in Ulster, a resistance organisation came into being: under Carson, its organiser was Captain James Craig. In September 1912, hundreds of thousands of people packed Belfast to sign the famous Solemn League and Covenant, being convinced in their consciences "that Home Rule would be disastrous to the well-being of Ulster as well as the whole of Ireland, subversive of our civil and religious freedom, destructive of our citizenship, and perilous to the unity of the Empire".

The aspirations of the Nationalists were violently in collision with the determination of the Unionists to resist change, but there was common ground. Each side maintained that its view should be accepted by the whole of Ireland. In none of the four provinces was there any thought of partition.

Despite the frenzied efforts of the Unionists, of the Conservative Party in the Commons and of the House of Lords, the third Home Rule Bill ended its tumultuous career on September 18th 1914. The new machinery of the Parliament Act of 1911 had been used to break the deadlock between Lords and Commons. Distinguished political figures had preached treason, a group of British officers had come close to mutiny and the bitter fight which endured for two and a half years brought Ireland and England to the verge of civil war. Both the Ulster Volunteers and the Irish Volunteers had succeeded in running guns on the grand scale and in Dublin there were casualties. As the whole of Europe exploded into conflict, the danger of civil war disappeared. The Act, together with an Amending Bill which provided for the exclusion of either four or six of the Ulster counties from its operation but which had not been debated, was put in cold storage for the duration of the war.

Redmond and the Irish Parliamentary Party were proud of their achievement and most Irish people were satisfied, but for Tom Clarke, Padraic Pearse and their friends in the Irish Republican Brotherhood, for Arthur Griffith and the Sinn Fein Party, and for many of the Irish Volunteers the measure did not go nearly far enough. Its passage had taken too long and Nationalist ambitions had run ahead of it. Ireland would have powers comparable only to those of a county council. Worse was the threatened division of the country. That even one Irish county might be stripped out of the national entity was intolerable.

The Volunteers had been formed without Redmond's knowledge, but he soon arranged to share in their control and this connection with the Irish Parliamentary Party was welcomed. In elated mood, he now offered the Volunteers as a Home Guard for

Ireland, to release British soldiers for service elsewhere. Many
Volunteers enlisted in the British Army, believing that Britain's
readiness to stand up for Belgium augured a new attitude towards
small, independent nations, but they were not allowed to form
Irish regiments with their own colours—as were the troops raised
in Ulster. Redmond's magnanimity split the Volunteers. Those
who followed him became the National Volunteers; the hard
core, maintaining that Britain's war was no concern of theirs,
retained the name of Irish Volunteers and sought to take advantage of her preoccupation with Europe. Those who did accept
that Britain's war was their concern were disillusioned and many
were to turn their weapons against her in years to come.

Britain's vaunted object of protecting little Belgium had an
ironical ring for those who resented passionately her occupation
of Ireland. England might argue that possession entitled her to the
fealty of the Irish, that Ireland was as much a part of the United
Kingdom as Lancashire. But no privileged class had been planted
in Lancashire. The police in Lancashire were not armed, nor
were they housed in fortified barracks. They did not have the
duty of garnering information which might have political
significance, however trivial, and feeding it into the greedy maw
of a vast administrative octopus like Dublin Castle. In short,
Ireland was an occupied country. Most of the population,
politically unsophisticated, accepted the system they were born
into, and only when injustice bore more heavily than usual upon
them did they protest. More often, they scraped together enough
money to leave Ireland for ever.

They sang proud and plaintive ballads about heroes of the past
but did not recognise in the latest generation of dissidents the
likeness to those of whom they sang. They did not understand
Griffith's elaborate formula for freedom. Griffith had to wait until
after the Easter Rising of 1916 to see Sinn Fein come into its own.
In Dublin, people laughed when Pearse proclaimed the Republic
of Ireland from the steps of the General Post Office, and jeered
when the brave rebels were compelled to surrender. Nevertheless,
admiration began to creep in as it was realised that this small band
of men had held out against the power of Britain for nearly a

week, then indignation flared as Sir John Maxwell carried through a pitiless series of executions, even propping the severely wounded Connolly in a chair to receive the death blast.

The British seized on the name of Sinn Fein as a label for the insurrectionists, to suggest that the Rising was the work of an obscure group of fanatics. Instead, for the first time, Griffith's political philosophy was linked with the physical force movement and Ireland was presented with a name that was also a slogan for revolution.

Although he was a Volunteer, Griffith had not been informed of the insurrection plan. His disapproval of violence was well known. Eoin MacNeill, Griffith's friend and Chief of Staff of the Volunteers, was also kept in ignorance by the IRB who were the real power behind the Volunteers. Most of the officers were IRB men; the Rising had been planned by the Supreme Council of the Brotherhood to which Connolly, scheming his own insurrection, had been co-opted and they had provided the members of the Provisional Government established under the Proclamation.

Griffith had always realised that some blood would be spilled when Ireland attempted to establish her own sovereignty, knew that only the sacrifice of lives would spur the people from their acquiescent rut, and he saw, with Yeats, the "terrible beauty" that was born of the Rising. He had tried to join the men in the Post Office but they turned him away. The brave garrison, among them Sean MacDiarmada, Griffith's colleague on *Nationality* and a signatory of the Proclamation, saw Griffith not as a soldier but as a man whose destiny lay in the leadership of Ireland's own government.

When they were gone, those young men, cut down by Maxwell's firing squads in Kilmainham Gaol or packed off to English prisons and internment camps, the pendulum swung back from physical force to the political arena. The Supreme Council of the IRB had been wiped out. In time, they would be replaced, but until then there was no question of further armed rebellion. Had their lives been spared, or had they been shot at once in a white heat of anger, their venture might have failed, but the executions were cold-bloodedly protracted over many days. In the House of Commons, Redmond and Dillon denounced the men of the Rising and called for stern measures. Soon, Redmond changed his plea and urged mercy. So, too, did Carson, leader of the intransigent Ulstermen.

The attitude of the Irish Parliamentary Party lost them ground in their confused electorate. They had shown themselves to be Members of the British Parliament first and Irishmen second. Prime Minister Asquith himself visited Ireland and announced in the Commons that the existing machinery of government had broken down and that the Government were ready to take another look at the pigeon-holed Home Rule Act. This in itself seemed a justification for the Rising, and the Irish people, recognising the achievement of the young revolutionaries, began to look for an alternative to the Irish Parliamentary Party. They found it in Sinn Fein, whose policy was well-thought out, essentially moderate, and required the withdrawal of Irish elected representatives from Westminster and the establishment of a sovereign parliament.

In the aftermath of the Rising, both Arthur Griffith and Eoin MacNeill were, predictably, arrested. MacNeill was in a difficult position. As Chief of Staff of the Volunteers, this eminent academic gave the Irish Volunteers a cachet of respectability. He was ready to use the Volunteers against England only if an attempt were made to impose conscription in Ireland; he opposed their use in rebellion. For that reason he was excluded from the councils of the IRB and, when he learned of their plans, he tried to stop them. Partially he succeeded, so that simultaneous risings elsewhere in the country did not take place.

Griffith, MacNeill, and hundreds more who had not taken part in the Rising but were under suspicion, were packed off to internment in England under the Defence of the Realm regulations. In Reading Gaol Griffith proved a lively companion and worked hard to keep up the morale of his fellows. He wrote in vehement indignation to an Irish Parliamentary Party MP named Lynch who tried to take up the cudgels on his behalf in the House of Commons, resenting especially Lynch's attempt to dissociate him from the events of Easter week.

As leader of the Parliamentary Party, Redmond turned down the Home Rule offer resulting from Asquith's visit to Dublin. Sir Edward Carson, now the British Attorney-General, ensured that any legislation would not apply to six of the nine Ulster counties and Redmond withdrew in disgust from the negotiations with Lloyd George, so soon to become Prime Minister. Redmond's party was losing popularity rapidly but he was a patriotic Irishman who battled for the release of his countrymen held in English gaols and strenuously opposed plans to apply conscription in Ireland.

One of Lloyd George's first acts as Prime Minister was to release the Irish political prisoners who had not been court-martialled and sentenced, and Griffith was able to spend the Christmas of 1916 with his wife and children. At forty-five, founder of Sinn Fein which was soon to score its first political success, Griffith found himself regarded almost as an elder states-man. He recognised that the Rising had brough history forward, that Ireland now had an opportunity to implement his proposals to take over the functions of government from within the country. Language was ever his weapon, and soon his weekly *Nationality* began to appear again. He was well known now and Sinn Fein was a household name.

Although he no longer pushed his Hungarian dual monarchy model, Griffith still saw Ireland as a co-equal partner with Great Britain under the Monarch's aegis. His moderate views attracted people who, before the executions, the failure of Redmond to get Home Rule a further hearing and the prospect of conscription, had been content to jog acquiescently along, many of them afraid to risk their material well-being for the sake of a dream. Griffith was a visionary but he was a practical man. He did not offer a dream but a constructive policy. Sinn Fein's branches proliferated; there was an organisation.

The Easter Rising had been a cheeky shot across the bows of the British battleship and the gunners were not done yet. But they needed a new command, more guns and a strategy. It was the strategy that Sinn Fein offered and it was inevitable now that a link with the physical force movement should be forged. From

their inception the Volunteers had appreciated the need for
political motivation and they had welcomed Redmond's penetra-
tion of the movement. Not only had he failed them, he had
divided them.

When Count Plunkett contested and won Roscommon at a by-
election as an independent, he announced that he would not take
his seat at Westminster. The Parliamentary Party suffered a
second reverse when Joseph McGuinness, then in prison in
England, won Longford. In May 1917 an alarmed British
Government offered immediate Home Rule but again the six
counties in the north-east were to be excluded, this time for a
period of five years after which a final decision would be made.
Redmond declined but agreed instead to a Convention at which
all political parties and factions should be represented. Lloyd
George promised legislation based on the Convention's report,
and as an earnest of good intention, released those men who were
still serving sentences in England.

Back they came and the mockery which had accompanied
their departure was gone for ever. The most tumultuous reception
was reserved for Eamon de Valera. Already the stamp of a leader
was apparent, and he became a national figure when, shortly
afterwards, he won East Clare at a by-election. His growing
stature impressed Arthur Griffith, the man who had once seen
himself as William Rooney's lieutenant, and all the loyalty that his
square frame contained was soon to be directed to Eamon de
Valera.

Convinced that national aspirations would be lost in a welter of
words, Sinn Fein and the Volunteers ignored the grand-scale
Convention convened by Lloyd George and held their own
assemblies. First came the Sinn Fein *Ard Fheis* at the Mansion
House, Dublin, in October 1917. This was a watershed in Irish
history for on this occasion all the streams of thought flowed
together to form a single formidable cataract. Beneath the surface
was a turbulent rivalry of currents but these intermingled as they
raced along the parched watercourse towards independence and
freedom.

All were agreed that Ireland should be a sovereign state but the form it was to take was not settled. A republic had been trenchantly proclaimed at Easter 1916, but Sinn Fein still stood for an unbroken link with the Crown, not from any sense of loyalty but simply because, as Griffith had always seen, there was no hope of persuading the Unionists of the north-east to enter a republic. A formula was devised to paper across the crack. It fell neatly into two parts: "Sinn Fein aims at securing international recognition of Ireland as an independent Irish Republic. Having achieved that status the Irish people may by referendum freely choose their own form of government."

Six months previously, in April 1917, the United States of America had entered the European war and the Irish believed that when the rights of small nations came to be considered at the peace table their nationhood would be recognised. This was to prove illusory and the republic was yet thirty years away.

Not unwillingly, Griffith yielded the presidency of Sinn Fein to de Valera. While he accepted that physical force was now necessary, he knew that he was not the man to direct it. De Valera had been the most successful commandant of the Rising, had shrewd political insight, an authoritative presence and an aloof but compelling quality which marked him as a leader. Griffith was naturally uneasy when drastic changes were made in the constitution of Sinn Fein but his basic concept, that of an Irish constituent assembly in control of all the functions of government, was retained. For the first time Dail Eireann was mentioned.

The *Ard Fheis* set a seal on the name of Sinn Fein as the symbol for revolution. Since the Rising the name had been applied to all those who opposed the Parliamentary Party, whether or not they were followers of Arthur Griffith. Some had objected to the misnomer, but now Sinn Fein was embarked upon a republican course; it was interlinked with the Volunteers and, through some of the Volunteers, with the IRB. The fast rising Michael Collins, whom Griffith had first met when Collins proposed Joseph McGuinness as a candidate for the Longford by-election, won a seat on the Sinn Fein executive and so gave the IRB a place. De Valera had not rejoined the Irish Republican Brotherhood.

The fusion of the political and physical force movements was completed when, the day after the Sinn Fein *Ard Fheis*, de Valera was elected President of the Volunteers.

Desperate for soldiers, the British Cabinet decided upon a Military Service Bill extending conscription. Whether or not the measure should apply to Ireland was the subject of harassed debate in the British Cabinet meetings of early 1918. They took advice from as many informed quarters as possible and their deliberations were soon common knowledge in Dublin. Opposition blew up like a line squall. When the Bill was introduced, Dillon, now leader of the Parliamentary Party, and Devlin appeared with Griffith and de Valera at a protest meeting in Dublin and the Catholic hierarchy, which had rumbled with admonition against revolutionary activity until now, denounced conscription.

Lloyd George was determined to push the Bill through but was mindful also that he had pledged himself to introduce Home Rule legislation in terms of the Convention's report, which had been received in early April. Conscription would cause tumult in Ireland but the British Government believed that if the troublesome Sinn Fein leaders could be got out of the way the unpopular measure could be enforced. Ministers seemed totally unaware that the most moderate of Irishmen were affronted by the intention to conscript their young men, that any remaining residue of goodwill towards Britain was being dissipated. A revolutionary mood was in the air and this should have been the time to conciliate, not alienate, the moderates.

Field-Marshal Lord French, more optimistic than others of the Cabinet's advisers that conscription would work in Ireland, was appointed Lord Lieutenant and given a free hand. Within a week he had arrested as many Sinn Fein leaders as he could lay hands on. Lord French and the British Government had misread the country's mood and the Sinn Fein leaders knew it. Though Michael Collins gave them ample warning of the impending arrests, they allowed themselves to be taken. Far from easing the path to conscription by removing these men, Britain made it more difficult for herself.

The British Government had an almost paranoic fear that Sinn

Fein would intrigue with Germany. A spate of rumours and some flimsy evidence, mostly harking back to 1916, allowed Ministers to persuade themselves that there was a "German Plot": some of the Cabinet believed it. Anyway, it came at a convenient time and Griffith, de Valera, Plunkett and others, including several militant Irishwomen, were packed off to England. What the Irish people thought of the episode was made plain in June, when Arthur Griffith, at the time in gaol in England, won a by-election in the Ulster county of Cavan.

Sinn Fein was now the party of the moment. Indignant about conscription, the Parliamentary Party quit Westminster, but they had left it too late. The Party had simply worn out.

Conscription was deferred in favour of a campaign to enlist volunteers. This failed but, with the war's end in November 1918, the issue died, and the Home Rule question was again shelved. In the December general election Sinn Fein were victorious in 73 out of 105 constituencies. Only six seats were held by the once-powerful Parliamentary Party. Using Britain's election machinery, Ireland had, in effect, elected a parliament of her own. The revolutionary movement no longer comprised a handful of extremists, it had absorbed vast numbers of the people.

3

DAIL EIREANN met for the first time on January 21st 1919 and confirmed the establishment of a republic in terms of the Proclamation of 1916. In a sense, there had been continuity of government since then, for the Irish Republican Brotherhood had maintained secretly the Provisional Government established by the signatories of the Proclamation. It was a frail link, but it is this link which enables the Irish Republic of today to trace its history through to that momentous Easter. De Valera being regrettably absent in Lincoln Gaol, Cathal Brugha was elected temporary President of the Dail.

Of those entitled to take their seat in Dail Eireann more than forty were still in prison. Two more, Collins and Boland, were prowling round Lincoln Gaol working out how to release de Valera. The remaining twenty-seven, enthusiastic, inexperienced, almost unable to believe that they were setting up a sovereign state, decided to send delegates to the Peace Conference in Paris. International recognition was believed to be crucial and here was the opportunity. Had not President Wilson pushed to the forefront the right of small nations to govern themselves? As yet, they were untutored in the ways of diplomacy and they did not see that a unilateral declaration of independence from one of the major powers at the peace table, resisted by that power, could hardly be accepted by the Allies. Ireland was, in fact, pre-empting the decision they were asking the great powers to make.

In the insistent declaration of a republic lay the blade which was later to divide the Irish independence fighters. For many it meant there could be no going back; for others the second part of the Sinn Fein formula—"having achieved that status, the Irish people may by referendum freely choose their own form of Government"—still had significance. At the Sinn Fein *Ard Fheis* de Valera had declared that "the only banner under which our freedom can be won at the present time is the Republican banner". But he acknowledged that others might prefer some other form of government. "This is not the time for discussion on the best forms of Government," he added. "This is the time to get freedom. Then we can settle by the most democratic means what particular form of government we may have." And he made it clear that a monarchy involving an English sovereign was not part of his thinking.

Arthur Griffith was one of the absentees from the first Dail. He was in Gloucester Prison, where he was as cheerful a leader as he had been at Reading. But he, too, was thinking of forms of government for Ireland and in a handwritten journal which he edited, the *Gloucester Diamond*, he argued that a limited monarchy was the best form of government. It is interesting to speculate upon the attitude he might have taken to the emphatic declaration of a republic had he been able to attend Dail Eireann. True, he had acquiesced in the Sinn Fein formula and the Dail was seeking no more than to achieve international recognition of a republic. Nevertheless, it is probable that he would have suggested that the Dail leave itself room to manœuvre in any future negotiations. But he had complete confidence in de Valera and was prepared to follow with exactitude the line his leader drew.

In March 1919 the British Government decided to release the "German Plot" prisoners and Arthur Griffith returned to Ireland. Padraic Colum relates how, as a matter of principle, he extracted from the authorities money for sustenance of the Irish prisoners and used the whole of it to tip the "cabbie" who drove them to the station.[3]

The amnesty also allowed de Valera to emerge from hiding and it was announced that his return to Dublin was to be made the occasion of a state welcome. Immediately the British authorities banned all processions and assemblies in Dublin. It was apparent that defiance would mean bloodshed. A meeting of the available members of the old Sinn Fein executive and of Brugha's temporary cabinet was called, with Arthur Griffith presiding.

Michael Collins, in belligerent mood, challenged the right of the executive to countermand a decision made by the Irish Volunteers, the "proper body" to make it, he claimed. Collins saw no good in maintaining the simmering situation. He wanted to turn on the heat and let the pot boil over. The sooner the issue was forced the better, he contended.

Quietly, Griffith denied Collins's argument. He held that the decision belonged to the meeting, and himself opposed the provocative plan. It was left that Griffith should consult the man most concerned. De Valera immediately wrote to the executive that the occasion was "scarcely one on which we would be justified in risking the lives of citizens".

He had already made up his mind to travel to the United States, intent upon securing international recognition of the new Irish Government in spite of the snub at Versailles. Irish-Americans were bringing pressure to bear on their Government, and already the House of Representatives had passed a resolution in support of self-determination for Ireland.

In April, before his departure, de Valera was elected President of the Executive Council of the Dail and appointed the team which was to guide the country through horrifying days to a crucial moment of decision. Arthur Griffith became Minister for Home Affairs. Among his colleagues was Michael Collins who, as Minister for Finance, was to organise a national loan. A huge amount of money was to be raised by Collins in Ireland and by de Valera in America, and this transformed the Irish scene in British eyes. Without money the Irish Volunteers were little but a nuisance and Dail Eireann a bunch of immature young men playing politicians. Money changed all that.

Far from playing at politics, the Dail, which in September was proscribed and had to go underground, set itself up as an alternative government. Though many of its members were on the run, Dail Eireann met frequently and became a functioning legislative body. Most local authorities were soon to be controlled by Sinn Fein, whose representatives swept the board in local elections as they had in the national general election. They were a vital part in Arthur Griffith's scheme to establish a sovereign state from within, and the Dail Minister for Local Government, W. T. Cosgrave, worked unremittingly to incorporate them within the new state system. When all the Departments were working, the Irish people found that they had two governments. Most of the administrative functions of Dublin Castle were matched, and while some Dail Ministers like Lawrence Ginnell, Minister for Propaganda, were concerned for the moment, others such as Eoin MacNeill, Minister for Industries, and Robert Barton, Minister for Agriculture, were planning far ahead. The majority of the people preferred to deal with their own new Administration rather than with the Irish Government, as the Castle Administration was called, and even Loyalists took their cases to the Dail courts, which were more effectual in the embattled days to come than were the regular courts.

Already the gun, so soon and for so long to be Ireland's ugly symbol, was being put to its deadly purpose. The first real incident of the Irish War of Independence occurred on January 21st 1919, the day of the Dail's opening meeting. At Soloheadbeg in Tipperary two policemen guarding a load of gelignite were ambushed and killed, From the beginning Lloyd George had intended that the Irish should shoot first. Like most of the Royal Irish Constabulary, the two men who died had done an honest job.

Generally the RIC were well-liked. If they sent off to Dublin Castle reports about fervent young men who were preaching subversion and creating a bit of a nuisance, it was just part of the job. Certainly they never considered that keeping law and order, which most did with the utmost tact, made them enemies of their own country. They were bewildered to find themselves ostracised by decree of the Dail.

This was a cruel but shrewd blow, not merely a matter of punishing those who were held to be minor traitors but a calculated move to disrupt the RIC, to fragment it so that it ceased to be an effective weapon in the hands of the British, compelling them to bring in the troops. Throughout the bitter struggle the Irish Volunteers, become the Irish Republican Army, insisted that it was a war they were fighting, while Britain maintained an elaborate fiction that it was a case of police action combating lawlessness. So any Irish soldier who killed, no matter what the odds against him, was tabbed a murderer and risked the gallows.

The British answer to the weakening of the RIC was to raise a small army and to send it to Ireland in the guise of temporary constables.

When de Valera left the country for America, he nominated the reliable Arthur Griffith as Deputy President of the Dail. Griffith, once more compelled to take the leading rôle, lamented his going. However valuable de Valera's mission to the United States, Arthur Griffith was convinced that he was needed in Ireland. Only with the greatest reluctance were the Cabinet persuaded to let the Dail President go.

De Valera, unknown until the Easter Rising, seemed to personify the independence movement. Arthur Griffith was someone whom the people seemed always to have known and admired without feeling close to him. At forty-seven, he was more than ten years older than the Dail President and nearly twenty years Collins's senior. No one expected fireworks of Arthur Griffith, nor saw him as the leader of a violent campaign to seize independence. He was a solid, stable, stubborn man who could be depended upon to chip, chip quietly at the barrier to Irish freedom. Logical himself, he expected reason to prevail in the end. But freedom would not be enough, nor would the political system now being developed. The country would need an economic policy, and in June 1920 Griffith instituted an inquiry into Irish natural resources and industries.

But even as he sought to compose a careful fugue of government, the tempo of violence quickened as a strident symphony, The lives and freedom of all the Irish leaders were threatened by the men of G. Division of the Dublin Metropolitan Police. Collins, whose Intelligence network had begun to undermine the very foundations of Dublin Castle, had the more dangerous ones "executed". In Cork the Lord Mayor, MacCurtain, was murdered by the Black and Tans. Throughout 1920 and until the Truce in July of the following year, killing and burning became commonplace.

In December 1920 a Bill introduced by the Lloyd George Government became law. This Government of Ireland Act, known since as the Act of Partition, replaced the 1914 Act which had left the problem of the northern counties to be settled later. This was the Act which created the division of Ireland that exists today and it was hardly to be wondered that it was no inducement to the fighting Irish to come to terms with Great Britain.

For the Unionists of the Six Counties the new legislation spelled security and so, after fifty years, it has proved. The policy of discriminating against Catholics began, even before the Bill was passed, with the expulsion of thousands of Catholic workers from the Belfast shipyards. In Belfast and elsewhere there was violence and death and this led to the Belfast Boycott, applying to all goods manufactured in Belfast, decreed by the Dail in August 1920. Although he finally accepted the necessity for it, Griffith was dubious. Ireland was still one country and the Irish Nationalists, by no means all Catholics, intended to keep it so. To boycott a section of the country was to imply recognition that it lay across the other side of a border.

Only a few days before the Act became law, the British Government put out peace feelers. Arthur Griffith was in prison, arrested on November 26th, with Eoin MacNeill and Eamonn Duggan, following Bloody Sunday when Collins's men killed eleven British Intelligence officers and the irate Black and Tans turned machine-guns on a football crowd at Croke Park. The arrests had not been authorised by the British Government who, with peace proposals in mind, were not anxious to detain essentially political leaders. General Boyd was rebuked by Lloyd George but not until December 29th, by which time de Valera was back in Ireland. Boyd claimed that the arrest of the Irish leaders was for their own protection. Whether or not Lloyd George accepted this, he made no move to release them.

For Griffith prison was almost a respite. He relaxed and his biographer tells us that "not only was he genial, but it was noted by some around him that he had an air as if things were going well".[4]

A few days after their arrest, Griffith and MacNeill were visited in Mountjoy Prison by Lloyd George's emissary, Australian Archbishop Clune. The Archbishop also was able to see Collins, though Griffith had advised Collins not to put himself in jeopardy. Based on a letter by General Cockerill to *The Times*, the proposals brought by Clune seemed to Griffith to require no surrender of principle on Ireland's part.

Collins, in the absence of both the President and his Deputy, was acting President of the Dail for the time being. When he met the Archbishop on December 4th, they agreed a formula which subsequently Collins put in writing. This read simply, "If it is understood that the acts of violence (attacks, counter attacks, reprisals, arrests, pursuits) are called off on both sides, we are agreeable to issue the necessary instructions on our side, it being understood that the entire Dail shall be free to meet, and that its peaceful activities be not interfered with."

A telegram from Father O'Flanagan, Vice-President of Sinn Fein but not in the councils of the Irish leaders, and an ill-judged resolution by the Galway County Council, both advocating a cessation of hostilities, persuaded Lloyd George that he might drive a harder bargain and Sir Hamar Greenwood, Chief Secretary for Ireland and convenor of the Black and Tans, convinced the Cabinet to insist upon a surrender of arms. In the House of Commons Lloyd George proclaimed that Cork and Tipperary were to be placed under martial law. This followed the ambush at Kilmichael, planned and led by one of the best of the Irish guerrilla leaders, Tom Barry. Eighteen Auxiliaries, members of an ex-officer force formed in August 1920 to reinforce the Black and Tans, were killed. On December 10th, Auxiliaries and Black and Tans ran amok in Cork and burned the heart of the city.

Despite all this the negotiations continued, with Archbishop Clune seeing Griffith in Mountjoy on both 13th and 14th December, but it was obvious now that Lloyd George's attitude had hardened. The British were not prepared to recognise Dail Eireann and they insisted on the surrender of arms. Griffith told the Archbishop that under no circumstance would the Irish surrender their arms and that no truce was possible unless all members of the Dail were enabled to meet. Otherwise, he said, there would not be a truce but a surrender. At least one member of the British Cabinet, Montagu, agreed with Griffith's interpretation; a truce, he argued, was a stand-to-arms. Inevitably the secret negotiations broke down.

On his return from America at Christmas, 1920, de Valera resumed his presidency and the war went on. Collins kept the incarcerated Griffith in touch with events and relayed Griffith's own messages. March saw the beginning of a strange obsession which was to become perhaps the one blemish on the selfless career of Arthur Griffith. This was his inexplicable hatred of Erskine Childers, the man who had run the guns to Howth in 1914, appointed at this time as Director of Publicity in place of Desmond Fitzgerald, who was also in gaol.

Within prison walls Griffith was in no position to fulfil his ministerial duties but he remained as always a profound political thinker. Sometimes he had visitors on missions similar to that of Archbishop Clune, and in March 1921 he sent out a public statement: "Any peace proposals between the British Government and Ireland should be addressed, not to the Government's prisoners but to Dail Eireann." He also prepared for consideration by the Dail "An Address to the Elected Representatives of Other Nations". Recognition by the outside world was still of paramount importance. Britain would find it difficult to hold out against the considered opinion of the world. Already the British Cabinet were apprehensive of American intervention and leading churchmen, both in England and in Ireland, were using all their influence to try to stop the ugly struggle.

But it all went on. The Mayor of Limerick was murdered, there were hangings and firing squads and reprisal executions by the IRA; martial law had been extended right across the southern belt of the country. And yet straws of peace were in the wind. In April, Lord Derby paid de Valera an unavailing visit, and in May Sir James Craig, Carson's successor as leader of the Ulster Unionists, also met the President in Dublin.

On May 19th the election for the Northern Parliament

established by the new Act took place in the Six Counties. Inevitably the Unionists coasted home, winning 40 of the 52 seats, but the minority elected six Sinn Fein representatives, among them Collins, de Valera and Griffith. These six, and six Nationalists led by Devlin, declined to take their seats, although the Nationalists did so later. Thus a substantial part of the electorate was not represented in the new Parliament and, indeed, did not recognise its right to exist. This refusal of a large minority to accept that they belonged to the new Six County State, or even that the State itself was valid, was a powerful irritant which aggravated the deep-rooted differences in Ulster. The Unionists, then as now, insisted that the minority in a democratic state must accept the rule of the majority, forgetting that it was only their own intransigence as a minority which brought the State into existence.

Five days after the Northern elections the voters in the Twenty-six Counties went to the polls. They had no intention of setting up a Southern Parliament subordinate to Westminster, but the machinery was useful for electing the second Dail which, naturally, included the six Sinn Fein representatives from the Six Counties.

The King's moving address at the opening of the Northern Parliament on June 22nd, which Field Marshal Smuts had a hand in drafting, opened the way to fresh negotiations which ended in a truce signed at the Mansion house on July 8th. There was no surrender of arms and the Dail was to meet unhindered. Peace could have been as easily made in the previous December, before steps had been taken to draw a boundary line around six of the thirty-two counties of Ireland.

Lloyd George's first proposal was that he should meet Craig and de Valera in London. No truce was suggested. The President's careful reply insisted on the principle of national self-determination. He also stated that he wanted first to consult other Irish leaders—meaning Unionists of North and South, Lord Midleton, Sir Maurice Dockrell, Sir Robert Woods, Andrew Jameson and Sir James Craig. His invitation made it clear that he was the spokesman for the Irish nation and that he wanted from them "the views of a certain section of our people of whom you are representative".

Craig declined the invitation but the others met on July 4th, adjourning the meeting until 8th while Midleton went to ask Lloyd George to agree to a truce. On July 5th, Smuts arrived and tried to convince de Valera that Ireland would be better off as a dominion than as a republic. De Valera was impressed with the man but not with the argument. Midleton returned with an affirmative reply from Lloyd George and the last difficulties were worked out with Macready at the meeting on July 8th.

Arthur Griffith, released on June 30th, attended the meetings of July 4th and 8th and also met Smuts whom, though Griffith said little, he impressed. In his memoirs Macready wrote of Griffith: "A square, squat figure, rather huddled up in his chair, hardly uttering a word, and then only a monosyllable, in whose eyes one could read nothing of what might be passing through his mind. During that hour I understood how it was that Arthur Griffith became a great leader of the Irish."

4

When he went to meet Lloyd George, de Valera took with him Count Plunkett, Austin Stack, Erskine Childers, Robert Barton and Arthur Griffith. Collins, it appears, was hurt that he was not included. On four occasions de Valera and Lloyd George conferred in London, each consulting his colleagues between meetings. Later, Lloyd George reported to the Cabinet that de Valera wanted a republic and had been told it was impossible. He believed that both de Valera and Craig were anxious for a settlement but afraid of their respective supporters.

Craig almost wrecked the talks by issuing a statement claiming the six counties also had a right to self-determination. This drew a strong protest from de Valera. The claim was not admissible and in a letter to Lloyd George de Valera reiterated that Ireland "would be willing to sanction any measure of local autonomy which they might desire, provided that it were just and were consistent with the unity and integrity of our island".

"The unity and integrity of our island." These were the telling words. De Valera saw no point in continuing the conversation if the British Government supported Craig's claim.

The proposals which, at de Valera's insistence, Lloyd George put in writing, were an advance on the Home Rule Bill of 1914 but far from satisfactory to the Irish. They offered dominion status but with conditions attached which all but contradicted it. By implication, the British Government were not prepared to gainsay the determination of the northern Unionists to maintain the newly created border.

De Valera returned with his entourage to Dublin, taking the proposals with him but with no intention of recommending them to his Cabinet or the Dail. On August 10th, in a long reply, de Valera rejected the proposals after consultation with the Cabinet and on 26th the Dail confirmed their action. All members of the Dail had now been released, although it was with some reluctance that the British Cabinet agreed to remove the rope from around Sean McEoin's neck. McEoin was acknowledged by his opponents as the most chivalrous of the guerrilla leaders. It was he who now nominated de Valera as President of the Republic of Ireland.

In rejecting the British proposals, de Valera gave Lloyd George an inkling of the solution he had in mind. It was the kind of inspired compromise which one might have expected British statesmen to grasp, but it was not until a quarter of a century later, in turbulent India, that de Valera's formula was adopted.

Making it clear that Ireland's sovereignty was paramount, de Valera stated that he would be ready to recommend "a certain treaty of free association with the British Commonwealth group, as with a partial League of Nations". This alternative to dominion status, which he phrased with deliberate vagueness, was put forward only if it would ensure the allegiance of "the present dissenting minority".

A long argument by letter and telegram persisted between Lloyd George and de Valera, with the latter claiming that he was head of a sovereign state and the former declining to accept either the title or the state.

The Irish had on their side a factor of which they were probably unaware—the British Government's apprehension of public opinion at home. De Valera had pushed them into a corner. Lloyd George explained to a Conference of Ministers at Gairloch, on September 21st, that "if they could enter a conference without the risk of recognising an Irish Republic, all would be well, and if the conference failed the Republic would never have been recognised by us".[5] At the same time, the public had "set its heart on a conference", and if it fell through merely because the Government insisted on recognition of the Crown as a pre-liminary condition, the Government might well lose support. This was probably why, having almost given up in exasperation, Lloyd George made one more attempt, offering with ingenious ambiguity "to meet your delegates as spokesmen of the people whom you represent with a view to ascertaining how the association of Ireland with the community of nations known as the British Empire may best be reconciled with Irish national aspirations".

De Valera accepted the invitation in a skilful reply: "Our respective positions have been stated and understood, and we agree that conference, not correspondence, is the most practical and hopeful way to understanding."

The Conference began in London on October 11th 1921. Arthur Griffith led the Irish Delegation. His colleagues were Michael Collins, Robert Barton, Eamonn Duggan and George Gavan Duffy. It was rather a lightweight team and suffered inevitably from de Valera's absence. There were good reasons for the President's remaining at home, but better ones perhaps for his going as leader of the delegation. As early as August 23rd, he had indicated to the Dail that he did not mean to go and later prevailed over the reluctance of his Cabinet to accept his decision. W. T. Cosgrave brought up the question again when the Dail met in private but the Deputies were satisfied with the President's reasoning.

When he was involved in negotiations, Lord Birkenhead liked to have some idea of the opposition beforehand and a civil servant prepared an *aide memoire* for him: "All the delegates with the exception of Gavan Duffy will be very nervous and ill at ease," it ran. "They have never been in conference with men of experience before . . . In overcoming their nervousness they may be a bit rude and extravagant in speech. They recognise their great responsibilities and this, of course, adds to their nervousness."

The thumbnail sketch of Arthur Griffith was in some ways wide of the mark: "Will be historical, probably even more so than de Valera; will start somewhere about A.D. 1100 and argue up to the sovereign independent right of every nation; will set out to show that Ireland is a nation; usually silent; not a good speaker, but said to be a fair conversationalist; will be ill at ease; is more clever than de Valera, but not so attractive; is the real power in Sinn Fein." That Griffith should have been described as the real power in Sinn Fein four years after the merger with the physical force movement did not say much for the civil servant responsible.

Politically Arthur Griffith was probably the most experienced member of the Dail Cabinet. Although he held tenaciously to his convictions, he was also a man who could see both sides of a question and was more likely than de Valera to yield some ground, provided that his principles were not breached and the concession was reasonable. He sympathised with the republican aims of his younger colleagues, but he was not committed to a republican form of government and in his heart still felt that his dual monarchy theory was the best solution in all the circumstances. Both de Valera and he accepted that to sever completely the tie with Britain would alienate the Six Counties. De Valera's answer was to offer an arrangement of external association with Britain and a degree of local autonomy; he would not accept allegiance to the Crown. Griffith saw that the sentiment of the Northern Protestants was too strong to be so easily overcome.

Thinking on a different level from either of them, Collins was ready to accept a compromise if need be, so long as the British were got out of Ireland and unity with the North could be engineered. The Republic might then evolve. Had he lived, Collins might well have altered his views. One thing was certain: with the Irish Republic Brotherhood behind him, Collins was in a position to exert great influence. Of this de Valera was somewhat apprehensive and it was also one of the reasons for Cathal Brugha's increasingly marked hostility to the "Big Fellow".

Collins did not want to be a member of the delegation and agreed to go only because it was his duty, but de Valera felt that his republican ardour had cooled. The President knew that Griffith, now Minister for External Affairs, would do his best to persuade the British to accept his external association plan, but he was no more than a luke-warm republican. Neither could be said to represent the more extreme republican viewpoint. An externally associated republic was in itself a compromise and . de Valera had had to convince Brugha and Austin Stack, his

Minister for Home Affairs, that his scheme in no way attenuated the republican ideal. Brugha himself refused to be a delegate and was in any case so single-minded that it is doubtful if negotiations of any kind would have been possible.

Eoin MacNeill and W. T. Cosgrave were both moderates. So it was that Robert Barton was chosen as delegate and Erskine Childers appointed principal secretary. Duggan and Gavan Duffy were chosen for their legal experience and were needed to offset to some extent the brilliant Lord Chancellor of England, Lord Birkenhead.

Exactly what powers the delegates had is still controversial. Much hinges on this point. In private session the Dail gave them full powers and it was given to the Press that they were plenipotentiaries. De Valera wanted the British to treat them as such and described them as Envoys Plenipotentiary from the elected Government of the Republic of Ireland. In the President's view, if the delegation's credentials were accepted by the British, then he had succeeded in getting some recognition of the Republic. In fact, the British waved the documents aside and this also became a point of contention later on.

The delegates also had instructions from the Cabinet which provided firstly that they had full powers as stated in their credentials and secondly that, before taking decisions on main questions, they should refer to the Cabinet in Dublin and await their reply. The instructions specifically stated that "the complete text of the draft treaty about to be signed will be similarly submitted to Dublin and reply awaited". De Valera's intention, his biographers tell us, was to strengthen their hands.[6] He saw that, faced with the experienced British, the tyro negotiators might be out-manœuvred and that, away from the arena, the Dublin Cabinet could ensure that they recovered their position. Nevertheless, the instructions were contradictory and put the delegates in the difficult position of having to conduct negotiations as plenipotentiaries when in fact they were not. Too much need not be made of this for, although in the end Lloyd George used the plenipotentiary status of the Irish delegates to urge them to a decision, at the outset he stated that he and his colleagues were bound by certain limitations and surmised that the Irishmen were in the same position.

Quoting from notes made by the Dail Minister for Publicity, Desmond Fitzgerald, Padraic Colum argues that Griffith knew that ultimately any decision must be his responsibility, that he would follow instructions as nearly as possible but that he must be the judge. Griffith and his colleagues had been given full powers by the Dail: "The Ministry could make recommendations to them but not charge them with instructions."[7]

Griffith made it plain that he regarded the instructions handed to him by de Valera as guide-lines only. On their interpretation hangs the whole question of whether or not the plenipotentiaries took more upon themselves than they were entitled to do. It is impossible to say that one was right, the other wrong. The truth is that a dichotomy persisted throughout the whole revolutionary period. It went back at least to the Easter Rising, was epitomised in the formula arrived at during the Sinn Fein *Ard Fheis* of 1917 and was carried into the negotiations. It led to the Civil War and a trace of it remains today.

De Valera's external association plan was an attempt to bridge the gap. Over-simplified, the position was that extremists and moderates had come together to achieve a common purpose, but the end of the line for some was only a halt for others.

Arthur Griffith went to London briefed to obtain from the British what he knew, and de Valera knew, to be almost impossible, recognition of a republican government embracing all thirty-two counties of their land.

It is worth quoting, perhaps, a comment made by Piaras Beaslai, one of Collins's earlier biographers: "In passing it may be remarked that nothing could well be less democratic in practice than the Government which we recognised as the Government of the Irish Republic. The legislative body was composed exclusively of one party. The people knew nothing of what passed at the Dail, and were required to accept its decisions blindly. The members of the Dail knew next to nothing of what the Ministry were doing and also accepted its decisions blindly. Over the Ministry and the Dail, and consequently over the fate of

3

the people of Ireland, Mr de Valera claimed and exerted an autocratic authority."[8]

There was just a faint hope that the British might have imagination enough to accept de Valera's radical proposal. In the Dail he admitted that there would have to be a compromise. For him external association was a compromise; for men like Brugha and Stack it was a compromise. But Collins did not take it very seriously and Griffith was convinced that the British would dismiss it out of hand. He made no secret of his own belief that it would be wrong to "break on the Crown", that if acceptance of the Crown were to prove the issue that determined peace or war, he would not opt for war. Throughout the negotiations his tactics were to make partition the crucial question.

On October 11th the Irish delegates first confronted the British representatives, Lloyd George, Austen Chamberlain, Lord Birkenhead, Sir Laming Worthington-Evans, Winston Churchill and Sir Hamar Greenwood, with the Attorney-General, Lord Hewart, at hand to help with legal questions.

They were some of the ablest men of their time. Their experience spanned the breadth of the world, they were accustomed to commerce with astute statesmen of countless nationalities and they had led Great Britain through the most crucial war in history. Hardened by adversity, made ruthless by the necessity to commit hundreds of thousands of men to muddy graves, and cynical because they had seen so often behind the masks of the reputedly great, these British political warriors were a formidable team. The ritual and the techniques of government and diplomacy had been grained into their instincts, and yet they were hidebound, steeped in the religion of British imperialism.

Lloyd George and his team were ready to concede more freedom to Ireland than had their predecessors in centuries of misrule. It is true they had been forced into this position by the Irish themselves and by the backlash of public opinion that sprang from the brutality of the men they had sent to put down independence. It is also true that the British delegates came to the Conference table in no vindictive spirit, but upon one issue they were implacable: Ireland must remain within the British Empire and must, if only to secure Britain's defence, swear allegiance to the British King, his heirs and successors.

On October 14th the Ulster question seeped into the conference. Griffith claimed that only the Belfast business men really wanted separation, that so long as England supported them they would not co-operate. Left to themselves, the Irish could work out a solution. Apparently sympathetic, Lloyd George told him the British Government stood behind Ulster "only in the sense that it could not allow civil war at its door", but it is doubtful that he could have held his coalition Cabinet together had he withdrawn support from Ulster.

The Irish tactics were to hear the British ideas first and to keep their own proposals under the covers until they were sure of their ground. This was why in the early sessions Griffith deliberately "waffled", to Lloyd George's intense irritation. At first, indeed, he had not been fully briefed on the Ulster "solution", but even when de Valera's instructions reached him, he talked only of allowing the South to make a "fair proposal" to the North and, in the event of its failing, to come to some kind of arrangement for a plebiscite, with the people voting by parishes. Lloyd George admitted that the border was a compromise and went on, "No compromise is logically defensible."

No mention of external association, even of a republic, was made by the Irish delegates at this stage and one can see now that their reticence in the early negotiations allowed the British to take the initiative. They had the further advantage of having the rest of the Cabinet close at hand. While Griffith reported constantly to de Valera and received his comments, the British team were able to confer with their colleagues and from British Cabinet records it is evident that each move was carefully worked out beforehand, that tactics were changed and adapted as need be. Although Lloyd George did most of the talking, he, too, was sticking to a brief.

On October 19th, the Pope telegraphed King George V wishing the Conference well. Taking exception to the King's published reply, which referred to the troubles *in* Ireland and spoke of *my* people, de Valera sent his own telegram to the Pope, to make sure he understood the true position. Though somewhat annoyed himself by what he considered an inopportune intervention by the President, Griffith defended him stoutly to an apparently incensed Lloyd George. But the Prime Minister soon shed his anger and rather plaintively pointed out the political risk that he and his Government were bravely running by negotiating with the Irish.

Point blank, Lloyd George fired three questions. Was Ireland prepared to belong to the Empire, to swear allegiance to the King and to provide defence facilities? This was on Friday, October 21st, and Griffith promised to table written proposals on the following Monday. Then, adroitly, he turned to the British attitude on Ulster.

The written proposals took the Irish case a step further but were still deliberately imprecise. Neither the Crown nor the Republic was specifically mentioned.

"On the one hand Ireland will consent to adhere for all purposes of agreed concern to the League of Sovereign States associated and known as the British Commonwealth of Nations. On the other hand, Ireland calls upon Great Britain to renounce all claims to authority over Ireland and Irish affairs." Somewhat sourly, Lloyd George had already defined the Irish standpoint as "that their independence should be admitted in the morning and that they should vote themselves into the Empire in the afternoon".[9]

The Irish document charged the British Government with responsibility for the "unnatural and indefensible dismemberment" of Ireland. It was proposed to deal with this "in the first instance by meeting the elected representatives of our countrymen in the area and forming an agreement with them safeguarding any lawful interests peculiar to the area. Should we fail to come to an agreement, and we are confident we shall not fail, then freedom of choice must be given to electorates within the area."

Lloyd George pressed Griffith hard on the question of Ireland's status. Would Ireland accept the same status as Canada? How did Griffith distinguish between association and belonging? Would the Irish be British subjects or foreigners? Lloyd George seemed bewildered by the external association concept which was now emerging, but he understood it well enough to sum up the Irish proposals for his colleagues:

1. Irish not to be aliens but there is to be common and interchangeable citizenship.
2. They will come in to the mechanism of the Empire and take part in the Empire's common purposes, e.g. defence of British and Irish coast, though they boggle over joining in a war on behalf of the Dominions.
3. They agree in principle that British Government should occupy their ports for Imperial defence, even if the exercise of that right involved war. They do not, however, accept the Crown. The head of the State would be chosen by them.

When he had arrived for the Conference, Arthur Griffith had been in carefree mood, paying a nostalgic visit to Reading Gaol, though he did not go in, and enjoying Gilbert and Sullivan at the theatre, but already, after two weeks, the strain of the negotiations was beginning to tell. Aged fifty now, and perhaps already showing signs of the illness which was to kill him within ten months, he began to look much older. His face was furrowed and haggard. His colleagues too were tense. All knew that beneath the smooth surface of unanimity ran currents of conflict.

When de Valera wrote warningly from Dublin that there was "no question of our asking the Irish people to enter an arrangement which could make them subject to the Crown, or demand from them allegiance to the British King", he angered the delegates. It was not an unreasonable letter, but to the hard-pressed delegation it seemed too easy for de Valera, who in the same letter reiterated his reluctance to join in the Conference himself, to sit back in Dublin and write in terms which restricted their freedom of action. The whole delegation wrote protesting against interference with their powers as plenipotentiaries and pointing out that "obviously any form of association necessitates discussion of some form or another of the head of the Association".

De Valera answered in placating vein and, perhaps rather unfortunately, avoided any mention of the contradiction between the plenary powers received from the Dail and the constraining instructions that he himself had given them.

In order to explore the Ulster situation the British delegated Chamberlain and Hewart, the Attorney-General, to see Griffith and Collins at a private meeting and Chamberlain informed his colleagues that the Irish had given satisfactory replies on safeguards and autonomy for Ulster. They were, however, "inexorable that they must not leave homogeneous Catholic areas in Ulster". This inexorability was to lead Collins into devious paths a few months later and was probably the reason for the killing of Sir Henry Wilson in June 1922.

If homogeneous Catholic areas were not to be left in Ulster, it followed that the Irish offer of autonomy applied to an area less than the Six Counties. Churchill had replied at once that the British Government were not free to abandon the 1920 Act; they would nevertheless recommend to the Six Counties that they accepted an arrangement similar to that which now applied, except that their Belfast Parliament should be subordinate to Dublin instead of Westminster.

British tactics were to first obtain Irish agreement to their other proposals and then to approach Craig. In this way, the Irish plenipotentiaries would have to accept the Crown or break off the negotiations on the Crown issue. Griffith reported to de Valera that the delegates had not held out much hope for this new British proposal but "between ourselves, thought it might be a possible basis".

Griffith's written proposals were rejected by the British. "No man can be a subject of two states," they answered. But the Irish idea was not dual citizenship but reciprocal citizenship. They insisted upon a sovereign state linked with, but not part of, the circle of countries making up the British Empire. They would recognise the Crown as "symbol and accepted head of the combination of signatory states", but only if Ireland were "free and undivided". So Griffith and his colleagues flicked the coin back to the Six Counties side.

Canny Lloyd George now persuaded Griffith that the real opposition came from the die-hards in and out of the House of

Commons. To help him move this faction towards acceptance of a reunified Ireland, he needed certain written assurances from Griffith, who informed his colleagues that he proposed to co-operate. He would send a letter, in his own name. Quite rightly, the rest of the delegation objected. They also saw that deliberate ambiguities in the letter, intended by Griffith to protect the Irish position, could be turned to undermine it. The letter was amended. It included the phrase "free association with the British Common-wealth", but the British wanted *with* altered to *within*, which was not the same thing at all. After a good deal of argument, the compromise reached was "free association with the other states associated within the British Commonwealth". A very clever, if trivial-seeming, play of words which did not help the Irish cause.

It was Lloyd George's belief that the Irish would finally accept allegiance to the Crown and would remain within the Empire—if Tyrone and Fermanagh were ceded to them, or if there were a plebiscite. He told Lord Riddell, according to Riddell's Diary, "If the matter can be settled on those lines, I am not prepared to consider civil war." Griffith thought the British Government were prepared to settle the Ulster problem first or, if they failed, to resign. On the question of a republic, it seemed to him that the still ambiguous formula accepted by both sides did not preclude de Valera's external association solution.

At this point the Cabinet in Dublin and the delegation in London seemed at one. To the President's relief, Cathal Brugha, who of the Cabinet was least likely to accept a compromise, agreed that recognition of the King as head of a Commonwealth with which Ireland would be associated, but of which she would not be part, implied no allegiance to the Crown. Ireland would not be a subsidiary of a giant company but would enter into a business arrangement, running her own affairs but in some matters complying with the policy of the group.

Through his trusted Assistant Cabinet Secretary, Tom Jones, Lloyd George advised Griffith early in November that he had failed to budge an obstinate Craig. He did not mention that until now Craig had had no inkling that his Six County area was a pawn in the game. Lloyd George would make one more attempt to win over Craig and, if he failed, would resign as he had promised. Gloomily, he reminded the Irish that this would mean a Conservative and Unionist Government under Bonar Law, who would take a much tougher line altogether. For Ireland's sake it might be better if Lloyd George did not resign after all. A better solution might be the setting up of a Boundary Commission, whose findings doubtless would favour the South.

An uneasy de Valera bade Griffith be careful. By this time there were no plenary sessions and Griffith and Collins did most of the negotiating. It has been suggested that this was a deliberate tactic of Lloyd George to split the Irish delegation in which some signs of differences had already appeared. But this is unlikely. Before the Conference began, Lloyd George put it to his Cabinet that it was likely to drag on for weeks, that sub-committees would be necessary to deal with detail and that "some questions might with advantage be remitted to individuals". Chamberlain, Churchill, Birkenhead and Lloyd George himself, with Tom Jones as a go-between, singly or in pairs tended to deal with Collins and Griffith as the senior plenipotentiaries. To Lloyd George this was a practical way of dealing with the complex issues. Tom Jones approached Griffith again, on November 9th, with the Boundary Commission suggestion in more concrete form. The purpose of the Commission, Griffith informed his chief, would be "to give us the districts in which we are a majority". Would the Irish support this proposal? Griffith told Jones that it was "their proposal, not ours", but he agreed that if Lloyd George wanted to use it as a tactical manœuvre the Irish would not "queer his position". He seemed to have given nothing away but, in effect, he had released Lloyd George from his pledge to resign if Ulster remained unyielding and had recognised the Boundary Commission as a practical alternative.

Craig still resisted the Cabinet's arguments. He suggested that if the South were to become a dominion the North could become another, separate dominion. If ever there were a case for an all-Ireland Parliament the machinery of the 1920 Act would be sufficient to establish it. Lloyd George's answer to this sounded a note so true that it is astonishing he allowed it to die away unheard. "Such a partition must militate with increasing force against the ultimate unity of Ireland," and he added with devastating foresight, "Frontiers once established harden into permanence." He pointed out that to the majority of Irish people the border was intolerable, "nor could we conscientiously attempt to enforce it. It would be fatal to the purpose of a lasting settlement on which the negotiations from the outset have been steadily directed." The Lloyd George Government should have kept to that. It is because they did not that the Irish people today lay upon Britain the responsibility for that border.

Whether or not Lloyd George had misunderstood Griffith's promise not to queer his position on Ulster, the Prime Minister informed Chamberlain that the Irish leader had pledged that at no stage of the negotiations would the Irish break on Ulster. Fatally, Griffith initialled a note which seemed innocuous but in fact committed him to the Boundary Commission solution. It seemed so unimportant that he did not mention it to the rest of the delegation.

On November 10th, Tom Jones delivered a rough draft of British proposals prepared in the light of discussions so far. They stipulated that Ireland was to become a self-governing dominion but as any reference to the Crown was omitted the Irish delegates did not lose hope. An all-Ireland Parliament was provided for and, even though the Six Counties were to be allowed to opt out, this was encouraging.

De Valera now advised his team to put fresh proposals, "as far as possible our final word". Griffith and Childers quarrelled violently over the drafting of these proposals. Childers, becoming more and more disquieted as he sensed the readiness of Griffith and Collins to concede the Republic, protested that too many concessions had been made. Griffith's dislike of Childers had been mounting. Though Childers was doing no more than his duty in reporting negotiations and sending minutes of meetings to de Valera, Griffith felt that he was under surveillance and was suspicious of Childers's influence with de Valera. In Griffith's mind Childers was no Irishman but an English apostate. On this occasion Griffith apologised but his dislike still festered.

The Irish Memorandum nearly put an end to the Conference. Lloyd George felt that he had got no further. Only the intervention of Tom Jones, with tactful suggestions of misinterpretation of words, saved the day. Griffith pinpointed the British difficulty for de Valera: without Irish agreement to enter the Empire there was no hope of any progress with Craig.

On November 23rd and 24th there were long discussions, with Griffith brilliantly arguing the case for external association in which he himself did not altogether believe. Finally it was agreed that the Irish should draft a formula expressing "the limited sense in which they were prepared to recognise the Crown". On the Ulster question Griffith said simply that they would accept the British proposals if Ulster did.

Griffith returned to Ireland, for the first time since the negotiations began, to attend a Cabinet meeting on November 25th. Collins had returned regularly to Dublin and the other delegates also had made frequent visits. Together de Valera and Griffith drove in the Dublin Hills discussing the whole situation, and in the meeting on the 25th of November the formula was agreed.

The delegates crossed to London again. Griffith presented the formula, together with a note in which he claimed that the British analogy of Ireland with Canada was false because of Ireland's proximity to England. The Crown would "continue to possess the real power of oppression and veto which Ireland knows".

His argument fell to the ground when at Chequers on November 28th Lloyd George invited Griffith and Duggan to insert any phrase which would ensure that the parallel with Canada was exact. The British Prime Minister also redrafted the Oath, putting allegiance to the Irish Constitution first and the King second—but, first or second, allegiance was nevertheless demanded.

Again the plenipotentiaries returned to Ireland, with a fresh draft of Britain's proposals for a treaty. They had won a lot of ground from the British and Griffith was convinced that no more could be achieved. There was a bitter Cabinet session. Griffith maintained that to refuse allegiance would spell the end of an all-Ireland Parliament but de Valera pointed out that he had won neither the Republic nor unity. At this meeting, Cathal Brugha, referring to the fact that Griffith and Collins had conducted most of the negotiations without the rest of the delegation, made his famous gibe—the British Government had selected their men. Brugha did not mean to impugn the honesty of his colleagues, only to suggest that they were the least determined to fight for a republic, but Griffith was deeply hurt by what he believed to be an assault on his integrity. With Collins, too, the allegation rankled. It was easy for de Valera, Brugha and Stack, all of whom had declined to be members of the delegation, to sit back in Dublin and criticise. Only de Valera had any notion of the task the plenipotentiaries had undertaken. De Valera did contemplate going to London himself but this he believed would have given the appearance of over-anxiety to come to terms. At the time this must have seemed valid thinking, but the President was ready to face a renewal of the war and could hardly have failed to convince the British delegation of this. Had he joined in the negotiations he would have realised that the British would not budge on the Crown and he would have agreed to what Griffith and his colleagues ultimately accepted, or broken off the negotiations on that intractable issue.

The delegation returned to London; Griffith, Collins and Duggan in one party, Barton, Gavan Duffy and Childers in another. The delegation had split down the seam which had been under strain almost from the beginning. Griffith had agreed to tell the British that their terms, particularly the Oath, were unacceptable. He himself was not enthusiastic about the British proposals but did not feel that there would be dishonour in accepting them. He put it to his Cabinet colleagues that the decision should lie with Dail Eireann and declared that, unless he secured amendments, he would not *sign* an agreement but would submit the proposals to the Dail. He was still adamant that he would not break the negotiations on the Crown question and the Cabinet were in agreement that if there were to be a break it should be on the other issue—partition.

News of the Dail Cabinet's attitude had been noised abroad and there was generally little hope that agreement would now be reached. The wearisome debate went on with Griffith trying to angle the argument towards Ulster. Impulsive words from Gavan Duffy frustrated him. "Our difficulty," said Gavan Duffy, "is to come into the Empire . . ." "In that case it's war," Lloyd George rejoined, but he did not throw in his hand. He was sure Griffith had been won over and he finally persuaded Collins to see him. But Collins still insisted on knowing whether the North would come in to an all-Ireland Parliament, and although he did not seem to mind if Ireland were to become a dominion, he wanted an oath which did not trumpet the concession. His last-minute stubbornness angered Lloyd George who, however, took a moderate line at a Cabinet meeting later, and a genuine effort was made to modify the Oath.

In the afternoon Collins, Griffith and Barton met Lloyd George, Churchill, Birkenhead and Chamberlain. Griffith said he would accept inclusion in the Empire provided Ulster came in. Collins was even more insistent on an answer from Craig. But now Lloyd George attacked Griffith at his weak spot, his unflagging code of honour. Griffith wanted Lloyd George to ask Craig: "If Sinn Fein accepts the Government conditions for the creation of the Irish Free State will Ulster accept unity?" At once the Prime Minister accused Griffith of going back on his word. Griffith had already accepted the Boundary Commission alternative, he claimed, and he flourished the document Griffith had so casually initialled on November 12th.

A lesser man than Griffith would have laughed it off and felt no dishonour. The promise had been given only to help Lloyd George with his tactics of the moment. But Griffith saw now how the promise could be interpreted and he could not go back on his word. He had accepted the Empire; now he had also accepted a Boundary Commission as an alternative to an immediately united Ireland. On neither issue could he break.

There were minor concessions by the British on defence and trade and an offer of full fiscal powers which Colum tells us "meant more to Arthur Griffith than the presence or absence of the Crown in an Irish Constitution".[10] Lloyd George declared that the British had gone through the document and met the

Irish fairly: were they now prepared to stand by this Agreement whichever choice Ulster made?

Griffith alone agreed and Lloyd George put pressure on the others. Sir James Craig was to have an answer that night—Craig, who had haunted the Conference from afar and gained his own way entirely. The Irish plenipotentiaries had to decide at once whether or not to sign. If they refused, it would be war within three days.

That evening, there was bitter division in the Irish ranks, but in the end, they signed—2.10 a.m. on December 6th 1921. Of the plenipotentiaries the last to give way were Barton and Gavan Duffy. Erskine Childers fought against the Agreement to the end, but not even he remembered the instructions to consult Dublin before they signed.

A long and skilful campaign had been fought by Lloyd George and in the end he had accelerated the discussions to a theatrical climax. It was his threat of immediate war which finally broke the resolve of the plenipotentiaries. He was as ready to renew the war to keep the Empire intact as de Valera was ready to face it to get out of the Empire. There is ample evidence in British Cabinet records that Britain intended to fight if Ireland refused to stay in the Empire. In preliminary drafts[11] of a letter to Craig, urging the North to enter an all-Ireland Parliament, statements (omitted in the letter itself) underline British fears that an Irish Republic was a mortal danger to the Empire.

The British Government believed that, unless there was a settlement, "a civil war will ensue, convulsing the whole Anglo-Saxon world, devastating Ireland, and in the end leaving the problem further from solution than ever". Settlement would only be made possible by "a final abandonment, by all sections including the extremists, of their claim to separation from the British Empire". If this failed and the conflict were resumed, "Britain will make whatever effort may be necessary to make her future safe".

There can be no doubt that Lloyd George's threat of war was not a bluff, but the words "immediate and terrible" probably were. So was the whole ambience of urgency.

It is probable that massive military strength would have been employed and there would no longer have been the pretence of police action. It is not in the least likely that the British troops would have opened an attack. They would have been simply an occupation force—until, as was inevitable, the Irish attacked them. The hope was that the British public would see that their Government had done all they could to reconcile the intransigent Irish and so would condone the reopening of the struggle.

Neither Collins nor Mulcahy, the Irish Chief of Staff, believed that Ireland could be geared up again to make a very effective answer to a new military occupation of their country. Nor did they feel that the brave and weary people should suffer more. None had more concern for the Irish people than de Valera, and in a way he was spared the need to make a terrible decision by the action of the plenipotentiaries in signing the Treaty without reference to him and arranging for the terms to be published before he had even seen them. Nevertheless, it came as a shattering blow. His anger is easy to understand, but then so is the torment of the plenipotentiaries.

De Valera's first thought was to sack Griffith, Collins and Barton from the Cabinet but he accepted Cosgrave's plea that first they should be heard when the full Cabinet met on December 8th. In a stormy session Cosgrave sided with the plenipotentiaries and so gave them a majority within the Cabinet. Griffith intended to recommend the Treaty to the Dail and was supremely confident that he could carry the day. Indeed, in a letter to Lloyd George[12] on the day of the Cabinet rumpus, he referred to a meeting with Southern Unionists the previous night. He had assured them that they should be represented in both houses of Parliament and he declared to Lloyd George: "We desire to secure the willing co-operation of Unionists in common with all other sections of the Irish nation in raising the structure and shaping the destiny of the Irish Free State."

From the outset of the Dail debate, Griffith maintained that neither the Irish nor the British negotiators had committed their respective Parliaments. Ratification would be required both at Westminster and in the Dail. He was wounded by de Valera's charge of disloyalty, yet he did not lose his admiration for the President and, outwardly at least, remained imperturbable as always. The long and demanding negotiations had wearied him and it was hard to have to tune-up his mind again to sustain the ordeal of the Dail. That he could do so was because he was satisfied that he had fought as hard as he could and in the end had done well.

5

As THE tortuous debate wore on, Arthur Griffith became more and more frustrated. De Valera's alternative, his Document No. 2, was produced when the Dail was in private session and upon its rejection its author declared it withdrawn. The terms were not to be made public. Griffith's objection was that the Treaty and those who had signed it were being flayed in public, yet the people were not allowed to know anything of the President's suggested alternative, an alternative which to many was as much a compromise as the Treaty itself.

When he moved the motion, "That Dail Eireann approves of the Treaty between Great Britain and Ireland signed on December 6th 1921," Arthur Griffith declared that as far as possible he would respect the President's wishes, but that he would not hide from the public his proposed alternative. He agreed that the Treaty was not ideal but it was honourable. "And now by that Treaty I am going to stand," he said pugnaciously, adding, "It is for the Irish people—who are our masters, not our servants as some think—it is for the Irish people to say whether it is good enough." He spoke, not eloquently, but earnestly, with great feeling and great dignity. Concluding, he made this appeal: "Let us stand as free partners, equal with England, and make after seven hundred years the greatest revolution that has ever been made in the history of the world—a revolution of seeing the two countries standing not apart as enemies, but standing together as equals and as friends. I ask you therefore to pass this resolution."

Almost all that Griffith had striven for had come to his grasp with the signing of the Treaty. True, six counties were to be severed from the rest of Ireland, but he believed their restoration would not be long in coming. Ireland was free and independent. She need no longer lean on the crutch of history but, entering a new age, build a stable, prosperous and tolerant nation.

De Valera answered him with bleak conviction. "I am as anxious as anyone for the material prosperity of Ireland and the Irish people, but I cannot do anything that would make the Irish people hang their heads."

In the next days, except for a break from December 22nd to January 3rd, every Deputy in the House spoke. The seven women deputies were all among the fiercest critics of the plenipotentiaries. Few of the speakers reached grandeur or nobility. Some voiced stubborn passion which no logic would ever touch, some were witty, some vituperative and malicious, but little new was left to say. Kevin O'Higgins, an assistant Minister, soon to become the strong man of the State, delivered a well-proportioned speech which put the issues with great clarity. Before him, Erskine Childers argued emotionally but with deep pessimism. Robert Barton almost tore himself apart, so agonising was his admission that he had broken his oath to the Republic in choosing the lesser of the outrages forced upon him. Duggan was cool and practical. He had signed the Treaty "deliberately, with the fullest consciousness of my responsibilities to you who sent me there, to the country, to the movement and to the dead". He maintained that they had been sent to find a compromise.

Fiery Miss Mary MacSwiney vowed that if the Treaty went through she would teach rebellion. "It was a minority that fought in 1916," she cried. "It is always a minority that saves the soul of a nation in its hour of need."

As the split in the Dail widened, one group of deputies worked out an ingenious but thoroughly unworkable plan to save the day. They proposed that those against the Treaty abstain from voting and allow a Provisional Government to come into existence. Its powers should derive from the Dail, of which de Valera should continue to be President. Griffith and Collins agreed to this curious arrangement but de Valera, sensibly, had no time for it.

The President circulated copies of a new version of his Document No. 2, intending to put it in as an amendment to Griffith's motion. Griffith suggested tartly that it should be handed to the Press and that night, exasperated by de Valera's tactics, himself released it to the Press.

Another tactical ploy of de Valera's was a proposal to resign with his Cabinet and then to stand for re-election when Griffith had made his final speech for the Treaty. The contest would have become a personal issue instead of a vote on the Treaty, and there were many, including Griffith himself, who would have found it painful to vote against the man who had knit the whole independence movement together and who was to every man and woman in the Dail an inspired leader.

But Griffith's motion stood. On the last day of the long debate, Cathal Brugha, having first attacked Collins with vast bitterness, appealed to Griffith (and the other plenipotentiaries) to abstain from voting. If he did this his name would live for ever in Ireland.

Arthur Griffith replied characteristically, "I cannot accept the invitation of the Minister of Defence to dishonour my signature and become immortalised in Irish history," and came emphatically to Collins's defence. Throughout the debate the strain on both Griffith and de Valera had been intense. Each was occasionally testy; de Valera sometimes sniped disagreeably and once Griffith let fly unreasonably at Erskine Childers. The sincerity and conviction of Griffith's final speech, his immense dignity, transcended all that had gone before. Whenever he had spoken in the debate his words had been deeply felt and concise. De Valera had a more difficult task, for he was trying to win unanimous support for a concept which the experienced British Ministers had failed to comprehend and the merits of which were not to be grasped for years to come. For many it was all too subtle and too often the President became bogged down in words. There was no answer to Griffith's challenge: "Is the Irish nation to be the dead past or the prophetic future?"

The vote was taken. Sixty-four Deputies approved the Treaty and fifty-seven voted against it. Two days later, de Valera resigned with his Cabinet. He made it clear that the vote meant only that "a certain resolution" had been approved. The Republic still existed and could be disestablished only by the vote of the people. The Dail remained the supreme Government.

So deeply grained was the affection for de Valera that he was almost re-elected President on a motion put by Mrs Clarke. It was lost by two votes only. Had de Valera won that election the result would virtually have annulled the earlier vote for the Treaty and it would have been almost impossible for Griffith and his supporters to have gone away and set up another Government in opposition.

Arthur Griffith had said that he did not think de Valera should have allowed his name to go forward and immediately the vote was taken he was full of concern. He wanted it known that the vote was not against de Valera but for the Treaty. "I want to say now that there is scarcely a man I have ever met in my life that I have more love and respect for than President de Valera. I am thoroughly sorry to see him placed in such a position. We want him with us."

De Valera was gracious in reply. He hoped nobody would talk of fratricidal strife. "We have got a nation that knows how to conduct itself," he said, and he promised, "We will not interfere with you, except when we find that you are going to do something that will definitely injure the Irish nation."

The split was complete but at least it appeared that the opponents of the Treaty would form themselves into a constitutional opposition. No one knew quite what form the Government should now take. Griffith had undertaken that the Republic should remain in being until an election could be held, but he had every intention also of implementing the Treaty and setting up the Free State.

The man who had always looked for a leader to whom he could become a trusted lieutenant now succeeded his old chief, who led his followers from the Chamber, allowing the pro-Treaty section to elect Griffith unopposed. It was a sad moment for Arthur Griffith to watch the departing figure of the disappointed de Valera. In his closing speech of the Treaty debate Griffith had referred to "the infamous Act of Union". Since that Act "our country has been ravished and ravaged; we have had the emigrant ship and the famine and the prison cell and the scaffold all through that one hundred and twenty years, because you have had the English Army in occupation here."

The Treaty meant an end to the occupation, but, he said, "It has no more finality than that we are the final generation on the face of the earth." De Valera and his followers could not see this. Griffith had recognised the shape of history. History has a length and a breadth and it cannot be telescoped, but the pattern is endless and constantly changing. Ireland would find her true destiny. To Arthur Griffith the Republic had been a symbol for the fight for freedom. Now it was a form of government which would come in time if the people wanted it. To Eamon de Valera it was sacrosanct.

And so Arthur Griffith became President of the Republic of Ireland. He announced his Cabinet, Michael Collins (Finance), Gavan Duffy (Foreign Affairs), Duggan (Home Affairs), Kevin O'Higgins (Economic Affairs), W. T. Cosgrave (Local Government), and Richard Mulcahy (Defence). The Opposition returned to the Chamber and de Valera made a magnanimous statement. But when Erskine Childers pressed him on his "curious and ambiguous situation" Griffith's dislike exploded: "I will not reply to any damned Englishman in this Assembly."

Some of the ambiguity to which Childers had alluded dissolved with the election of Michael Collins as Chairman of the Provisional Government which was to bring the Free State into being. This new body was in effect a working party to accept the transfer of powers from the British Administration and to prepare for future government. It was born of "a meeting of members of Parliament elected for Constituencies in Southern Ireland since the passing of the Government of Ireland Act, 1920".[13] At this meeting the Treaty was ratified. This "Parliament" did not meet again. Dail Eireann was still the sovereign body and, in theory at least, the Provisional Government was responsible to it. Several of the Provisional Government Ministers held the same portfolios in Griffith's administration and were therefore responsible to themselves, a situation which provoked some devious, if rather comical, situations in days to come. It was a clumsy, anomalous arrangment which held great danger. On the anti-Treaty side, too, there was a prickly dualism; the gap between the extreme republicans and those who would accept some form of external association with the British Commonwealth was hazardously bridged.

The task now faced by Arthur Griffith was momentous. He began with the remnants of an underground government which had functioned with staggering efficacy as an alternative to the British administration. He had now to draft a constitution and build a permanent system of government which would allow Ireland to take an equal place with other nations. The people of Ireland were immensely relieved that there was peace at last and there was little doubt that the majority supported the Treaty. But there was confusion and some disillusionment with all the men who almost overnight had become politicians. Extensive damage had to be repaired, an economy built up and, above all, democracy had to be protected from the many who were determined to go their own way in defiance of the democratic ideal.

Anti-Treaty feeling was strong at the Sinn Fein Ard Fheis on February 21st but Collins and de Valera agreed that there should be no vote on the Treaty and that the general election should be deferred for three months. There was little concord in the agreement. Both men were serving their own purposes. De Valera believed the new Constitution would simply reflect the Treaty, and that, given time, the people would realise that the Republic they had been promised had been written down to a satellite of the British Empire. They would be jolted out of their euphoric state and set their principles before peace. Collins had no fear of losing the people's support but he needed time to try to swing the army to his side.

It was not long before a large section of the IRA, heedless of the Cabinet's prohibition, held an Army Convention at which the authority of the Minister for Defence and the Chief of Staff was rejected. The IRA had taken a two-part oath, first to the Republic and then to the Dail. Re-affirming their Oath of allegiance to the Republic, those present reverted to their old authority, their own Executive.

Meanwhile, the British Forces handed over their establishments to whichever faction of the theoretically still-unified IRA had control of the area. Civil war was now a frightening spectre and moderates on both sides attempted to exorcise it. At Limerick a clash was only just averted. McEoin had something like a mutiny to deal with at Athlone. On April 14th the Army Executive seized the Four Courts and other public buildings and there was a threat of government by military junta.

Arthur Griffith must have watched with anguish the movement he had constructed, and which had served as the vehicle to carry the independence movement forward, broken and abandoned. He was disappointed that Collins had agreed to postpone the elections and, although he resisted deliberate attempts to sour their partner-ship, from this time became increasingly critical of Collins's manœuvres. For the younger man the riven IRA was a personal tragedy and he was prepared to risk a great deal to try to restore harmony. He believed that personal loyalty and friendship would win through. Promising them that the Treaty was but the first step to the Republic they had fought for, if only they exercised patience, he tried to convince the dissenters that they should accept the situation. In doing so he strained other loyalties and put almost unbearable tension on his own honour.

The Dail had quarrelled over the Treaty almost entirely on the issue of the Crown and the Republic. Partition, which in the long term was a much more vexed question, had been neglected. For Griffith it was a much more significant point and Collins, too, was preoccupied with the enigma of the North. On January 21st, they concluded an agreement with Sir James Craig which became known as the Craig–Collins Pact. In return for Craig's promise to protect the Catholic minority in the Six Counties the Belfast Boycott, which was at the root of so much of the bloody feuding in the North, was to be lifted. The British Cabinet welcomed the agreement, but it soon curdled. Clashes on the border resulted in fatalities, a Catholic family were murdered in Belfast and retaliation against a Protestant family was just as fearful.

Like Collins, Griffith was grieved by the coldness of friends, but he looked at the situation very differently. For one thing, he had not shared danger in action with the men whom Collins was so reluctant to hurt; more germane was his own straightforward character. He did not bend to the expedient as Collins often did and, although he was a sensitive man with deep-lying emotions, he was capable of steely self-control.

Ireland would be nothing if it were not a democracy, in Griffith's view, and he would not tolerate those who flouted the majority vote of the Dail. Nor was he prepared to countenance an army which existed outside the control of the Government. He respected his opponents and understood their hostility, but expected it to be expressed in the constitutional setting of Dail Eireann. The formation by de Valera of *Cumann na Poblachta*, or League of the Republic, suggested that the former President also proposed to adopt a constitutional approach, in opposition, but speeches he made in the country at this time appeared to urge armed resistance at whatever cost. De Valera was shocked, nevertheless, when Rory O'Connor repudiated the Dail, including himself. "Some of us are no more prepared to stand for de Valera than for the Treaty," said O'Connor. In the Dail itself, Liam Mellows declared that the IRA would have to be separated from the Dail. Its function was to sustain the Republic. Yet, at this stage, Dail Eireann was still the Parliament of the Republic, though in truth not very convincingly.

There was now as much danger of a civil war on a north–south axis as there was between the quarrelling factions of the IRA, and on both sides of the border there were extremists who, for different reasons, would have welcomed it. IRA forces were moved to the North to protect the Catholic-Nationalist minority who were having a grim time, especially in Belfast. Collins, without Griffith's knowledge, helped them with guns. Craig introduced severe measures to deal with men found in possession of firearms or explosives, and prohibited drilling and the wearing of unauthorised uniforms. The measures seemed designed to stop the IRA rather than the Orange extremists and the appointment as military adviser of the arch intriguer, Sir Henry Wilson, rooted suspicion deep in Collins's mind.

He had already charged Craig with breaking the pact, but a second agreement was reached in London between Griffith,

Collins and Duggan on the one hand and Craig and Lord Londonderry on the other. Under this agreement IRA activities in the Six Counties were to cease and Craig was to reorganise the police force to include Catholics in some areas—although, in fact, Catholics had not been precluded from the police. But murder continued. The IRA Executive reimposed the Belfast Boycott. This was a political decision which they had no right to make, but they were in a position to enforce it. Three days after the Agreement was signed, de Valera also wrote it off as "already a scrap of paper". Certainly there were few indications on either side that it could endure.

On April 1st, the Treaty having been ratified at Westminster, all powers were now officially transferred to the Provisional Government and Ireland was in control of her own finances. Churchill expressed the confidence of the British Cabinet in the Irish leaders but, within days, was writing to Collins to tell him that if he could not deal with the situation, the British Government would have to step in. Collins half-believed that the British were looking for an opportunity to reoccupy the country. In fact, the British wanted only to be done with the Irish problem, but they were not prepared to make further concessions. Churchill explained to his Cabinet colleagues that "Mr Arthur Griffith and Mr Michael Collins considered it vital and indispensable to the success of the policy of the Treaty to avoid striking the first blow against the Republicans, or any preparatory steps which might be regarded as provocative". He added, "Any British military or police support at the present stage would prove disastrous to the Provisional Government."

If Britain had interfered she would have found that the ranks of the Irish had closed again. Griffith and Collins had accepted a hard-driven bargain primarily to rid Ireland of the British. They did not want them back. The British were afraid that the Provisional Government might be overthrown and an Irish Republican Government set up before elections could be held. "The mere fact of its being brought into being would constitute a state of war between it and the British Empire," the British Cabinet agreed.

Griffith entertained the same fears and the strain was telling on him, especially as Collins seemed to be working on quite another plane. "Ireland is yours for the making. Make it," Collins exhorted the people, and Griffith wondered why Collins did not get on with it but seemed obsessed with re-establishing the old rapport with his estranged friends. Even the seizure of the Four Courts was tolerated, though it was a gauntlet flung down in the faces both of the Provisional Government and Dail Eireann.

It is difficult to see how Rory O'Connor and his men could have been thrown out of the building without precipitating civil war, and it is doubtful if the new National Army was strong enough to accomplish it. Collins still believed that if he could bring the two parts of the army together, the National Army and the Executive forces, a political settlement would be possible. De Valera had not moved out of the political sphere and the Dail still functioned, though it was an acrimonious assembly.

The Executive forces were playing a powerful, if negative, political game. Both Griffith and Collins had a hard time of it when they addressed meetings in the country. Several times their meetings were proclaimed by local leaders. In Sligo, Sean McEoin out-manœuvred the local leader, Liam Pilkington, and then, with a gun in each hand, stood guard at a window above the street while Griffith addressed the crowd. At that meeting Griffith declared determinedly, "We have won the right of the Irish people to rule their own country and I am not going to surrender that right to any junta."

On May 1st, the efforts of Collins and moderates on both sides produced some kind of agreement between them, but Rory O'Connor repudiated what came to be called the "Army Document". The same day, the Executive forces financed themselves by concerted raids on banks throughout the country.

A Dail Committee also sought a basis for agreement. They came near to a formula and asked Collins and de Valera to try to make the idea workable. What resulted was the Collins–de Valera Pact, providing for a coalition government. At the forthcoming election there would be a National Coalition Panel, the number from each party being in proportion to their present strength in the Dail. The Executive would comprise the President, the Minister of Defence (who was to represent the Army) and nine other ministers, five from the pro-Treaty section and four from the anti-Treaty group. This meant virtually an agreed election, though the Agreement did stipulate that candidates representing other groups were free to stand against Panel candidates.

The Pact angered Griffith. "You have given them everything," he accused Collins. Alarmed, the British Government sent for the Irish leaders.

"What am I going to tell these men?" demanded Griffith. But he went to London with Collins, Cosgrave and O'Higgins, with Dermot O'Hegarty as secretary. So well did they put their case that Churchill was able to explain it to his colleagues with some measure of sympathy. Although he denounced the Pact, which he saw as a threat to democracy, he said that "the idea was to try and get a non-party Government so as to secure tranquillity in Ireland and at a later date stage a proper election on the main issue. The June election would not be one in which the Irish people could be regarded as arming the Parliament to carry out the Treaty."[14]

The snag in the Collins–de Valera Pact was the new Constitution, upon which a distinguished committee under the chairmanship of Darrell Figgis had been working for some time. There could be no doubt that, unless that Constitution absolved de Valera and his supporters from any oath of fealty to the British King and any written acceptance of the Treaty, they would not take their seats in the Dail. The British supposed that after the election the curious duality of government would cease and, indeed, Griffith had agreed to keep the Republic alive only until the election. De Valera's belief was that the Pact over-rode that earlier statement, that the Dail would continue as a Republican assembly and, he hoped, that the Provisional Government would fade quietly away. Churchill, it seems, had recognised that the present dichotomy was to continue until a "proper election" was held. This could mean a postponement of but a few months, since the Treaty allowed the Provisional Government to exist until twelve months after the date of the Treaty. The kernel of it all was that, whenever the election came, the Constitution had to be in accordance with the Treaty.

Accused by Lloyd George of swerving from the path laid down by the Treaty, Griffith in high indignation argued that the Pact was a domestic matter. It would not prevent the operation of the Treaty. But the work of the Irish constitutional draftsmen was, in Churchill's words, "a negation of the Treaty". He told the Cabinet, "The distance between their Constitution and the Treaty is almost as great as when the Prime Minister began his negotiations with Mr de Valera."[15]

Churchill was not insensitive to the dilemma of the Irish leaders, who had explained to him that under any other conditions a free election would be impossible, but he had no intention of allowing the Irish one iota of freedom more than was prescribed by the Treaty. The Irish must be held to their bargain. At the same time, he believed that the lives of the Irish leaders were in danger and he was "anxious not to put upon them more than they could bear". The trouble was that the Constitution the Irish wanted was unacceptable. Birkenhead, once the implacable opponent of Irish separatism, was more sympathetic to the men who had signed the Treaty than were most of his colleagues. He knew the complexity of drafting a constitution which would accurately interpret the Treaty and Churchill, too, saw that "the Constitution adjusted to our view might prove insuperable to them when they return to Ireland".

Lloyd George gave his own diagnosis: "If they made the Constitution conform to our view, de Valera would not be able to accept it and the Pact would be broken."[16] This has been interpreted as the synopsis of a plan of campaign to smash the Pact, but it was no more than a percipient observation. The Pact was objectionable because it could only be carried through in breach of the Treaty. Pact or no pact, the Constitution as drafted could not be permitted. It was purely republican in character and but thinly veiled, pronounced Lloyd George: "It did not comply with the Treaty in substance or in form." He had no wish to be confronted with the larger issue of the Republic versus the Empire, an issue which could be resolved only by force of arms.

This, he was sure, would be the consequence if the Constitution were not made to conform with the Treaty.

In answer to the British memorandum of criticism, the Irish presented their own observations in a document of immense dignity. They argued that the other British dominions had power to alter their constitutions to suit their own traditions and conditions, and submitted that their Constitution was one "which the Dominion of Canada could not be debarred from adopting".[17]

Collins, perhaps looking over his shoulder at the Pact, snapped at Lloyd George that the British Government were behaving like Shylocks in "demanding the fulfilment of the letter of the bond".[18] The Prime Minister believed that Griffith knew the choice was between the Treaty and de Valera. Collins, however, "still appeared to think he could carry the others along with him".

To the British Government, it seemed that they were right back to the arguments of the previous November and December, that again the negotiations would have to be manœuvred so that the break came on the Crown and not on Ulster, where they felt their case was less secure, but Griffith removed all their fears in his answer to the several points the British Prime Minister had put to him.

In a letter which resounded with sincerity Arthur Griffith first set the record straight:

"Before taking up the specific questions you have put, I think that, in view of the atmosphere which seems to have gathered from the course of events, there is one thing I should make perfectly clear. The draft Constitution which we have submitted was prepared wholly by a committee of persons appointed for the purpose by the Provisional Government. Every member of that committee was an actual supporter of the Treaty." He explained that the committee had no instructions other than to prepare by a certain time a draft constitution "within the Treaty". It was, he went on, "the work of an independent Committee acting upon their own independent interpretation of the Treaty and approaching it with minds biassed in its favour".[19]

To each of Lloyd George's questions he gave an explicit and careful answer, concluding, "In so far as it can be shown that the draft Constitution is in conflict with the Treaty, we are prepared to make such amendments as will reconcile its terms with those of the Treaty."

Interestingly, not one of Lloyd George's questions had concerned, even remotely, the Ulster problem, although throughout the flurry of argument on the Constitution Griffith and Collins had reverted again and again to the uproar in Belfast. In Cabinet, Lloyd George had complained that the draft Constitution did not recognise the position of Ulster but, he said, "this point differed from the others and was not so clearly a breach of the Treaty".

The Irish leaders saw the turmoil in Ulster as a bar to any progress in the South and placed the responsibility for keeping order squarely on Great Britain. They pressed for an impartial enquiry, believing that the 48,000 "Specials", who were being employed in lieu of troops, were themselves fermenting much of the trouble. The British Government, on the other hand, suspected IRA activity, but there was no gainsaying the fact that most of those who had died were Catholics. Craig was sent for, to discuss "the best way of crushing out this disorder", for Lloyd George "wished the whole world, whether Catholic or Protestant, to feel that the British Government was doing its utmost impartially to deal with the situation".

Collins and Griffith returned to Dublin, the latter hopeful that something would be done to alleviate the plight of the minority in the North, the former, mistrustful of the British, planning his own course of action. Arthur Griffith was a weary man. The long negotiations culminating in the Treaty, the acrimonious marathon in the Dail and constant sniping in later sessions, the division of the army and the dissidents in the Four Courts, the strain of setting up a government in a country on the edge of civil war, frequent journeys to London and endless discussions with the British Government, the Ulster problem, and the Constitution squabble with the British, all vitiated the strength of this homely man who looked like a grocer but possessed one of the finest minds in the land.

Now he was faced with an election which, because of the Collins–de Valera Pact, was so arranged that all the old opponents

could be expected to come flooding back. Or would they? He had
no intention of sustaining the paradox of the two governments.
If the people supported the Treaty, as he was convinced they
would, there was no bar to setting up the Free State. He had
promised his wife to retire from politics by August, but he knew
he would be needed beyond then.

Speaking at Cork on June 14th, two days before the election,
Collins implied that the Pact with de Valera was dead. He knew
very well that the Constitution he had finally accepted would be
anathema to de Valera.

The result of the election, although emphatically endorsing the
Treaty, indicated a high degree of disenchantment with the
quarrelling heroes of both sides. Of 620,283 votes cast, non-Panel
candidates gained 247,226, a few thousand more than Griffith's
pro-Treaty party and almost twice the number received by the
anti-Treaty party. Because of the arguments in London, publication of the Constitution was delayed until the morning of the
election and it is impossible to guess what effect it may have had.

Arthur Griffith never took his seat in the new Dail. By now he
knew that civil war was inevitable. "Pierce, we will have to
fight," he told Piaras Beaslai, Collins's biographer.

Momentous happenings jostled one another through the next
few days. Sir Henry Wilson was shot dead on June 22nd by two
members of the IRA's London battalion. After an emergency
Conference of Ministers, Lloyd George sent a stiff protest, drafted
by Churchill, to Michael Collins. On June 26th, men from the
Four Courts raided a garage to commandeer transport for the
North. Their leader was arrested by the National Army and in
retaliation the Four Courts garrison kidnapped General J. J.
O'Connell, the National Army's Deputy Chief of Staff.

These events at last goaded the Provisional Government and
the Dail Cabinet to action. Arthur Griffith would have acted much
earlier, not because he had become suddenly belligerent, but because he knew that there was no hope of constitutional government while a dissident section of the IRA, however outraged by
the retreat from the Republic, occupied a great public building
and attempted to impose its own rule on the country. He had

stood aside while Collins sought reconciliation, but the men in the Four Courts were irreconcilable. The British had challenged him to govern his country, claimed that the Treaty he had signed was being flung aside; now they charged against him, or against Collins as Chairman of the Provisional Government, the indirect responsibility for Sir Henry Wilson's death.

Griffith recognised Britain's right to be indignant. He, too, was outraged that a minority were frustrating the claim, so stoutly established, that given freedom Ireland could rule herself wisely and well. What little hope there had been of a rapprochement with the North, which might one day lead to unity, had been dissipated. There was even a danger that Britain would move to lance the Four Courts sore, and such intervention would inevitably mean the mending of the army split—and war. Macready and his troops were still in Dublin. Already the British Government had refrained from attacking the Four Courts only on Macready's advice.

It was to be expected that the Executive forces would accuse their opponents of jumping to Churchill's command, but the British ultimatum was scarcely mentioned at the meeting when action was decided upon. Nevertheless, British guns were borrowed and it was these which reduced the Four Courts garrison to surrender. Griffith and his colleagues believed that once this focus of rebellion, for so they saw it, was eliminated, there would be no further obstacle to the establishment of orderly government, but they were prepared to fight on if need be.

The fight did go on—for nine weary months. It seemed to those who fought for their ideal of a Republic, whatever it cost, that they were threatened with British domination for ever. Yet, most of them lived to see their Republic restored when they were still in early middle age. In the end, Ireland took the stepping-stones course which Collins had advocated.

But many of Ireland's finest young men, who had fought together with fiery valour to win their country's freedom, died at each other's hands. Irish families, close and affectionate, were sundered and charred ruins littered the countryside. Eamon de Valera, who at first had remained aloof from the Executive forces, joined them once the battle had broken out. For him, as much as for Griffith and Collins, the tragedy of it all was beyond calculation.

Griffith lived in the Government building; his bed was in the Council room. He seemed to have aged. His face was grey and lined and his old geniality had deserted him. He could not sleep. This quiet, stubborn, thoughtful, honourable man, still only fifty-one years of age, must have looked back in these last weeks of his life to those early days of discussion and debate with young and enthusiastic friends, days of meditation and writing. Perhaps he recalled the hopes he had held for William Rooney and transferred later to Eamon de Valera. Remembering the founding of Sinn Fein and its slow development until it finally gave shape and cohesion to a revolutionary movement and provided the organs of government by which that movement succeeded, he must have been bewildered at the irony of his position now as leader of an Ireland torn by civil war.

His friend and physician, Oliver St John Gogarty, prescribed a week in a nursing home to allow him to recoup some of his spent energies, but on August 12th 1922 Arthur Griffith was overwhelmed by a cerebral haemorrhage or, as some now think, by a coronary thrombosis.

Stunned by grief into lapidary stillness, a great crowd watched Michael Collins, proudly uniformed as Commander-in-Chief of the Irish National Army, lead the black procession to Glasnevin. Arthur Griffith was buried as Head of State, but an anomaly still persisted. The new Dail had not yet met. He was still President of the Republic of Ireland. To the British Cabinet he was "merely President of the Dail", though "connected with a Government which was fighting a loyal battle so far as the Crown was concerned", and so the King was advised to send, not an official expression of condolences, but a personal message to Mrs Griffith, while the Prime Minister and the other Treaty signatories sent an official one to Michael Collins as Chairman of the Provisional Government. Lloyd George reminded his Cabinet of "the firm and loyal attitude towards the Treaty displayed throughout by Mr Griffith". He might have added that during the negotiations

Arthur Griffith

Michael Collins

Arthur Griffith had evidenced a kind of integrity that was beyond Lloyd George himself.

Eamon de Valera heard of Griffith's death with sorrow, but he could not forgive him for, as he believed, putting peace before principle. He did not see then, and perhaps never did see, that Arthur Griffith laid the solid foundation upon which he himself was to help build the Irish nation.

In the words with which Padraic Colum completes his poetical biography, "each and every change that has been made in its polity since an Irish state was set up has been made possible by the terms of the Treaty to which Arthur Griffith was the first Irish signatory".

MICHAEL
COLLINS

I

SWIFT AND strident communications have in our turbulent age transformed that over-rated revolutionary, Che Guevara, into the martyred idol of a generation of young people. In his day, the exploits of Michael Collins engaged the admiration of the young but no evanescent cult focused upon his name, which will be remembered, not with names like Guevara, but rather with those of Garibaldi or Mazzini or Kosciuszko.

Collins was the one man without whom the Irish Revolution probably would not have succeeded. Other men were almost as essential to success: the distant magnetism of de Valera drew disparate elements together and gave them inspired, if frail, homogeneity; the political philosophy of Arthur Griffith was the foundation upon which the cause was built and his sagacity gave it durability; but neither was a man of action, well though de Valera acquitted himself in the 1916 Rising. The dynamism of Cathal Brugha, the cool planning of Richard Mulcahy, the inspirational guerrilla leadership of Tom Barry, Sean McEoin, Michael Brennan, Liam Lynch and others were all vital to the movement. But only Collins was quite irreplaceable, only he had that extraordinary amalgam of courage, ruthlessness, energy, organisational flair, audacity, cunning and compassion of the complete revolutionary. He was as dazzlingly conspiratorial as Mazzini, and his generalship, clandestine though his campaign was, had something of Garibaldi's passionate grandeur. He was achingly Irish.

Yet it is only in recent years that his achievements have begun to be seen in perspective. For long he was a ghost in the shadows and it seemed that, almost deliberately, some had turned the light away from him, resenting the persistent ambience of his great personality.

Though he had political awareness from a singularly early age, unlike some of his revolutionary contemporaries he was never a fanatic. His emotions were powerful and sometimes burst from him, his determination to win Ireland's freedom smouldered in him like a banked fire, but he was not a zealot, half in love with death, like Pearse or Brugha. Throughout his short life his actions were governed by a shrewd, almost a calculating brain reinforced by an inflexible will. Able to stand back in judgment from himself and his work, he made himself professional in all that he attempted. What he might have achieved had he lived can only be guessed at; as it was, he was the mainspring of Ireland's battle for independence and, at the end of it, held his own in argument with some of the shrewdest and most experienced statesmen of the twentieth century.

Youngest of eight children, Michael Collins was born on October 16th 1890 at Sam's Cross near Clonakilty. His father was then seventy-five, his mother, an O'Brien, forty years younger. The families of both had been rooted for generations in West Cork, a remote and beautiful region, forbidding to a stranger, with hardy people, self-sufficient and proud. Michael Collins the father was a life-long, self-taught scholar, as many men are who live in lonely places, and the old man imbued in his son a love of knowledge which he never forsook. The boy read hard and deeply. From his father he heard stories of Ireland's heroes and his first teacher, Denis Lyons, for whom Collins never lost his affection, gently awakened the boy's patriotic instincts, pointed him in the direction from which he was never to diverge. This was not unusual; there were in the Ireland of the day many far-sighted teachers like Lyons, many receptive boys like Michael Collins. It was a time, as never before, to look to Ireland's future.

The fall of Parnell in 1890, which had split the Irish Parliamentary Party, and the failure of Gladstone's final attempt to push through a Home Rule Bill in 1893 had led men like Arthur Griffith to lose hope of any amelioration of Ireland's plight by the Westminster parliamentarians. Douglas Hyde and Eoin MacNeill founded the

Gaelic League in 1893. Intended to revive the Irish language, the League inspired a literary revival which threw up some of the greatest writers of our epoch and caught the imaginations of the people. Griffith's Sinn Fein came into being in 1905 and the Irish Republican Brotherhood had sprung to life again.

In little more than a decade came disillusionment, the breaking of the old political pattern and the beginning of the new, a resurgence of the national culture, and with it the remembrance of past glories, the revitalisation of a physical force movement in the tradition of Wolfe Tone's United Irishmen of the 1798 rebellion. Little wonder, then, that thoughtful men with dreams of freedom sought to mould eager and intelligent youth. Ireland's English masters missed the portents. They saw Ireland as a useful but eccentric old cart-horse instead of the mettlesome half-tamed creature that she was, tried to rule her with a whip and a handful of hay and never expected her to savage the harness and kick the cart to pieces.

When, at the age of sixteen, Michael Collins won his way into the postal service and was appointed to London, his education for the task of which he had yet but an inkling was already well advanced. He had lived his young life within the comforting boundaries of religion and strong family tradition, among a proud people in their ruggedly secluded countryside. Yet he had known already the touch of fine minds and his own had responded, reaching constantly for knowledge. Already the frame that was to earn him the soubriquet "The Big Fellow" was taking shape and, for all his love of books, the Gaelic Athletic Association probably meant more to him at this time than the Gaelic League, both of which he was soon to join.

At first the lonely vastness of London subdued his normally boisterous spirits but he soon made a niche for himself in the Irish Community and gravitated naturally towards those with political leanings. In 1909, at the age of nineteen, he was sworn into the Irish Republican Brotherhood and the secret loyalties the movement engendered in him became in time possibly the strongest force in his life.

His years in London overflowed with activities; he attended

evening classes, played football and hurling, became secretary of
both the Gaelic Athletic Association and the Gaelic League, but,
above all, the IRB engaged his time and energies. His flair for
organisation was noted and he soon gained promotion within the
movement.

He did not stay long in the Post Office, and went from one job to
another, learning all the time. Like his father, he was gifted with
mathematical agility, like him he enjoyed philosophy, economics
and the use of words. Rumbustious, occasionally wayward, he
loved to use his strength, especially to wrestle, and took a satanic
delight in overwhelming his friends. Sometimes he hurt them and
remorse sprang quickly.

With the onset of the First World War Collins was in a dilemma.
The idea of joining the British Army was repugnant to him yet the
mystique of war was attractive and he did not wish to seem a
coward. In January 1916, aware that plans were in the making, he
returned to Dublin to work with the dedicated minority who saw
in England's preoccupation with Europe an opportunity to strike
for Ireland's independence. Asquith's Home Rule Bill, which
might in 1912 have satisfied all but a few fanatics, was now in cold
storage for the duration of the war. The Ulster question was still
unresolved.

Collins had been in England throughout the wearisome passage
of the Bill and, by the time it received the Royal Assent in September 1914, he, like his friends, was convinced that England's
politicians ultimately would bow to Unionist pressure and scrap
the measure. But for many young Irishmen the Government of
Ireland Act had been overtaken by the swift changes of the times
and they themselves had matured quickly. The Act already had a
musty look, the freedom it conferred seemed faded.

They were the boys born in those years when rain fell upon the
desert and all was green. Like Collins, they had grown up in an
atmosphere of revivalist fervour, and their minds had been shaped
by idealists like Lyons. Now they were men and their mentors were
not so very much older than they. At Easter 1916 one of those
idealists, Padraic Pearse, read from the portico of the GPO in
Dublin the brave proclamation of the Irish Republic. Michael

Collins followed Pearse into the Post Office and five tragic days later, when the inevitable end came, marched with him from the inferno into the hands of the British Army. Collins served as a staff captain through the Rising, fighting close to Sean MacDiarmada, one of the seven signatories of the Proclamation, whom he hero-worshipped.

MacDiarmada, six years older than Collins, died with the other six signatories and seven more men of the Rising at the hands of Sir John Maxwell's merciless firing squad.

Narrowly escaping execution himself, Collins was interned first at Stafford and then at Frongoch in North Wales, where the countryside must have reminded him a little of West Cork. It was there, in what became a revolutionaries' university, that Collins emerged as a leader, there that he attracted to him men who were to give him an extraordinary loyalty and who became members of the team which undermined British power in Dublin. The men of Frongoch were released by Lloyd George at Christmas 1916: the Welsh Wizard was anxious to try and recover some of the goodwill lost in Ireland by Maxwell's marathon of executions and to take the chill off American opinion. He was also well aware that Frongoch was a breeding ground of revolution and that the British taxpayer was meeting the cost of it. (Prisoners serving sentence, among them Eamon de Valera, were not released until June 1917.)

Back in Ireland, Collins set about rebuilding the broken Irish Republican Brotherhood with the help of his close friend Harry Boland, Thomas Ashe, Diarmuid Lynch and Con Collins. The vital secrets necessary to its restructuring were held in the indomitable hands of Mrs Kathleen Clarke, widow of Tom Clarke who had been largely responsible for resuscitating the organisation a few years earlier.

Clandestine politics earned Collins no bread and butter and he was lucky to be appointed secretary to the Irish National Aid Association which had set out to help families impoverished by the Rising. The interviewing committee were impressed by his ability, nettled by his apparent conceit of himself, but Collins's friends had worked hard on his behalf and he got the job. The work gave him opportunities to make new contacts and extend his influence but he gave it up gladly enough little more than a year later.

It was a time when events moved swiftly. The United States of America entered the war in April 1917, and the British Government, eager that the Americans should relieve as much as possible the fearful strain of the war effort, sought to check the drain on American goodwill caused by their Irish policy. The decline of the Irish Parliamentary Party, hastened by Redmond's denunciation in the Commons of the Easter Rising, and the minatory rise of Sinn Fein spurred Lloyd George to make the Home Rule offer which Redmond turned down in favour of the alternative of a grand Convention. This long drawn-out Assembly, which handed in a voluminous report many months later, was spurned by Sinn Fein who were no longer interested in crumbs of comfort tossed them in expediency. Nor did they want the stale half loaf of Home Rule. They wanted the whole loaf of Irish sovereignty and were ready to smash the baker's window to get it.

On October 26th 1917 Eamon de Valera was elected President of Sinn Fein, its founder, Arthur Griffith, standing selflessly but advisedly aside. Collins was barely acquainted with de Valera but he knew that he had done well during the Rising and that in Dartmoor and Lewes prisons his stoical resistance to authority and his quiet concern for the welfare of his comrades had earned him many admirers. His austere, stubborn conviction, a quality of permanence about the man, impressed the younger Collins, who now joined him on the Sinn Fein Executive. De Valera was also made President of the Volunteers, and this dual appointment succeeded in uniting many divers views.

At the Ard Fheis the three strands of the Irish independence movement became one, but it was a curious threading because of the secret nature of the Irish Republican Brotherhood. The IRB, with its interlocking regional circles, was a powerful influence in the Volunteers, which put Cathal Brugha, the new Chief of Staff, in a difficult position. Brugha had no time for secret movements. De Valera, too, though once a hesitant member, preferred to remain outside.

Collins was now a member of the Supreme Council of the IRB

and was to enjoy increasing power in the movement. He shouldered power lightly and his use of it was to sour his relationship with Brugha. As Director of Organisation and, later, of Intelligence also, he was Brugha's subordinate, but the older man could never be sure to what extent Collins's influence pervaded the Volunteers, and Collins often made decisions in his secret rôle which impinged upon Brugha's area of authority.

Sinn Fein, no longer an underpowered vehicle for Arthur Griffith's political theories, germane though they were, but now re-engined to carry a broader and longer load, was pledged to "securing the international recognition of Ireland as an independent Irish Republic". America's participation in the European war seemed to offer Ireland the hope of international recognition when the war was over and the statesmen of Europe and America planned the world of the future. Many young Irishmen were fighting for Britain in the belief that her benevolence towards Belgium would encompass Ireland as well.

To Collins, de Valera and the others who were planning independence in their own way, this was misplaced confidence. They would not help England either voluntarily or under compulsion in any circumstances. More and more, it seemed likely that Britain would attempt to bolster her flagging armies by conscripting young Irishmen. The British Cabinet spent hour upon divided hour of discussion on the subject, tempted on the one hand by the possibility of 150,000 vigorous new troops, apprehensive on the other that the trouble which inevitably would ensue in Ireland would not be worth it. Complicating the issue was the factor of public opinion in Britain. Hostility could be expected if young boys and older men were conscripted, while the Irish who, in British eyes, had been born British by virtue of ancient conquest, were exempt.

In Dublin the dilemma of the Cabinet was an open secret. On April 10th 1918 the Military Service Bill was introduced in the House of Commons and the Irish Parliamentary Party, led by Dillon, marched protestingly out. They carried their protest to the Mansion House in Dublin where they joined forces in an anticonscription meeting with Sinn Fein. They were supported by the

Catholic hierarchy whose intervention decided the British Government to notify their Representative at the Vatican "of any case that might come to light of the improper interference of the Irish priesthood in secular affairs, and more particularly the recent promise of absolution to persons engaged in resistance to the Military Service Act".[1]

The British discovered that the Sinn Fein leaders who were most likely to resist conscription, with or without absolution from their priests, were also implicated in the famous "German Plot". Collins received a copy of the list of those proscribed almost as soon as the authorities in Dublin Castle. It came from Eamon Broy, a detective in the Castle, the first of his several contacts there.

De Valera, Griffith, Plunkett and other political leaders decided to ignore Collins's warning in order to make capital out of their imprisonment. The physical force men like Collins himself, Richard Mulcahy, Cathal Brugha and Harry Boland avoided arrest. They had a job to do.

2

THE REMOVAL of the political leaders opened up Collins's path to power. He had never been very convinced that the Easter Rising, doomed as it was from the beginning, had been a very efficient revolutionary operation. But, because of the Rising and its aftermath, the independence movement now had the people's support and Collins meant to use it. With his usual thoroughness he was reorganising the Volunteers throughout the country, his whole object being to ensure that when the struggle began it could be sustained for as long as was necessary. He knew everything about every Volunteer unit in Ireland, exactly what arms and ammunition they had, who their officers were, even how many bicycles they had. Directives flowed from his office. Always there was a personal note, sometimes caustic if he suspected inefficiency or lack of enthusiasm, usually brief but encouraging. And stealthily he built up his Intelligence network, spreading it not just in Dublin but throughout the country. The number of people who worked for him in this way, often unknown to their family and friends, eventually ran into hundreds.

He did not concern himself with the running of Sinn Fein which, in the absence of most of its leaders, seemed to him to carry too much dead wood. Quietly his friend Harry Boland was working to revitalise the organisation.

Although the Military Service Act of 1918 was never applied in Ireland, the fact that the British Government had taken the necessary powers to conscript Irishmen was not to be forgiven. The whole business had been clumsily handled by war-weary leaders who saw the shadows of defeat beginning to lengthen and gave scant consideration to the feelings of the people. And the people showed their feelings through the ballot boxes.

Michael Collins was one of the sixty-nine Sinn Fein candidates elected to Westminster in the General Election of December 1918. Four of them each represented two constituencies. The electors knew that they were pledged to secure a republican government for Ireland and that no successful Sinn Fein candidate would take his seat in the Commons.

There was no doubt in the minds of the successful Sinn Fein candidates that Eamon de Valera was the man they wanted for President of Dail Eireann. In Lincoln Gaol, de Valera missed the first meeting of Dail Eireann on January 21st 1919, but his captivity on this occasion was almost at an end. De Valera had ingeniously established communication with Dublin and, with his astute co-operation from the inside, Collins, Boland and Frank Kelly were to engineer his escape on February 3rd. Two other prisoners, Sean McGarry and Sean Milroy, also escaped and were spirited by Collins across the country.

In his absence, Collins was elected Minister for Home Affairs, and a few weeks later became Minister for Finance. The British Government tolerated its Irish rival until September, probably because of Ireland's claim to be represented at the Peace Conference. When the American President declined to support the claim, the Dail was suppressed and thenceforward became in its own country a Government in exile.

By this time, its various Ministers had established Departments designed to take over the administrative functions controlled from Dublin Castle. For two years, while Ireland blazed, the carbon copy government operated more effectively than the Castle-based Irish Government. Exemplifying this incredible success was the Irish loan, master-minded in Ireland by Collins, who himself sat at a table in the street selling bonds. In Ireland alone, well over £300,000 was raised and in America, where de Valera made the loan his responsibility, the amount was about five million dollars.

After his escape from Lincoln de Valera had remained in hiding until the British Government amnestied their political prisoners in March 1919 and enabled him to return to Dublin. On April 1st he was elected President of Dail Eireann and, on April 10th, his resolution to ostracise the men of the Royal Irish Constabulary was passed by the Dail.

Collins was critical of men of the South Tipperary Brigade of the Irish Republican Army who took matters into their own hands and ambushed and killed the two RIC constables at Soloheadbeg. According to Dan Breen, one of the ambush leaders, the killings were designed to fire the revolution for which they were becoming impatient, but Collins would rather the British had been provoked to shoot first. Sean Hogan, aged seventeen, one of the ambushers, was captured but brilliantly rescued from a train at Knocklong. Two more RIC men were killed as they fought to keep their prisoner.

If the Soloheadbeg ambush had been a dubious undertaking, the rescue of Sean Hogan was as brave as it was audacious. Together the two episodes established the pattern of conflict to come. Relieved that the first shots had been fired and appreciating the swing of public sympathy which followed the Knocklong rescue, Collins now set himself relentlessly to drive the British out of Ireland.

In May 1919 Harry Boland was smuggled to America to make preparations for de Valera's visit. Without his gingering influence the Sinn Fein leadership seemed less inclined to back the physical force side and Collins was exasperated. To his friend and protégé, Austin Stack, who was later to become an inveterate enemy, Collins wrote, "The position is intolerable—the policy now seems to be to squeeze out anyone who is tainted with strong fighting ideas," and, again, next day, "We have too many of the bargaining type already."[2]

The tempo soon quickened. There were attacks on RIC Barracks, ambushes in the country and in Dublin the battle of the Intelligence services began. The British Government never admitted that a state of war existed but maintained that they were taking police action to deal with civil disturbances, and thousands of mercenaries were brought in as temporary constables of the Royal Irish Constabulary. They made their appearance in March 1920, and because of their hybrid uniforms were soon nicknamed the Black and Tans, after a famous pack of hounds. Doubtless there were good men among them, but not many. A drunken, cut-throat gang, they fought by fire and murder. Just as ruthless, though generally braver and tougher, were the ex-officers who joined the auxiliary RIC, and were known, not very affectionately, as "Auxies".

These were the men who fought the IRA's outgunned flying columns, but their adversaries knew the terrain and were sheltered by a stubborn population taking indefatigable risks. The Irish learned from, and improved upon, the tactics of the Boer guerrillas. Houses and villages were burnt by Britain's emissaries, the heart of Cork was destroyed. Every incident sparked off reprisals. The Black and Tans killed without conscience and the IRA retaliated with little heed for the admonishments of their bishops. Neither side showed much pity and the chivalry of men like Sean McEoin only occasionally lightened the dreary picture of reprisal and counter-reprisal.

In Dublin the campaign was insidious and vicious. There, too, the IRA and the Black and Tans were in combat, but for the most part it was a duel between the Castle's Intelligence network and that of Collins. With spies and informers on either side, no one involved was safe. Experienced men of G. Division of the Dublin Metropolitan Police, some of whom knew many of the Irish leaders by sight, hunted their quarry. They constituted a threat and Collins destroyed them. A special financial investigator, briefed to locate the Irish Loan funds in bank accounts, was remorselessly shot down.

The British had the prisons and the gallows and in the name of affronted Society, British Society, they executed young Irishmen, like seventeen-year-old Kevin Barry, with the same ritual as they had dispatched Crippen. The Irish were in no position to arrange such elaborate rites and carried out death sentences by the gun wherever they found those condemned. The results looked much more like murder than the ceremonious execution by the hangman, and Collins, who ordered his famous "Squad" to carry out the death sentences, was regarded by the British as of the same ilk as Jack the Ripper. The price on his head reached £10,000, but it was not long before those who put it there were shaking his hand with warmth.

Collins's exploits in those years are legendary; his escapes from capture verged on the miraculous. Never for a moment was he safe, yet he did not operate from underground cellars nor resort to disguise. He carried out his multitudinous duties from offices in the city, met his friends, and sometimes his enemies, in bars and generally used a sturdy old bicycle for transport. He was always neatly but unostentatiously dressed, a large, friendly looking man who would probably run a small business somewhere.

He was fortunate that his enemies had no recent photograph of him and he was fortunate, too, in his friends. Men like Joe O'Reilly were near at hand as often as they could be and were ready to die for him. There were his followers in Dublin Castle who kept him informed so that if his office or a meeting place came under suspicion he quickly moved on. Four times the Minister of Finance moved his offices. His audacity stemmed from common sense: the obvious is most likely to be over looked and normal behaviour does not attract suspicion, but a man in thick disguise or hidden deep in a cellar is in no position to argue.

When his friend Harry Boland wrote anxiously from America, Collins reassured him. "I am in love with life as much as the next man," he wrote. "The escapes of others often chill me to the marrow. But for myself I take a logical view of things and act in accordance with what would seem to be a supersensitiveness."[3]

Despite the strain of ever-present danger, not only for himself but also for his friends, and the knowledge that if he were to be removed it would be extremely difficult for others to pick up the threads of his work, Collins brought a tremendous verve to the cause of Irish independence. Not one, but four onerous jobs were entrusted to him and, although he was well able to delegate responsibility and depended, indeed, upon a number of colleagues, no detail escaped his alert mind.

As Adjutant-General, Director of Organisation, Director of Intelligence and for some time Director of Purchases, every aspect of the Irish Republican Army was his concern. To some extent the functions overlapped. When the Director of Purchases was smuggling arms into the country he found it useful to be also head of Intelligence. And in his capacity of Minister of Finance he was able to cut corners in arranging payment. He cut corners often but carefully, like a shrewd racing driver, but this sometimes meant that he pre-empted the authority of others. Decisive, confident, he saw no point in wasting time, or risking a messenger and his message, in order to refer to the man who strictly had the right to make a certain decision. Most problems impinged upon one or other of his areas of authority and if they came to him he dealt with them. And because his was a robust, outgoing, colourful personality, though equally he could be described as reserved, introspective and tender, he attracted the attention of the Press who soon fashioned a romantic outlaw character for him. He was *the* leader of the revolution. Among the general public, among many within the independence movement itself, and in the British Cabinet, it was largely accepted that he was. In fact, although Collins was the driving force, the pivot of the revolutionary movement was Eamon de Valera, far away though he was most of the time.

What is now known as a "personality cult" was deplored by Brugha who, as Minister of Defence, was one of those to whom Collins should sometimes have deferred. Brugha did not underestimate Collins's abilities but he suspected that Collins revelled in the publicity, enjoyed being the Scarlet Pimpernel of the Irish Revolution. In this he was wrong. Collins did not seek self-advertisement, he simply had "star quality".

Cathal Brugha himself was a curious admixture of Collins and de Valera, having the adventurous spirit of the one and the austere, inflexible purpose of the other. He was not personally jealous of Collins but simply resented that one man attracted the attention when many good men were playing invaluable parts and were just as likely to end on the gallows as was Collins.

Until August 1920 a strange dichotomy existed in the independence movement. The Irish Republic Army owed allegiance only to its own Executive, an incongruous situation because the Irish Republic had already been proclaimed and Dail Eireann recognised as the instrument of government. With few exceptions, the members of the Dail were soldiers of the IRA, and conversely almost all the IRA leaders were members of the Dail.

In August 1920 the IRA took an Oath of allegiance to the Republic and the Dail, which was the Government of the Republic, so completing the powers of the underground State. Sir Hamar Greenwood, in the same month, introduced the Restoration of Order in Ireland Bill in the House of Commons: maintaining the fiction that the IRA were merely obstreperous civilians, the Bill nevertheless provided for them to be tried by secret military courts. It further provided for imprisonment on suspicion, curfews and restriction on the movement of traffic, and it substituted military courts of enquiry for coroners' inquests. Persistent verdicts of wilful murder by Crown forces brought in by Irish juries were annoying to the British Government and were likely to create an unfavourable impression overseas.

These measures, the British hoped, would enable them to deal effectively with the rank and file of the revolution. Political leaders like Griffith and MacNeill could be imprisoned—and were shortly afterwards. That left the most potent force, the hard, dangerous core of the Collins network to be dealt with.

A number of Intelligence officers were drafted in from Cairo. They adopted new names, wore civilian clothes, took ordinary lodgings and appeared to follow occupations which had nothing to do with soldiering. Known as the "Cairo gang", and in code as the "particular ones", they set about ferreting out their quarry. At first they had some success but they did not realise how formidably well informed their opponents were. Collins assembled dossiers on these men and he knew that they were also discovering a great deal about him and about his colleagues. Carefully they were preparing a trap and inevitably it would achieve its purpose unless the Irish moved first.

On this occasion Collins consulted Cathal Brugha who went carefully through the dossiers, putting aside some when he considered the evidence insufficient. Collins ordered the execution of the others. The arrangements were made by Dick McKee and Peadar Clancy who were betrayed and arrested at 2 a.m. on the morning of Sunday November 21st, a few hours before the informal executions were carried out. Eleven officers were killed and four wounded, shot down pitilessly on Bloody Sunday. The day was made bloodier in the afternoon when Black and Tans went to a football match at Croke Park and killed fourteen people, and, at the end of the day, McKee and Clancy were brutally done to death.

The British Government extracted the last ounce of propaganda from the liquidation of the spy ring and the public were persuaded that they were ordinary officers, "cadets" in fact, who had been foully murdered by the Irish terrorists. In reality, the Cabinet accepted the episode for what it was, a military defeat.

To the Irish people, who were living in the same tense circumstances as the people of occupied Europe in the years of World War II, in constant dread of raids and reprisals and the nocturnal clap of rifle butts on their doors, the execution of the "particular ones" meant much the same as the killing of a Gestapo squad by the Resistance meant to the French or Dutch. But even the Irish people at the time probably did not realise that the executions had been formally authorised by their Minister for Defence after proper consideration of the evidence presented to him.

Collins himself had no more compunction in ordering the killings than Maxwell had when he executed the Easter leaders. But a man who orders killings in cold blood needs steel in him, and this Collins had—so did every British Home Secretary in the days of capital punishment. It is a quality which judges, generals and most political leaders must own and must be prepared to use in the cause of duty. They can be magnanimous but never weak. This was why, within a year of Bloody Sunday, British statesmen were quite ready to accept Collins as an equal at the negotiation table.

Within days of Bloody Sunday, the Roman Catholic Archbishop of Perth brought peace proposals from Lloyd George to Arthur Griffith in Mountjoy Prison and later saw Collins. It was easy enough to find Collins if you knew how, Lloyd George realised. Because the surrender of arms was a condition, the proposals were unacceptable. At first the British Cabinet had favoured an amnesty to all members of the Dail. They believed there was now little prospect of capturing Collins and other wanted leaders in any event. But Greenwood persuaded his colleagues that the IRA would soon crack and they stiffened their attitude. Collins and Mulcahy were advised by Archbishop Clune to disappear for a while.

On December 12th and 13th Archbishop Clune had further interviews with Griffith, who got in touch with Collins. In a terse reply Collins said, "We have clearly demonstrated our willingness to have peace on honourable terms. Lloyd George insists upon capitulation."

Arthur Griffith believed that Lloyd George was anxious for peace but was hampered by his "diehards", but Collins suspected the Prime Minister of attempting to divide the Irish leaders. He did not like the combination of threatening utterances in public and conspiratorial blandishments.

The British Cabinet were reluctant to deal openly with Collins whom they had branded as an "organiser of murder", though Dr Clune had assured them that he was "the only one with whom effective business could be done".[4]

Sir Nevil Macready was agreeable to a truce without surrender of arms if it were politically expedient, but he was confident that the IRA would be broken within four months. The Cabinet decided that to offer a truce on these terms would be weakness and to defer the matter at least until elections could be held under the Government of Ireland Act which had just become law.

Asked if there would be intimidation if an election were held in February or March of 1921, Macready answered, "A general boycott at the point of the pistol, on the word of Michael Collins."

Lloyd George's rejoinder was enlightening: "If Michael Collins can stop three million people using their vote, it doesn't say much for the policy His Majesty's Government is now pursuing."

De Valera's return from America just before Christmas was discussed by the British Government and they gave orders that he was not to be arrested. His value to them was that, in the public mind, unlike Collins, he had no blood on his hands; he was a much more respectable person with whom to be seen in negotiation when the time came.

The President of the Dail was none too keen on the methods which had been employed in pursuit of independence. Ambushes in the countryside, and especially assassinations carried out by

Collins's men, were repugnant to him. He did not want the flag of the Republic to be sullied before it flew openly and triumphantly over the Capital. But de Valera was out of touch. The most graphic reports he had received could convey little of the atmosphere of terror or of the realities of the fighting. No tactics but those used could have succeeded. To have followed the lead of the Easter rebels and taken up defensive, challenging positions would have led only to further disaster, a much heavier loss of life and more destruction. Open battle on any scale also would have been suicidal. The Boers had given a lead in guerrilla warfare, the Irish took it a step further and the pattern has been emulated since by every country striking for independence.

On his return, de Valera decided that Collins should go to America. There was work for him to do there and some dispersal of leaders in perilous times was prudent. Again, the tensions in the Cabinet, between Brugha and Stack on the one hand and Collins on the other, contained their own dangers. But de Valera also wanted to get the revolution out of the backstreets and respectably into the open. That the British had made peace overtures at all suggested to de Valera that the Irish were in a sufficiently good position to carry the war into political terrain. He was appalled by the suffering inflicted upon his people in two years and doubted that they could for much longer endure the fire and death of the Black and Tan campaign. But he knew, too, that although a military defeat of England was impossible, the British Government was under strain. Politically they were insecure and the British people had been made restive and ashamed by the apparently never-ending struggle and the black tactics resorted to by their Government. Moreover, if the reunion of Ireland was to be achieved, the hostile element in the North East had to be won over. Loyalists in the South, too, would be needed in the new Ireland— if they were prepared to give their allegiance to it.

He made no drastic changes immediately. Collins declined to go to America and the President did not press the point. De Valera's biographers suggest that both Collins and de Valera changed their minds, Collins becoming reconciled to the idea of the American mission, de Valera deciding as the circumstances changed that he was after all more valuable in Ireland. At a meeting of the Dail on January 25th the twenty-four Deputies present were opposed to his soft-pedalling on military effort. They were men whose judgment he respected and who, he knew, had grown in experience. He took further soundings outside the Dail and saw in the end that the momentum of the war could not be lost now. At the same time, he was still insistent that the burden of the people should be lightened if possible.

More bitter retaliative months followed. Most of the southern area was under martial law and here "official" reprisals, which were little different from those which were officially "unofficial", were instituted. Houses of suspected Sinn Fein supporters were now burned under supervision. De Valera tried to win the support of the Catholic hierarchy, who were inclined to castigate both sides, but he was unable to convince them that the IRA were the military arm of a legitimate government.

In March the British Cabinet were divided on the question of offering a truce without surrender of arms and postponed a decision until after the elections held under the Government of Ireland Act. Lloyd George believed that it would take twelve more months to pacify Ireland but he was doubtful that he could carry public opinion with him for that time. He contemplated meeting Collins himself but shrank from this step. Although the British Government had it in mind that de Valera might be the man with no blood on his hands to whom they could talk without seeming to have truck with "murderers", they were still of the impression that Collins was *the* leader. But it was de Valera who interviewed the several emissaries who came to Ireland in the ensuing months, and it was to de Valera that Lloyd George, following the King's appeal for peace when he opened the new parliament in Belfast, sent his invitation to talk. Collins was sceptical and scarcely paused in planning measures to render Dublin Castle even more impotent than it had become already, but de Valera accepted the invitation. Griffith, MacNeill and other leaders were released from prison and on July 8th the Truce was signed, to become effective on July 11th. As easily the same terms could have been offered in the previous November.

Then followed the correspondence like a long game of chess between Lloyd George and de Valera, then stalemate resolved by an agreement to start another game. Lloyd George took his place at the board surrounded by his experienced colleagues, de Valera sent his friends to the game and stayed at home to master-mind tactics. His overall strategy had been carefully explained to the delegates who were to negotiate with the British.

Michael Collins accepted reluctantly his appointment as Griffith's deputy leader. He did not see himself as a statesman, even as a politician, and felt that as a soldier he should not be sent on an essentially political mission, but he was also a member of the Dail Cabinet, and Minister of Finance at that, so it was not unreasonable that he should be asked to go. If the negotiations failed and the war were resumed he would no longer be the mysterious Michael Collins of the past years. Every British soldier, every auxiliary policeman would know exactly what he looked like. Ever mistrustful of the British, he crossed to England doubtful that he would ever be allowed to return to Ireland. His own men travelled with him ready to die in his defence if need be, and at Croydon a light aircraft and its pilot stood by.

3

FROM THE moment the Conference began on October 11th 1921 Collins's life swung into a new orbit. The ten months he had left to him were in many ways the most demanding and the most interesting of his life. From a dedicated revolutionary ready to further his cause or protect the lives of his friends by calculated assassination, he was to become a political leader and a man of peace, ready to strike a bargain with the shrewd dealers of the international market place and alert to the prospects of driving harder bargains in days to come. But he did not slough off the old skin overnight; the conspirator in him lived to the end.

Collins very quickly won his diplomatic spurs. Early the British representatives realised that they were not dealing with a criminal gunman, as once they had convinced themselves he was, and as the talks went on he gained the respect of them all. Churchill and Birkenhead, each of whom had a flamboyantly adventurous streak as Collins did himself, were especially attracted to him and Birkenhead became a good friend. In the next few months, though neither could bring himself to depart from Britain's basic hard line on Ireland, both of these British statesmen showed considerable understanding of Ireland's problems at Cabinet meetings.

When the Ulster question was raised at the meeting of October 14th, Collins made his attitude plain. Lloyd George urged that "all the dominions had begun by being divided. Union was bound to come but it would never come if an attempt was made to force it from the first." At once Collins denied that this was a valid analogy. "The British have divided an ancient and historic State," he said.

On October 24th, following the seventh meeting of the two

sides, Lloyd George and Chamberlain continued the discussion with Griffith and Collins. Although Cathal Brugha was to charge bitterly that the British had broken up the plenary sessions so that they could work on the weakest members of the team, the truth was that Griffith and Collins were the obvious leaders and candid discussions between four men were likely to achieve more than formal conferences with all present.

At this first meeting Griffith said that the Irish "could not accept the Crown because they were Representatives of the Republic, but all else being satisfactory they would undertake to recommend it. Mr Collins had tried to whittle down this offer and when told that the Crown involved the Oath of Allegiance suggested an oath to the Constitution."

Had the British adopted this suggestion, Eamon de Valera might have seen his way clear to take his seat in the Dail very much sooner than he did. It is even possible that the Collins–de Valera Pact might have worked, in which case, instead of becoming a focal point for resistance to the Treaty, the Four Courts Garrison would have found themselves isolated. It would not seem a too drastic concession for the British to have made either at the time of the Treaty discussions or when the Constitution became the stumbling block to the Pact in June 1922.

Among themselves the British were uncertain as to which was the key issue, the Crown or Ulster. Lloyd George thought the only way to reconcile Ireland to the Crown was to secure Irish unity. He did not see this as a denial of autonomy to Ulster. Ireland would be a dominion with Dublin as its capital. Belfast would be subordinate to Dublin instead of to Westminster. Chamberlain thought the Crown would be the difficulty in any event. He was probably right, for the Irish delegates and the Dail accepted the ambiguous Boundary Commission solution with much less resistance than they did the Oath and with less suspicion of British intentions.

During the negotiations Collins was the principal spokesman on defence and finances. Vehemently he resisted the condition that Britain should have complete command of Ireland's coast and harbours. "Nothing else will do," said Lloyd George. Earlier,

Collins and Childers had had discussions with Admiral Beatty and Winston Churchill, and he fired at Lloyd George that Beatty had been much more reasonable than the Prime Minister. Ireland was prepared to give guarantees. She would do nothing "to imperil British security or British lives", but freedom to take every port and harbour was another matter.

Beatty had shown the Irish representatives charts with U-boat sinkings marked. His object was to show that unless Britain could hunt out the enemy submarines they could take refuge in Irish inlets. England would not accept Irish neutrality, Churchill said; her inactivity in war, yes, but not the prohibition of ports to the British Navy. In the end, the Treaty provided that in peacetime Britain should have the use of harbour facilities in Berehaven, Queenstown, Belfast Lough and Lough Swilly and in wartime such facilities as she required for the defence of Great Britain and Ireland.

Britain's conditions concerning defence and trade evoked caustic remarks from Collins. From the outset Griffith had laid down that, while there was no objection to free trade in English goods, Ireland must have protection against foreign goods sold by English merchants. Collins argued that the British delegates kept citing Canada as an example "then ran away from it", that in no wise was Ireland being offered the same status, the same freedom as Canada. When Lloyd George pointed out that trade questions were of vital concern to Ulster and could create such difficulties that Ulster would not enter a united parliament by consent—"and that is the only way you will ever get them"—Collins retorted, "We could destroy Ulster industry but we shall not. We are ready to give securities and to settle these securities beforehand—but we are being fooled."

It was at this meeting, on November 23rd, that Collins attacked the British Government for issuing a secret circular in Northern Ireland which related to the enrolment of a special defence force. To the embarrassment of the British Government the document came into Sinn Fein hands and was published. In fact, the circular, put out by Colonel Wickham, was unauthorised and the proposal illegal, but British Ministers thought it likely that Wickham had been given the go-ahead by someone higher up. Lloyd George explained to Collins that neither his Government nor General Tudor had authorised the circular. Collins was prepared to take Tudor's word but heatedly alleged that someone high up was behind it. Probably he had Sir Henry Wilson in mind, and he may well have been near the truth. He claimed that Craig and the Lord Mayor of Belfast could end disturbances in that city in twenty-four hours "if they were minded". How was it then, Chamberlain wanted to know, that Mr Collins and his friends were not able to secure observance of the Truce in the South? He did not question their good faith "but would invite them to remember that Sir James Craig met with equal difficulties".

Lloyd George proposed that Collins and Griffith meet Birkenhead to try to iron out the wrinkles of the discussion. Collins suggested that a constitutional lawyer should accompany Griffith. Birkenhead welcomed the idea but urged Collins to attend also. He expressed interest in a memorandum which Collins said he had been writing. "Who outside our six would guess the name of the writer?" commented Austen Chamberlain when he had read the memorandum, which was marked "Personal and unofficial".

For centuries, wrote Collins, England had striven to reduce Ireland to the position of an English province: "Ireland was to be used according to the Colonial policy to feed and enrich England." Ireland had never been a British colony but "a separate nation kept subject by a more powerful neighbour for that neighbour's own advantage". Now, after centuries of political struggle and armed conflict, Ireland had won independence. The business of the Conference, Collins believed, was "to state the form of the partnership or alliance in which two peoples of equal nationhood may be associated for the benefit of both".

He looked beyond Ireland: "While Anglo-Irish relations have taken on this aspect with an apparent suddenness which is almost bewildering to the ordinary British mind, it happens that at the same moment the relations between Great Britain and the Dominions have, by a different process, reached a stage in which the finding of a solution is almost as urgent in the interests of British security and world peace." The colonies had outgrown the mother country and were "restive under any appearance of parental restraint, though willing to co-operate with the parent on an equal footing in regard to all family affairs. Ireland as a separate nation would be also restive under any control from the neighbouring nation, but equally willing to co-operate in free association on all matters which would naturally be the *common concern* of two nations living so closely together."

Collins maintained that friendship and co-operation would be made possible only "by recognising without limitation the complete independence of the several countries". Ireland would be content to enter an association only if it were based "not on the present technical legal status of the Dominions, but on the real position they claim and have in fact secured".

"Such an association," Collins thought, "would be the pattern for national co-operation on a wider scale, and might form the nucleus of a real League of Nations of the world . . ."

He believed that America might well be inclined to enter such a League and pointed to Ireland's "powerful influence in consolidating the whole body, for Ireland is herself a mother country with world-wide influences . . ."

Concluding, he stated, "Mr Lloyd George's invitation to the Irish representatives to consider how association with the nations of the British Commonwealth can best be reconciled with Irish national aspirations, makes it necessary to consider how far the members of the group have attained to independent nationality and what further steps should be taken to declare and secure such a standard of independence."

This memorandum fitted well enough with de Valera's external association concept, but it could never have been written by de Valera, who was not interested in the progress of members of the British Commonwealth. Collins quite evidently was, and his ideas, which anticipated the Statute of Westminster to which his colleague, Kevin O'Higgins, made a notable contribution, suggest that he might well have been content with dominion status for Ireland if it enabled her to play an important rôle in Commonwealth and world affairs.

Acting on the Prime Minister's suggestion, Birkenhead met

Collins, Griffith and Barton; then on the following day, November 24th, he and Hewart conferred with Griffith, Collins, Gavan Duffy and Chartres. The British were still seeking a definition of external association and it was Chartres who put it in plain words: within Ireland the Crown would have no significance at all. It was now that Lloyd George began to turn nasty. Hewart had assured the Irishmen that they "must not suppose that the British Government were contemplating the alternative of war". Lloyd George hastily sent a note to put the Irish right. He inserted the words "with equanimity". So the threat of war still existed. This rather unusual incident does suggest that the threat of war was a bluff but it is a tiny indicator and there were much more potent pointers in the other direction.

The plenipotentiaries now returned to Dublin and came back to London with the formula agreed by the Dail Cabinet, but from that point, despite a game stand by Griffith, the Irish delegates began to lose ground. It was like the moment in a tennis match when after a close fought game one player senses victory, the other defeat. Collins attacked hard on trade and defence. Griffith wanted further discussion on the Oath and insisted that the action of the Crown in Ireland should be governed by the law and *practice* of the Crown in Canada. In effect, the argument had been conceded. The deadline crept in, December 6th. On that date Sir James Craig must have word, one way or the other. Why? Craig could wait, but somehow Lloyd George had injected urgency and haste into the negotiations.

They got down to discussing detail, safeguards for the Unionists in the South, fair treatment for dispossessed officials. Birkenhead said that he and Collins had discussed this. Collins had promised fair treatment. "Oh, yes!" Collins retorted, "There are even more disagreeable people, such as County Inspectors of Police, to be dealt with, but we quite agree that they must be treated fairly."

The Irish made one more attempt to modify the Oath. The wording hinted at desperation but it was ingenious and, again, could easily have been accepted by the British negotiators. It provided for Dail Deputies to promise allegiance, first to the Constitution of the Irish Free State, and then to the King *in acknowledgement of the Association of Ireland in a common citizenship* with

Britain and the Commonwealth. But the British were obstinate.

On Friday, December 2nd, at 8.45 p.m., Collins boarded the boat train at Euston. He had in his possession twenty copies of the proposed treaty. Just before the train left, he was handed twenty copies of the annex, in final form. Next morning saw the irretrievable division of the Dail Cabinet.

On their return to London, according to the British records, Collins said he was "fed up" with the differences in the delegation and sent Barton and Gavan Duffy to Lloyd George in the hope that he might convert them. Collins did not mention that, nettled by Brugha's charge of weakness, he was offering Barton and Duffy a chance to do better.

Griffith, Barton and Gavan Duffy met Lloyd George, Chamberlain, Birkenhead and Horne on the Sunday afternoon, December 4th, and the meeting broke up with Lloyd George threatening war. The Irish were to submit their formal rejection next morning. Persuaded by the ineluctable Tom Jones, Collins saw the Prime Minister early and argued through the case again. Lloyd George emerged in high dudgeon, C. P. Scott, then Editor of the *Manchester Guardian*, noted but the Prime Minister's account of the interview to his ministers shortly afterwards does not suggest this. He reported that Collins and Griffith were greatly disappointed by the rejection of the British proposals. Collins still felt that they should know whether or not Craig would accept a united Ireland but had seemed placated when Lloyd George reminded him of his own opinion that what was left of the North after the Boundary Commission had completed its work would not be economically viable.

Collins, however, still held out for Craig's answer when he, Griffith and Barton met Lloyd George, Chamberlain, Birkenhead and Churchill at three o'clock that afternoon. Griffith led off. If the Prime Minister could get an answer from Craig it might make the position easier. Collins thought it might help even if the answer were negative, "because it would put a stop to what is now happening in the two countries. We should have a Boundary Commission at once."

"I thought I had made the position clear," said Collins as Lloyd

George pressed for an answer. "You have our conditional agreement on the one side. It is just as easy to get Craig's conditional agreement on the other."

But Collins did not know about the document Griffith had initialled, in effect accepting that if Ulster declined to unite with the South the boundary would be revised by the Boundary Commission. Griffith did not argue any further and took very calmly Lloyd George's threat of war. Collins did not give his own pledge at that moment but decided to sign the Treaty document as he was returning to Hans Place and the desperate dispute which ended with all plenipotentiaries signing.

Michael Collins was under no illusion as to what had happened, but it was really no more than he had expected from the start. He had done all he could to gain the best possible bargain for Ireland; he believed the plenipotentiaries had done so. There would be a future in which much could be modified, whittled away, changed. But there would be a blazing row in Dublin.

He signed in an agony of foreboding but, when he returned to Dublin, was soon his resilient self and quickly began to gather support. As head of the Irish Republican Brotherhood he was in no weak position and at a meeting of the Supreme Council the line to be taken was agreed by all except Liam Lynch. The Supreme Council approved the Treaty and a directive went through the "centres" to all members of the organisation. Those who were also Dail Deputies were advised to vote as their consciences dictated but all other members were expected to adhere to the decision of the Supreme Council. Although the IRB was less powerful than in earlier years, the support of the Supreme Council enhanced Collins's confidence when he went to face his detractors in the Dail. Throughout the debate he was workmanlike and effective, though seldom eloquent.

When de Valera opened the proceedings by taking the plenipotentiaries to task for signing the Treaty without reference to him, it was Griffith who denied that they had exceeded their instructions, Collins, who pointed out that the Treaty instrument was not final, that it would have to be ratified both at Westminster and in Dublin. The plenipotentiaries had signed the document and agreed

James Craig (Lord Craigavon)

Eamon de Valera

to recommend it to the Dail—nothing more. He also argued that essentially the compromise lay in de Valera's acceptance of the invitation to a conference. Without that compromise there would have been no conference. He recommended the Treaty neither for more nor for less than it represented, and declared, "It gives us freedom, not the ultimate freedom that all nations desire and develop to, but the freedom to achieve it." Few, he thought, appreciated "the immense powers and liberties it secures".

Fifty years after that momentous debate in the Dail, when torment and hatred still possess the northern counties of Ireland, there is poignant relevance in Collins's words in that assembly: "What is the use of talking big phrases about not agreeing to the partition of our country," he demanded of his critics. "Surely we recognise that the North-east corner does exist, and surely our intention was that we should take such steps as would sooner or later lead to mutual understanding." He agreed that the arrangement under the Treaty was not ideal (and, indeed, it had even less to recommend it than he believed), but, he went on, "If our policy is, as has been stated, a policy of non-coercion, then let somebody else get a better way out of it."

Towards the end of the debate, which had become bogged down in a morass of repetitive and vituperative argument, Collins tried to save both the Treaty and its opponents' pride by proposing that they abstain from voting. This would enable the wishes of the people to be met and leave to the Treaty party "the shame and disgrace".

His proposal led to the curious plan to work the Treaty while keeping de Valera as President, a hopelessly impractical plan which yet demonstrated that much goodwill had not been dissipated. But much had. The scheme was rejected and Collins endured a spiteful attack from Seamus Robinson, who wanted to know whether there was any record of Collins ever firing a shot at an enemy of Ireland, and a further assault from Cathal Brugha.

Putting Collins firmly in his place as a subordinate officer, Brugha decried his reputation, his notoriety. "The Press and the people put him into a position which he never held; he was made a romantic figure, a mystical character such as this person certainly is not." It was an undeserved attack from a man who himself has become a legend. Collins listened without rancour and it was Arthur Griffith who set the record straight:

"He was the man whose matchless energy, whose indomitable will, carried Ireland through the terrible crisis; and though I have not now, and never had, an ambition about either political affairs or history, if my name is to go down in history, I want it associated with the name of Michael Collins. Michael Collins was the man who fought the Black and Tan terror for twelve months until England was forced to offer terms. That is all I have to say on the subject."

When the vote went narrowly for the Treaty, it was Collins who rose to make a plea for unity and especially for public safety. He was deeply moved and his words were clumsily put together.

"Now, in all countries in time of change—when countries are passing from peace to war or war to peace—they have their most trying time on an occasion like this. Whether we are right, or whether we are wrong, in the view of future generations, there is this—that we now are entitled to a chance."

There would be elements "that make for disorder and that make for chaos", and he suggested some kind of joint committee be formed to carry out all the arrangements that would be necessary. Warmly he spoke of Eamon de Valera: "He has exactly the same position in my heart now as he always had." The President was touched but, before he could reply, Miss Mary MacSwiney rejected the proposal out of hand.

4

A few days later, on January 14th, Michael Collins was elected Chairman of the Provisional Government. Griffith had earlier been elected President of the Republic which was to continue in being until elections could be held. And so these two men, the tiring elder statesman and the large and zestful revolutionary, together undertook the task of translating the terms of the Treaty into the Irish Free State. As Griffith had wished, his name will be forever associated with that of Michael Collins.

It was Collins who strode into Dublin Castle, the one-time powerhouse of British colonialism in Ireland and, in Irish eyes, monstrous symbol of repression, and formally took over the administration of Ireland from the Lord Lieutenant, Lord Fitzalan. With his Ministers, he then met the administrative heads of department, many of them men who in their own way had loved Ireland and had done their best for her. Towards them Collins behaved with kindliness and tact. There was no malice in the man.

Almost in spite of himself, he had become a politician but he had always been mistrustful of politicians and in a way was mistrustful of himself in that rôle. "The more the rigmarole of my life continues to encompass politics, the more uneasy I feel. I am a soldier . . ." he wrote to his friend O'Kane.[5] Yet there was in Collins, with his delight in secrecy and intrigue, very much the instinct of a politician.

He was well aware of the magnitude of the task of setting up the machinery of government for a new state, and it had to be done in the face of bitter opposition in the Dail and in a large section of an essentially politically motivated army. It was vital for the well-being of the new state that the Government had complete control of the army and Collins knew, too, that for even a fragile link to be established with the Six Counties, the first prerequisite was a harmonious and stable community within the main section of Ireland.

Although Collins and Griffith were pledged to set up the Irish Free State in compliance with the Treaty, neither saw this as more than a bivouac in "the march of a nation". The British Government laboured under the delusion that the pro-Treaty party had forsworn the republican doctrine, but Collins had always been, and was still, a thorough-going Republican at heart, while Griffith's long-advocated dual monarchy system had been devised not as an ideal form of government for Ireland, but as a practicable solution to the Ulster problem. Both believed that within a few moments of history the right form of government would evolve, but both believed that the key to their country's destiny would be found in the past, in a revival of the culture, language and traditions of the Gael, in ridding Ireland of the excrescences on her natural body induced by the British irritant.

This was no atavistic romanticism on Collins's part. What he wanted was a way of life that was Irish in character, based on a proven civilisation but set in a forward looking modern world. In *The Path to Freedom* he furnished a detailed blueprint for the country's economy, for the use and development of her resources. "What we must aim at," he wrote, "is the building up of a sound economic life in which great discrepancies cannot occur. We must not have the destitution of poverty at one end and at the other an excess of riches in the possession of a few individuals beyond what they can spend with satisfaction and justification." He hoped that the growing wealth of Ireland would be "diffused through all our people, all sharing in the growing prosperity, each receiving according to what each contributes in the making of that prosperity, so that the weal of all is assured."

And his conclusion was that "a prosperous Ireland will mean a united Ireland. With equitable taxation and flourishing trade our North-east countrymen will need no persuasion to come and share in the healthy economic life of the country."

The first step towards a *rapprochement* with the North came with the Craig–Collins Agreement signed in London in late January. Collins promised to end the Belfast Boycott in return for Craig's undertaking to protect the Catholic minority in the Six Counties. Craig also agreed to facilitate the re-employment of 9,000 Catholic workers who had been thrown out of their jobs, and it was decided that the Boundary Commission arrangement should be altered. A representative from each side would meet and report to Craig and Collins, who would endeavour to reach a final agreement. The two men were also to devise a better mechanism than the Council of Ireland, provided for by the 1920 Act, to deal with problems affecting all Ireland.[6]

The agreement very quickly wore thin. Violent clashes occurred in border areas and in Belfast the religious vendetta became pitiless. The British Cabinet were informed that the outrages were mostly against Catholics. Anger grew in the South and Collins was almost beside himself with anxiety. In the next few months the plight of his fellow Catholics in Northern Ireland obsessed him almost to the exclusion of all else. Especially he was soured by the British Government's financing of the new Special Constabulary in the North, a force whose reputation remains unsavoury to this day. It is difficult to apportion responsibility, for there was provocation on both sides. The IRA was 8,000 strong in the Six Counties and reinforcements were moving up from the South. Their retaliation was often as macabre as the acts of their opposite numbers, but the fact remains that far more Catholics than Protestants lost their lives.

In February, Collins sought to negotiate further with Craig but Craig declined while Ulster Specials taken in a clash at Clones were held prisoner. An enquiry into this affair proposed by the British Government was cancelled on Churchill's advice. In view of the disturbances in Belfast, he did not think it worthwhile to proceed.

Churchill had informed Craig that he intended to address a formal letter inviting Northern Ireland to enter into negotiations with the South, but pending the liquidation of the "situation at Limerick", he did not propose to press the matter. Once this situation was cleared up, however, he would "not be disposed to accept a simple refusal from the Northern Government, in view of the heavy obligations in regard to troops and Special Constabulary which we are incurring on their behalf".[7]

The "situation at Limerick" arose when the Provisional Government ordered Michael Brennan to march in from Clare and take over posts which the British were evacuating, to prevent anti-Treaty forces from securing them. The two IRA factions seemed bent on fighting it out while British troops still in the city remained as uncomfortable witnesses. An agreement was reached but Brennan felt he had been let down by Collins, to whom he went ready to resign. Collins was short with him and Brennan tore up his resignation but felt that Collins and Mulcahy were counting too much on IRB ties to hold the loyalty of Liam Lynch who was left in charge.

Collins had little time to deal with the recalcitrant IRA leaders and left this to the very efficient but more austere Mulcahy, the Minister of Defence. The majority of the old IRA Headquarters staff supported the Treaty or, at any rate, followed Collins, but those who did not were no less his friends and he could not believe that in the end they would lift a hand against him. Mulcahy, too, counted a good deal on old loyalties, particularly those engendered within the secret Irish Republican Brotherhood, but he did not have the extraordinary magnetism of Collins and was altogether more unbending.

In January, under pressure, Mulcahy had agreed to the holding of an Army Convention within two months, but by March he had to admit to the Cabinet he could give no guarantee that "if their Convention was held there would not be set up a body regarding itself as a government not responsible to the people". Accordingly, the Dail Cabinet banned the Convention, which had the undesired effect of driving many of the moderates on to the side of the extremists. The Convention was held in spite of the edict but pro-Treaty members did not attend. An Executive was elected which, two days later, repudiated the authority of the Minister of Defence and Chief of Staff and demanded that recruitment to the Civil Guard and the Provisional Government's new National Army should cease.

To Griffith this was the usurpation of civil authority by the army and he believed it was of the utmost importance to eliminate such a form of opposition, by force of arms if need be. In theory Griffith was right; sooner or later, it was imperative that the army become the instrument of the State; but a revolutionary army comprises individuals who have taken up arms, not as a career, but to over-turn a government which they believe to be oppressive and to re-place it with a government which is acceptable to their consciences. Only when this has been achieved are they prepared to become the servants of the civil power they have set up. In the transitionary period, as happened in Ireland, it is probable that the legislature and the army are nearly synonymous.

Griffith and Collins both knew this, but Griffith had grown up in the political wing of the independence movement and, indeed, only accepted the employment of physical force as a last resort. In his mind the achievement of the Treaty had been accepted demo-cratically by a majority both in the Cabinet and the Dail, and the army should now stand aside. Collins, on the other hand, had come up through the physical force movement, he understood the feelings of the dissenters and, but for his experience in the Treaty negotiations, might well have stood with them. Collins's attitude was based on what he believed to be a correct judgment rather than upon principle. At the same time, his imagination was ranging ahead and he saw the Republic evolving a step at a time, a design which had convinced many who might otherwise have opposed the Treaty that he was right. Yet, as we have seen, he seems also to have been fascinated by the thought of playing a part—as Kevin O'Higgins one day was to play a part—in the restructuring of the British Commonwealth.

Collins was confident that he could win the dissenters over. He was so sure he was right that he could not believe his intelligent friends would not eventually see it too. With all his energy and guile he tried to heal the break between the two factions of the IRA. He did not move against the Executive, even when in April they seized the Four Courts. The last thing he wanted was to antagonise them.

One thing which drew them together was the Ulster situation.

Deceiving Griffith as well as the British, Collins was soon embroiled with Liam Lynch and others in sending succour to the
North. By agreement, Lynch, who was hostile to the Treaty
though as yet classed as a moderate, sent rifles to the North which
Collins then replaced with British rifles supplied to the Provisional
Government. Neither Griffith nor de Valera was capable of this
kind of double dealing which certainly justifies the charge, often
levelled at him by his critics, that Collins put expediency before
principle. Ironically, when anti-Treaty forces captured a large
quantity of arms at Clonmel, General Tudor reported to the
British Government that they were now "in relatively a better
position than the forces of the Provisional Government who were
complaining of the niggardly distribution of arms to them".[8]

Collins had lost all faith in Craig's ability to control the situation
in Northern Ireland and accused him of doing nothing to implement his promise to restore jobs to the 9,000 Catholic workers.
Craig's Government introduced legislation to deal with men
caught with arms or explosives and to prohibit unlawful drilling
and the wearing of unauthorised uniforms. But many of the
Orange extremists were camouflaged as Specials, so the legislation
bore more heavily on the IRA. Sir Henry Wilson's appointment as
military adviser to Craig's Government aroused the deepest mis-
trust in Collins, and it was a curiously provocative move for Craig
to make since he was fearful of civil war developing on a north–
south axis. Britain inevitably would have been drawn in and
extremists on both sides would have welcomed this. In the South
the intervention of Britain would have mended the split in the
IRA and killed the Treaty; for the Northern extremists it would
mean, they believed, that the Border would become a permanent
barrier.

Determined to avoid this situation which, in his surreptitious
campaign to help his fellow Catholics, he was doing much to
provoke, Collins did not close any doors in Craig's face. On
March 28th, Craig refuted Collins's accusations that he had not
implemented his promises of January and counter-charged that
Collins had kept quiet "about the agreement with Lloyd George
that large territories were involved in the Boundary Commission

and not merely the boundary line". Craig blamed the disorders on the South, and unemployment on the disorders. The 9,000 Catholics were only some of 60,000 unemployed.

Two days later Craig and Collins met again in London and a second Agreement was signed by Craig and Lord Londonderry, and by Collins, Griffith and Duggan. It was countersigned by the British. On the one side it was agreed that the IRA should cease its activities in the North, on the other hand the Belfast police were to be reorganised. In mixed districts half the police were to be Catholics, a rather unlikely provision which, could it have been implemented and sustained, might have obviated a great deal of trouble. The British contribution was £500,000 for unemployment relief, a measure to ease the pressure on Craig to have Catholic workers reinstated in accordance with his undertaking to Collins.

On April 4th, Craig wrote Collins,[9] "I am glad to say that the effect of our Agreement is beginning to be felt." Unemployment was to be relieved by means of a programme of public works. One third of the money available was to be spent in Catholic areas. Steps were being taken to deal promptly with serious crime and he sought Collins's co-operation in setting up a Catholic Police Committee. He reminded Collins of his promise to release sixteen prisoners and requested action on the Belfast Boycott. A strong appeal had been made to 2,000 business men to re-engage Catholic employees but their willingness to do so was qualified by the need for a trade revival. He was sure Collins would recognise that he was "energetically carrying out the spirit as well as the letter of our Agreement". The Boycott, however, was operated by the Army Executive and, even had he wanted to, Collins could do little about it.

General Macready was convinced at this time that the Free State—as he prematurely called it—had no army to speak of and so there would be no civil war. He reported also that there would be little support for Collins and his followers when the election was held.[10] It was little wonder that the British Government were becoming anxious.

The inadequacy of the Provisional Government's Army may

well have been a factor in their allowing the occupation of the Four
Courts to continue with impunity but, much more to the point,
was Collins's unwillingness to precipitate a fight with his friends.
Nevertheless, his fellow-feeling was under strain for, since the
beginning of April, there had been constant attacks on Dail
troops and military posts in Dublin and elsewhere. Several men
had been killed. Post offices and shops had been raided. But it was
difficult to know how many of these incidents were the responsibility of lawless opportunists.

Between Collins and Griffith there was not the close sympathy
of a few months earlier. The older man could not understand the
prevaricating attitude of the other. But on their frequent excur-
sions to London, whenever they met Craig or British Ministers,
they presented a united front, with Griffith supporting Collins
rather than the reverse. He was later to argue tenaciously to justify
the Collins–de Valera Pact of which he altogether disapproved.

For Collins it brought near realisation his hope to see the IRA
restored to its former homogeneous self and an end to the skir-
mishes between the two factions throughout the country. Some
were mild affairs such as the protracted struggle at Kilkenny in
early May. There the air was hideous with the sound of rifles and
machine-guns but there was little risk except to the birds. No one
was killed. But there were tragic incidents too, such as the murder
of pro-Treaty Brigadier-General Adamson in Athlone, a deed
which was repudiated by the anti-Treaty garrison.

An attempt to bring about a peaceful settlement was made by the
Archbishop of Dublin at the end of April. This failed but a group
of officers representing both sides produced what came to be called
the Army Document. To avert what they believed would be "the
greatest calamity in Irish history" they advocated "unification of
forces on the basis of our present national position in the best interests of Ireland" and, admitting that "the majority of the people
of Ireland are willing to accept the Treaty", they introduced the
idea of an agreed election. Three days later, despite Rory
O'Connor's repudiation of the Document, a four-day truce,
afterwards extended indefinitely was agreed upon by three members of the Army Executive and three representatives of the

Provisional Government's National Army. At the same time, a peace committee of ten members of the Dail was formed.

The Dail Committee met unsuccessfully several times. Michael Collins, in an interview, declared, "If this Conference fails there will be no other." It did not fail altogether; the representatives tried to hammer out an agreement on the basis of an agreed election and a coalition government, but somehow they could not get the mould right. Collins and de Valera were asked to see if they could.

Already the idea of an agreed election had alarmed the British Government. As Churchill put it to his colleagues, "In signing the Irish Treaty we thought we were dealing with the plenipotentiaries of the Irish people." He went on: "Even when serious opposition to the Treaty developed in the Dail, we hoped that an immediate vote of the Irish people would be taken which would result in a substantial majority for the acceptance of the Treaty."

Instead, the Ministers of the Provisional Government had given "hardly any thought to the essential measure of going to the Irish people for their opinion of the Treaty". They lived "far too much in the narrow circle of their own associates and late associates" and had "rather adopted the rôle of a passive sufferer under the tyranny of the extremist party". It was a view which Arthur Griffith shared, though he would have died on the rack rather than admit it to Churchill.

Churchill had written to Collins pointing out that an agreed election "would be received with world-wide ridicule and reprobation", but Collins was much more concerned with preventing a civil war in Ireland than with the views of the world. On May 20th the Collins–de Valera Pact emerged. There was to be a National Coalition Panel of Sinn Fein candidates, the number from each party to be in the same proportion as the party was at present represented in the Dail. A coalition government would follow, with an elected President, a Minister of Defence who would represent the Army, and nine other ministers, five from the majority party, four from the minority. The justification of the arrangement was that "the national position requires the entrusting of the government of the country into the joint hands of those who have been the strength of the national situation during the last few years without prejudice to their present respective positions".

The Pact meant that in no constituency would the electors be able to choose between a pro-Treaty and an anti-Treaty candidate, but they could, if they wished, vote for any other candidate instead of a member of Sinn Fein, for the Pact did provide that "every and any interest is free to go up and contest the election equally with the Sinn Fein Panel".

5

It was "an arrangement full of disaster," Churchill told his Cabinet colleagues. "It prevented an expression of opinion on the Treaty; it gave the Provisional Government no further representation of strength or authority from the Irish people; it left the Government in its present weak and helpless position; it ruptured Article 17 of the Treaty."[11]

This last point was the real nub. Article 17 required every member of the Provisional Government to have signified in writing his or her acceptance of the Treaty. It could be argued that once the Irish Free State was constituted this condition no longer applied, but then, under Article 4, the much argued Oath to be taken by Members of the Parliament of the Irish Free State was clearly set down. De Valera and his followers would certainly decline to comply with the conditions of either Article 17 or Article 4. Unless they did so, then the Irish were in breach of the Treaty.

The Dail grasped eagerly at this straw of peace and the people were much less bothered by any limitation on their choice at the polls than they were relieved by the prospect of an end to disorder. That Michael Collins and Eamon de Valera had reached agreement augured well for the future peace of Ireland. Collins recommended the agreement at the Sinn Fein Ard Fheis on May 23rd, declaring its value to be, not so much that it secured unity in the Dail, but that it secured unity in the country.

Both men must have been confident of their grounds in reaching agreement and this could mean only one thing—that the Constitution of the Irish Free State did not cut across the principles to which de Valera and his followers held so strongly. The Constitution was the key to the Pact; but the key would only turn if the British Government did not file it down. The peace of Ireland was once more in the hands of the British Government and they had a magnificent opportunity to compromise on the form of the Constitution for the sake of internal peace in Ireland. But, of course, they did not. The last word had been said on December 6th 1921 and there was to be no going back on it. Inevitably this would destroy the Collins–de Valera Pact.

The Pact, in the view of the British Government, had aggravated the disturbances in the North. The Craig–Collins Agreement was dead. "Sir James Craig had made a great effort to help," Churchill said, "but after the de Valera–Collins Pact he had gone over to the other side. Sir James Craig had been willing to go to great lengths and while he could not stand for unity he would resign rather than stand in its way." This rather noble sentiment was hardly likely to be put to the test; the Unionist majority were right behind Craig.

Britain now had nineteen battalions in the North and there were 48,000 Specials. A request from Craig for arms and munitions for them was to be met. "I am bound to say that we could do no less having regard to the gathering of the forces from the South and the ferocious steps used against Ulster," declared Churchill, who was convinced that "had Collins taken strong steps and turned the Irregulars out of their Dublin strongholds the whole situation in Belfast would have improved, but having joined hands with avowed Republicans we could hardly wonder that the North had gone back to its extreme and violent position."

In a long interview with Lloyd George and Chamberlain, Collins and Griffith charged that the murders in Belfast were part of a deliberate war against Catholics. They talked, Lloyd George told the Cabinet, of the "extermination" of Catholics. The Prime Minister had countered with figures. Since December 6th 1921 80 Catholics had been killed and 188 wounded. "They are considerable figures," he admitted, "but they do not justify Mr Collins's description." Seventy-two Protestants also had been killed. Collins, who would talk of nothing else, claimed that "unless something were done the whole of Ireland would get out of hand".

In reply to this, Lloyd George quoted Lord Randolph Churchill's remark to Gladstone: "You call yourself a Government, whom do you govern?" and added the extraordinary comment: "You have handed over the government of Ireland to Erskine Childers." The tenacious opposition of Childers during the Treaty negotiations still rankled with Lloyd George, as indeed it did with Griffith, and the remark may have been meant to goad the Irish leader.

Collins and Griffith in their turn charged that Britain had "handed law and order over to Sir James Craig". They alleged, said Lloyd George, that the murders were committed by Specials in British pay. They urged Britain to proclaim martial law in Northern Ireland and to initiate an impartial enquiry.

The British Government were themselves not very happy about the Specials. Pointing out that they were not trained policemen, Griffith had said, "You might as well arm the East End," and Lloyd George told the Cabinet that the Fascisti in Italy was "a more exact analogy". He favoured an enquiry.

Collins, worried and exasperated, had said he was willing to give Ireland back "as a present" and that Lloyd George and de Valera should "share the government of Ireland between them", conveying, thought Chamberlain, that "one was as impossible as the other".

Pointedly, Chamberlain put it to Collins, "Supposing we were to give you this investigation would you be prepared to disavow the IRA in the Six Counties, to tell them and all persons affiliated to them that they were bound to obey the Northern Government pending the results of the Boundary Commission?" To this Collins had answered that he was prepared to carry out the Agreement with Craig of March 31st but not to "hold up the hands of the Ulster Government while Catholics were being murdered".

Shrewdly, Worthington-Evans hazarded that Collins was behind the IRA in the North but Chamberlain thought only that Collins "would not openly discourage them".

Almost as if he sympathised with Collins, Lloyd George told his colleagues: "He says, 'I can't leave these people unprotected with 48,000 Specials out against them.'" Unexpectedly, he came to the defence of the South a moment later in the discussion when

Churchill remarked that the temper of the English people was "high and rising", that the Government "would be told that they had been cheated by the South and that when loyal Ulstermen defended themselves we proposed an enquiry. The public would ask, 'What about an enquiry into the South?'" To this Lloyd George pointed out that one was a dominion and one was not.

Whatever may be said of Lloyd George's handling of the situation, indisputably he acknowledged the right that Ireland had won under the Treaty. If the measure of freedom was mean in the first place, it had been exactly prescribed, and he was not prepared to reduce it. As a dominion, Ireland was not to have courts of enquiry foisted on her.

In the North it was a different matter. Britain had accepted financial responsibility for law and order. Lloyd George was "profoundly concerned with the public presentation of the trouble when it came" and "not sure that Collins was not manoeuvring us into a position where our case was weak". The Prime Minister enlarged. Collins had challenged the British Government on the Ulster question. What was Britain's position? The victims of the first murders and, indeed, of most of the killings, were Catholics. No one had been punished, no enquiry made. Britain had armed 48,000 Protestants. "It would be a bad case," said Lloyd George simply, and added, "It is our business to maintain a stern impartiality between all races and creeds." He made clear the importance of public opinion in the dominions, in America and in the outside world. "If we broke on the issue of 'Republic versus Monarchy' we could count on solid support," he said, "but if we broke on Ulster we should get into the same atmosphere of doubtful responsibility as in the case of Reprisals."

The position as Lloyd George saw it was that the Irish had submitted a Constitution which was totally unacceptable, but any concession to the British on the issue of the Crown would mean the end of the Collins–de Valera Pact which Collins saw as the all-important factor in his task of reuniting the divided IRA. It was to his advantage to put pressure on Britain because of her implicit responsibility for the tragic events in Belfast. If he could force a showdown with Britain on Ulster, then any break would be held against her and the Crown problem would be discreetly shelved.

Subtle though he could be, it is very doubtful that Collins had worked out a plan such as Lloyd George envisaged. Collins was an Irishman to his bootstraps and he was distressed, even obsessed, by the plight of the minority in the North. He had accepted the Boundary Commission plan because Lloyd George had persuaded him that most of the Catholic-Nationalists would be removed from the ambit of the Belfast Parliament.

Lloyd George reminded his colleagues that "democratic communities were sentimental communities and that was why a policy of repression could not be carried through". It was rather late in the day to reach that conclusion, but the British Prime Minister was right. His solution was to take "such steps as would eliminate the Ulster issue and leave a clean issue of 'Republic versus British Empire'." He favoured a judicial enquiry. "Neither side would care to create evidence against itself and they might then be able for a time to stop the outrages and give time for the other issue to develop." He suggested that two judges, one Catholic and one Protestant, should conduct the enquiry.

Churchill did not see that an enquiry would help very much and suggested instead that part of Belfast be put under martial law.

"And the border too?" interjected Lloyd George.

"You have not enough troops for that," replied Churchill and added, "The border trouble starts in Belfast," and Birkenhead warned of trouble with the South if martial law were applied to the border.

On May 31st, Churchill spoke in the Commons on lines which he had indicated to the Cabinet the previous day. Griffith and Collins listened from the Strangers' Gallery. Earlier in the day, Collins had assured Churchill that his men had played no part in border incidents but, a few days later, believing he had been misled, Churchill sent the Irish leader an accusing telegram. "It must not be supposed that any part of the border can be kept in a continued state of disorder and alarm either by raids or by fire directed from your territory," warned Churchill. There had been a scattering of fire from the fort at Belleek in the direction of British troops who had used howitzers in reply. The tension then slackened, but the danger of British involvement remained acute.

Chamberlain was convinced that Collins and Griffith were using the situation in the North as a smoke screen for their republican Constitution, but he believed that "they had seen they must either quarrel with de Valera or with the British Government". Other members of the British Cabinet held more moderate views. Lloyd George himself explained that the attitude of the Irish representatives was that their position was made impossible by events in Ulster and Birkenhead thought they were bowing to their critics who could point to the fact that Britain was financing the Special Police as well as a large army. Churchill believed Sinn Fein and the IRA were deliberately making government impossible in the North and Sir Alfred Mond (later Lord Melchett) wondered whether Griffith and Collins were not paving the way for their own resignation.

H. A. L. Fisher thought the leaders from the South could not be expected to be co-operative while Britain failed to restore order in the North. This nettled Austen Chamberlain who wanted to know why Fisher "put Ulster in the Dock and ignored Southern Ireland". The British Cabinet were not sanguine of a settlement of the Constitution problem. Churchill declared emphatically that "We could not possibly give way on the question of requiring a declaration from all Members of the Coalition Government. With regard to the election itself, it would be better to wait until we knew the composition of the elected parliament and the method of its election before denouncing it. The more the fear of renewed warfare was present to the minds of the electors, the more likely were they to go to the Polls and support the Treaty."

Balfour, Lord President of the Council, took a nobler line; he did not mind "the parliament being a very imperfect one, but it would be a real tragedy if in days to come Irishmen asserted that the Constitution of their country had been adopted by a Parliament which did not truly represent Ireland".

The speculative discussion in the Cabinet went on and on. Lloyd George did not think the Constitution could be revised in time for the election. A questionnaire had been sent to the Irish leaders. If their answers were unsatisfactory, there would be a break with

Britain, if, on the other hand, they were satisfactory, then they would break with de Valera. Churchill pointed out that in the latter case the Irish leaders "would be making no new concessions but simply reasserting their concurrence in the Treaty". He believed the Constitution could be modified within a few days. Birkenhead thought "the Irish leaders had known long ago that they would have to break with de Valera", that "the slow but inevitable course of events was at last forcing the issue". But he favoured less stringent demands for revision of the Constitution and Lloyd George pointed out—and none was in a better position to recognise it than he—that too often the Crown had represented repression in Ireland.

Griffith took the points raised in his stride. He was unexpectedly willing to amend the Constitution to suit the British interpretation of the Treaty.

The long argument had delayed publication of the Constitution until the morning of the general election. The electorate really had no opportunity to assess it and the vote for the Panel and other candidates could be no more than an expression of opinion for or against the Treaty.

Collins saw that his Pact with de Valera was doomed and it was for this reason that, two days before the election, he made his famous and contentious speech at Cork: "I am not hampered now by being on a platform where there are coalitionists, and I can make a straight appeal to you to vote for the candidate you think best of."

Although he found the speech disquieting, de Valera still believed that the panel arrangement was to stand and, following the election, he waited for his recall to the Dail Cabinet.

No summons came, nor did the Dail assemble, for the quick rush of events led, in less than a fortnight, to the attack on the Four Courts garrison.

6

ON JUNE 22nd, Field Marshal Sir Henry Wilson was assassinated in London by Commandant Reginald Dunne and Volunteer Joseph Sullivan who subsequently were hanged. These men carried out an ordered execution in exactly the same way that Collins's squad did on many occasions during the struggle with Britain, though whether it was Collins who ordered the killing is still a matter for some conjecture; what evidence there is certainly points to it. Even by a process of elimination it is difficult to see who else could have been responsible. At the time, the British Government blamed Rory O'Connor's men in the Four Courts but O'Connor stoutly denied that they had anything to do with it. If they had, they would have admitted it.

The volatile Collins was tormented by the frequent and futile murders of Catholics in the North. Throughout the discussion with British ministers he constantly reverted to them and seemed almost impatient of the Constitution issue. Again and again, he insisted that the onus was upon Britain to restore order. Of Craig he was deeply distrustful but it was Wilson, master of intrigue and long-standing enemy, whom he saw as the master-mind behind the trouble. Not only were the lives of co-religionists at stake but sharpened hatreds were alienating the two parts of Ireland when Collins's overwhelming ambition was to make them one. More-over, the risk of war on a north–south axis was growing and this would wreck the Treaty and set back Collins's plans to move step by step towards an even less trammelled Ireland.

Collins's great swings of mood at this time were indicative of the tremendous pressures he was under. Despite months of tolerant and conciliatory conduct, he seemed to make no headway with his adversaries in the anti-Treaty party, there was no healing of the break in the IRA and even his great friend, Harry Boland, who equally was de Valera's friend, had taken the other side. "It has come to this! Of all things it has come to this," he was to write to Boland in deep distress.[12]

"We appealed to the soldiers to avoid strife, to let the old feelings of brotherhood and solidarity continue," wrote Collins.[13] "We met and made advances over and over again to the politicians, standing out alone on the one fundamental point on which we owed our unquestioned duty to the people—that we must maintain for them the position of freedom they had secured. We could get no guarantee that we would be allowed to carry out that duty."

Of the Pact with de Valera he wrote, "It was a last effort to prevent the use of force by Irishmen against Irishmen. We refrained from opposing the anti-Treaty Party at the elections. We stood aside from political conflict, so that, so far as we were concerned, our opponents might retain the full number of seats which they held in the previous Dail. And I undertook, with the approval of the Government, that they should hold four out of the nine offices in the new Ministry. They calculated that in this way they would have the same position in the new Dail as in the old. But their calculations were upset by the people themselves, and they then dropped all pretence of representing the people and turned definitely against them."

For months he had resisted the pressure of the British Government to take action against the recalcitrant Executive forces. Then he had come up against a blank wall of opposition to a Constitution which, over-optimistically it must be conceded, had seemed to him to offer a bridge across the seismic chasm which the shock waves of the Treaty had sliced through Ireland. And in the North the British Government made no effective move to halt the onslaught against the Catholic-Nationalist minority.

Collins may well have seen the removal of Sir Henry Wilson, whose malignant influence he felt certain was a powerful abrasive in the North, as a first step towards breaking out of the whole imbroglio and resorted, for the last time, to the method he had been forced to employ to destroy Ireland's enemies in the past. If this was so, he was letting an obsession get the better of him. Wilson had played an important part in organising the Specials in Belfast and, according to Thomas Jones, had attempted to buy surplus armaments, including aeroplanes and bombs, from the Disposals Board,[14] but devious though he was, he was too rigidly cast in the military mould to think of inciting the rabble of Belfast to murder. Collins himself had been underhand, deceiving the British Government, Griffith and perhaps even himself in his efforts to protect the minority in the North. It can be argued that the IRA units and their arms which Liam Lynch and he sent to the North merely aggravated the disturbances.

News of Wilson's death shocked the British Cabinet, who were shown by police chief Colonel Carter the actual guns used and documents discovered on Reginald Dunne. They were in no doubt that the Four Courts garrison had conspired to assassinate Wilson, and Churchill was deputed to draft a letter to Collins, as Chairman of the Provisional Government, in which it was stated that the ambiguous position of the IRA could no longer be ignored. "Still less", ran the letter, signed by Lloyd George, "can Mr Rory O'Connor be permitted to remain with his followers and his arsenal in open rebellion in the heart of Dublin in possession of the Courts of Justice, organising and sending out from the centre enterprises of murder, not only in the area of your Government, but also in the six Northern Counties and in Great Britain." The British Government had a right "to expect that the necessary action will be taken by your Government without delay". Lloyd George offered to place artillery at the disposal of the Provisional Government. In the Commons next day, Churchill even more trenchantly declared that if the occupation of the Four Courts were not brought to an end, the British Government would regard the Treaty as formally violated. Collins, already occupied with plans for securing the freedom of Dunne and Sullivan, was not impressed. Churchill could do his own dirty work, he commented savagely.

In their weekly report on Revolutionary Organisations in the United Kingdom, British Intelligence stated that Wilson's murder had caused "surprise and alarm in Sinn Fein circles". The extreme section "secretly expressed satisfaction", but "more moderate sections fear a revulsion of feeling on the part of the British people . . ." There had been raids on thirty known persons but with little result.

Arthur Griffith publicly declared his detestation of the deed: "Whether the assassination of Sir Henry Wilson was an act of private vengeance or had a pseudo-political aspect, I do not know. But it is a fundamental principle of civilised government that the assassination of a political opponent cannot be justified or condoned."

On June 26th, the day of Churchill's fulmination in the Commons, the second episode occurred which was to have a climactic impact on the course of events. Men from the Four Courts, led by Leo Henderson, the army Executive's "Director of Belfast Boycott", raided a garage to seize vehicles for use in the North. Troops from Beggar's Bush, the National Army H.Q., moved in and arrested Henderson. Almost at once, General J. J. O'Connell, the National Army Deputy Chief of Staff, was kidnapped and taken into the Four Courts, and this precipitated the decision of the Provisional Government to clear Rory O'Connor's men from them. Griffith presided over a meeting of Ministers of the Dail Cabinet and Provisional Government and National Army leaders, who came to the conclusion that an ultimatum should be delivered and that artillery should be borrowed from the British to carry out an effective attack if the Four Courts garrison proved obdurate.

The decision came as a relief to Griffith, who had seen from the beginning that the Government could not govern while an armed force occupied public buildings in the capital and anarchy held sway in the countryside. At the meeting he was restrained, allowing the others to come round to his way of thinking. For Collins the decision meant disappointment and sadness, but it seemed probable that the fight, if fight there were, would not go beyond Dublin, perhaps even beyond the Four Courts, for there had been a split in the army Executive itself, with Liam Lynch in particular taking a much more moderate line. Collins hoped that Lynch would in the end be moved by loyalty to the Irish Republican Brotherhood to exercise a restraining influence: he had already helped defuse the explosive situation in Limerick. But, unknown to Collins, at the last minute Lynch had promised full support to the Four Courts men. Collins was to be confronted, after all, by a united Executive.

At the fateful meeting the threat of the British Government to take action—it had nearly done so—was hardly mentioned, but the heavy pressure applied after Wilson's killing must have been in the minds of them all. Collins knew that the aim of the army Executive was to inveigle the British into armed intervention as a means of reuniting the IRA. The last thing Collins wanted was the return of British military rule. For him the Treaty represented a political beachhead from which a gradual offensive could be mounted and he had no intention of losing it.

To the extent that Wilson's assassination had produced a danger of British action, with inevitably another long struggle and the loss of all that had been won, it was a factor in the decision to oust O'Connor and his friends from the Four Courts, but the conviction of the anti-Treaty party, which has persisted—understandably enough—that the Provisional Government acted at the behest of the British Government, was ill-grounded. Griffith himself, who felt in no position to scorn the attitude of the British Government, told P. S. O'Hegarty, "When the garage was occupied, we nearly decided to move; but when O'Connell was kidnapped, we did decide to move and the order was given. Then came Churchill's speech and we wavered again. Some of us wanted to cancel it. But we said that we had either to go on or to abdicate, and finally we went on."[15]

Within two days, the beleaguered garrison in the Four Courts had been forced to surrender and the battle switched to the block of buildings in O'Connell Street which were also in the possession of the Executive forces. Again the borrowed British artillery compelled surrender, though most of the defenders had already gone. It was a costly victory the National Army won in Dublin. A vast explosion had ripped the dome off the lovely Four Courts building and destroyed the records of centuries. O'Connell Street was in a shambles and Cathal Brugha had died an indomitable death. Of him, Collins wrote, "When many of us are forgotten, Cathal

Brugha will be remembered."[16] It was a generous statement from the man whom Brugha had excoriated in the Dail.

Meanwhile, Liam Lynch had been arrested in Dublin during the Four Courts battle and released on the instructions of General Mulcahy because, like Collins, Mulcahy believed that Lynch would work for peace. But, in a statement issued from Mallow, Lynch made it clear that as Chief of Staff of the Executive forces he had every intention of resisting the Provisional Government and its troops. He was to prove the most obstinate opponent of all.

A few days later, on July 6th, the Provisional Government also issued a call to arms and, on July 12th, a Council of War was appointed. Collins became Commander-in-Chief of the National Army. He seemed to have thrown off the despondency of recent months, his vast reservoirs of energy seemed to fill again, and prevarication gave way to forthright action. No longer bogged down in politics, he set himself to his rôle of military commander with all his old verve.

In the next weeks the National Army commanders campaigned with overwhelming success through the countryside. They had several advantages: the big guns which had dominated the struggle in Dublin were employed again in Limerick, and possession of coastal shipping enabled them to make landings at Fenit, Cork and elsewhere. Generally, too, the Executive forces fought with less heart, not because they lacked either courage or conviction, but because their aim was simply to try to prevent the Treaty from being worked. They had not wished to push their opposition to the stage of life or death enmity if they could avoid it. Again, they did not enjoy the support of the people as they had done in Black and Tan days. This was disheartening. There was spirited opposition in places, but mostly the Executive troops abandoned the barracks they had held and destroyed them.

As yet there was little of the bitterness that followed the death of Collins and in many places the skirmishing was almost lighthearted. But lives were lost, lives valuable to Ireland, and there was much destruction, blamed very often upon Erskine Childers, who had become the Provisional Government's *bête noire*, though he was simply a propagandist and even in that rôle showed himself capable of paying a just tribute to the enemy.

On July 31st Harry Boland was killed by a trigger-happy soldier who may or may not have believed that Boland was attempting to escape after his arrest at a hotel in Skerries. Although they were far apart, geographically and cerebrally, Collins and de Valera shared a moment of grief.

"I'd send a wreath but I suppose they'd return it torn up," Collins wrote forlornly to his betrothed Kitty Kiernan.[17] He had on his mind, too, the fate of Dunne and Sullivan, destined to die on the scaffold on August 10th. He had been able to work out no way of rescuing them. Several plans had proved impracticable, even his own rather wild scheme to have a distinguished Briton captured and held as a hostage.

The war went on. Collins never lost touch with his friends on the other side. Always he hoped they would see reason and accept his terms, but he would not yield to them any longer. While they resisted he meant to drive them hard but never to use more force than was needed. At least he had the satisfaction of knowing that in Belfast the violence had almost ceased. Churchill opined that this "might be due to the fact that the gunmen are engaged in the South".[18] Some in the South attributed the peace to the removal of Wilson from the scene. Churchill had also remarked "increasing signs that justice was being meted out to Protestants and Catholics equally",[19] and that was a more likely explanation than either of the other two. The spectacle of civil war in the South had probably served also to damp the ardour of extremists on both sides.

Even now, Collins found time to look to the future and he proposed to send a delegation of officers to Switzerland to study the Swiss army system, believing that it could be a model for the Irish National Army. On August 9th he set out on a tour of inspection, but three days later Arthur Griffith died and Collins hastened back to Dublin from Tralee. Preoccupied with military matters, he had left the political sphere to Griffith, to Cosgrave who acted for Griffith during his last illness, and to the rising Kevin O'Higgins. Griffith's death stunned him, the more so because the older, more experienced and, it must be admitted, more honourable man had for some time been out of sympathy with the brilliant but sometimes wayward Collins.

After the funeral Collins sorrowfully resumed his tour. He must have wondered how many more victims the civil war would claim, for Griffith had worn himself out in the service of Ireland. Collins himself was unwell, and sometimes pessimistic about his own chances of survival. He wept for his friends. On his tour of the South he carried out his self-imposed tasks with customary thoroughness.

In the valley of Beal na mBlath, shortly after visiting his native Sam's Cross, his party was ambushed. One man was slightly wounded, Collins was killed. It was August 22nd 1922.

Even about the death of this legendary man mystery has been built up. The bullet which hit him was probably a richochet. That's not important—Collins was dead. What he might have achieved does not matter now, for much has been achieved by other men. But his dream of reuniting the two parts of Ireland has been overlaid by fifty years of prejudice and outbreaks of violence which have scarred the border even deeper into the soil of Ireland.

JAMES CRAIG
(LORD CRAIGAVON)

I

THE RESOLUTE personality of James Craig of Ulster dominated the Treaty negotiations of 1921, though he took no direct part in them. Both the British and the Irish negotiators wanted a united Ireland with a single parliament. But Craig, leader of the Ulster Unionists, would not have it, and he got his way. Lloyd George's final ultimatum to the Irish plenipotentiaries—sign or war would be resumed—was highlighted dramatically by the two letters that he held aloft, both addressed to Craig.

"It is a bargain between Sinn Fein and the British Government?" demanded the British Prime Minister. "I have to communicate with Sir James Craig tonight. Here are the alternative letters which I have prepared, one enclosing the Articles of Agreement reached by His Majesty's Government and yourselves, the other telling Sir James Craig that the Sinn Fein representatives refuse allegiance and refuse to come within the Empire and that I have therefore no proposals to make to him. If I send this letter it is war—and war within three days. Which of the two letters am I to send? That is the question you have to decide."

The plenipotentiaries signed and Mr Geoffrey Shakespeare (later Sir Geoffrey), for whom the train at Euston had been delayed and a destroyer held to rush him across the Irish Sea, sped on his mission. Sir James Craig and his Unionist Party had flatly refused to be part of a united Ireland; they were a minority party dominating four counties and retaining a grip on two more. How was it then that they exerted such leverage on the British Cabinet? How was it that the plenipotentiaries allowed themselves to be dictated to? Only Collins held out on this score. "You have our conditional agreement on the one side," he told Lloyd George. "It is just as easy to get Craig's conditional agreement on the other."

Griffith backed him up. Craig should be asked: "If Sinn Fein accepts the Government conditions for the creation of the Irish Free State will Ulster accept unity?" But Griffith spoke from a crumbling position, for he had made that fateful, too-easily misinterpreted promise to accept the British proposals for Ulster.

The Treaty applied to all thirty-two counties, but the Six Counties had the right to opt out and there was no doubt that they would do so. Only the meagre Boundary Commission provision remained of the plenipotentiaries' high hopes for a united Ireland. That was to come to nothing, and so for fifty years Ireland has been partitioned and the end of the border looks further away than ever. In fifty years nothing has changed.

Craig was the one man who at that critical time might conceivably have been able to change what has proved a tragic course of events, but there was never the slightest possibility that he would. Unionism is a stubborn doctrine and, recognising that all political doctrines arise from self-interest, a logical one.

Seventh of nine children, James Craig was born into a wealthy home in County Down on January 8th 1871. He was, therefore, almost the same age as Arthur Griffith who was born in March of the same year. By his own efforts, his father, the son of a bailiff, had amassed a fortune in the distillery trade and, like so many self-made men, saw no reason why his children should not make their way in the world as he had.

Like Eamon de Valera, Craig walked several miles to school, in his case a preparatory school. At the age of eleven he was sent to Merchiston Castle in Edinburgh. A cheerful, average boy, he enjoyed sport and excelled at nothing, though his masters recognised qualities of character which were to evidence themselves throughout his life. The family lived at Craigavon, the large, rather ugly house from which he was to take his title, but frequently visited Tyrella on Dundrum Bay about twenty miles south of Belfast. There he spent much of his time on his father's farm and acquired a knowledge of agriculture that was to stand him in good stead.

Leaving school at sixteen, he worked first in an office in Belfast, then in a London stockbroker's office, after which he set up his own stockbroker's business in Belfast. For eight years he went about his business with success, spent his leisure moments sailing and did not particularly interest himself in politics—he was not inherently a political animal. His appearance did not suggest that an astute mind lay behind it. Friendly and gregarious, he had the cheerful, sanguine countenance of a farmer, the features heavy, a high-bridged nose prominent over a thick moustache, and unusually large ears. Men tended to under-rate him, were taken by surprise when his shrewdness or his humour revealed themselves.

As a boy he had been half-inclined towards a military career and in January 1900, soon after the outbreak of the Boer War, volunteered for service with the Royal Irish Rifles. Seconded to the Imperial Yeomanry, he was a good and popular officer and a brave soldier. Taken prisoner, he elected to march with his men instead of riding with the other officers to the prison camp two hundred miles away. The march took a month.

Earlier, a splinter from an exploding gun had pierced an eardrum and in the prison camp the ear became very painful. His captors, unable to help, chivalrously put him across the border into Portuguese territory. On his recovery, though his ear troubled him for the rest of his life, he became a transport officer and his remarkable powers of organisation were amply demonstrated. Then, laid low with dysentery, he was invalided home in June 1901. Craig was not beaten and a few months later he sailed again for South Africa. This time he was not needed. The war, which the English had regarded almost as a joke in the beginning, but which had cost them dear in lives and money and dearer still in national prestige, at last was ended.

Captain James Craig did not re-open his broker's office. During his absence his father had died, making him a wealthy man. He could have led a life of leisure, but that was not his way: he needed a career which would stretch his resources and he began to think of a political life. The war had given him an awareness of Empire and pride in Ulster's part in it. Throughout his life Craig was first an Ulsterman then a Briton; he never thought of himself as an Irishman.

6

His brother's successful candidature at a by-election gave Craig his first opportunity to gain political experience and soon afterwards, in March 1903, the Unionists selected him to contest North Fermanagh. The seat was won narrowly by the candidate of a small land reform group led by Thomas Russell, but Craig impressed the electorate and the Unionist Party.

In 1905, at the age of thirty-four, James Craig married. He was then carefully nursing his home constituency of East Down, ready for the coming election, and his English bride found herself working in a politico-religious atmosphere such as she had never imagined. But she made the shock adjustments quickly and it proved that Craig, like de Valera, was to be supported through a difficult career by a splendid wife.

At the general election in January 1906, Craig won East Down from the sitting member, a Russellite. His purpose, St John Ervine tells us,[1] was "to settle the land question on equitable terms, to resist Home Rule, to secure better conditions of life for agricultural labourers, to knit the Empire more closely by means of preferential tariffs, and to maintain the Protestant religion in the place where it prevailed in Ireland. He was opposed to sectarian education." In short, it was the platform of an honest man with an eye to social injustice who, on fundamental issues, believed absolutely in the religious and political faiths into which he was born.

For some months before the election he had been a member of the standing committee of the Ulster Unionist Council, a body formed in December 1904 to bring under one umbrella the numerous Unionist associations. Its object was to guard the link with Britain and to stamp out any sign of life in the dormant dragon of Home Rule.

From the thin ranks of the Conservatives, decimated in that 1906 election, Craig had more opportunities to make his mark than might otherwise have been the case. He quickly became an adroit parliamentarian and his wit proved as quick and as sharp as that of the Nationalists who, deceived by his bucolic burliness, tried to bait him. The Nationalists themselves were in a difficult position, for their hopes of Home Rule were pinned on the Liberals, whose majority was so massive that they could afford to snap their fingers at Irish support and seemed to care less for the Home Rule cause than once they had. Some of their leaders, indeed, had expressed opposition to it, but Campbell-Bannerman, the Prime Minister, had publicly declared his belief in self-government for Ireland. Craig and his Unionist colleagues were uneasy but the Liberal Government concentrated upon bringing in a plethora of social legislation and the Home Rule pot simmered quietly without threatening to come to the boil.

As the Liberals were in a reforming mood, Craig battled to right some of the wrongs in Ireland. The schools troubled him deeply. Such heating as there was usually was paid for by the teachers from piddling salaries, or the children themselves heaved turf to school. Children sat in cold, overcrowded classrooms and were expected to do the school cleaning. Five times up to 1911, Craig tried to put through a Bill to improve these conditions; each time he was baulked. His campaign to improve the Poor Law also got nowhere.

He was trying to help the whole of Ireland, not just Ulster, but got unexpectedly little support from the Nationalists. They had bigger fish to fry, but the time to fry them was not yet. Meanwhile, they intended to keep in with the Liberals. In any case, they did not see eye to eye with Craig on education. Though a staunch Presbyterian, he was not anti-Catholic, and was opposed to schools run on sectarian lines. He believed that children should mix from an early age if religious barriers were ever to be broken down, but the Catholics, unfortunately, did not agree, nor do they today.

By 1909, though he persisted in his personal crusades, Craig had begun to watch the Home Rule pot more closely. Campbell-Bannerman had resigned, and died shortly afterwards. Asquith was Prime Minister and the zealous and ambitious Lloyd George had gone to the Exchequer. Arrogantly the House of Lords—but for whom Gladstone's Second Home Rule Bill would have been passed in 1893—had been blocking Liberal measures passed by the House of Commons. The Liberals were up in arms and their chance came when, in November 1909, the Lords rejected the Finance Bill—as Lloyd George (who didn't much care for the aristocracy anyway and who had raised their income tax to 1s 2d in the pound, throwing in surtax of 6d in the pound for good measure) hoped they would.

Asquith went to the country early in 1910 and was returned, but with ranks so depleted that he could survive only with the support of the Irish Nationalists. The price of that support was a Home Rule Bill. But the big issue for the Liberals was to overcome the permanent nuisance that the large Conservative majority in the Lords represented. On the death of Edward VII, soon after the election, party warfare had to be decently put in cold storage for a time, but before the year was out Parliament was again dissolved. King George V required the electorate's confirmation of his own consent to create a large number of Liberal peers if the Lords resisted reform. The electorate returned Liberals and Conservatives in almost equal numbers, so the victors were really Redmond's Irish Nationalists.

At each election Craig increased his majority. He was now a redoubtable politician and at Westminster it was thought that he would be given office once the Conservatives came to power. He played the political game hard but straight and, although a master of obstruction, was seldom out of order and asked innumerable, always pertinent questions. He was never disconcerted by interruption, criticism or derision.

Having completed his apprenticeship, he was ready to put his massive frame and his big mind in the way of Home Rule, which now looked menacing to the Irish Unionist Party. The fact that its introduction was a political expedient, with nothing of the honesty that prompted Gladstone's earlier crusade, aggravated the offence in Unionist eyes. Except as an aside, Asquith had not even mentioned Home Rule in the recent election campaign. But since Gladstone's two failures the possibility that something like this would happen had been in the back of Unionist minds and they had kept their resistance machinery under dust covers. The Ulster Unionist Council had knitted together the tangle of clubs which had sprung up in 1893 and had become a policy-making body working closely with the Irish Unionist Alliance, which covered the other three provinces, and the Unionist Defence League in London. A powerful ally, providing a mystical impetus, was the

Orange Order, founded in 1795; in its early days it was disreputable, and did not attract respectable members until 1885, when Gladstone became imbued with the ambition to cure the running sore of Ireland by giving her political independence.

The Parliament Act of 1911 clipped the arrogant wings of the Lords, which they sullenly preferred to sharing their gilded cage with a horde of new Liberal birds, and cleared the way for a Home Rule Bill. The new measure came at just the right time for the Irish Nationalists, who wore a nineteenth-century left-over air and were uneasily aware of a new spirit in their homeland which they did not really comprehend. Their success at this juncture seemed to assure them the support of the electorate for a long time to come.

In July 1911 Sir Edward Carson, a Southern Unionist, became leader of the Unionists in the House of Commons. A tall, powerful man, he had made his name as a barrister by ruthlessly tearing down the scintillating façade of Oscar Wilde. Like the other great advocates of his time, he had much of the actor in his make-up and this he carried into his political life, though as yet he had made no indelible mark. It was Craig who perceived in this darkly moody man, at once ascetic and temperamental, complex beyond even self-analysis, exactly the qualities needed to lead Unionists in resistance to repeal of the Union. That resistance inevitably would have its core in Ulster, but Carson had had little to do with the North and temperamentally seemed to have much more in common with the southern Irish. He seemed an unlikely choice to lead the Ulster people with their hectic emotions and lapidary Protestantism, but Craig was right; Carson burned his way into their confidence and affections. Craig himself was to prove the ideal adjutant, providing impeccable staffwork so that his leader's energies were not dissipated.

But first Carson wanted a sign. "What I am anxious about is to satisfy myself that the people really mean to resist. I am not for a mere game of bluff and unless men are prepared to make great sacrifices which they clearly understand the talk of resistance is no use."[2]

Craig's answer was to organise a massive demonstration of support. On September 23rd 50,000 men marched from the centre of Belfast to Craigavon, Craig's home, three miles away. They represented Orange lodges and Unionist clubs from the whole of the province. They were not from the land-owning classes but were ordinary working people shrewd, practical, obstinate people, moved by fears of religious discrimination and economic disadvantage.

These two strands were entwined but the one was much older than the other. There had been a time when both Catholics and Presbyterians were trammelled by the established Church and had drawn uneasily together in a common ambition for independence. The Society of United Irishmen of the late eighteenth century had included both sects and almost all the leaders of the rebellion of 1798 had been Presbyterians. After the Act of Union the industrial revolution reached Ireland and, while the South remained largely agrarian, great commercial interests became centred on Belfast. Strictures remained on the freedom of Catholics, and the Presbyterians, no longer "have nots", tended to side with the "haves". Catholic emancipation in 1829 set the Protestants on the defensive. Even before this, in rural areas where too many people contended for a living from too little land, it was inevitable that rivalries should follow the historical line of weakness, religious antagonism. Lawless action resulted and since lawlessness is better carried out clandestinely, secret societies came into being, Protestant and Catholic.

Harking back to Protestant William's victory over James II at the Battle of the Boyne, the Protestants felt that this demonstration of their supremacy should be forever remembered, and to William's "pious and immortal" memory they dedicated the Orange Society. Much more significant battles have become footnotes in history; the consequences of the Battle of the Boyne fill a bloody page. When the first Orange procession was held, on July 12th 1797, the demonstration was scorned by the Presbyterians whose sympathies lay with the United Irishmen. Not they but the episcopalian Church of Ireland provided the first members of the Orange Society, but soon the movement began to attract others, especially the tenant farmer class. But it was not until the first threat of a Home Rule Bill, by which time the early impetus of the Society had been lost, that the movement became respectable and metamorphosed into a political institution of the middle-classes. Their creed was Unionism and the Orange Society, with its atavistic allegiance to the long-dead William and its glowing expression of Protestant righteousness, provided an ideal framework.

The Ulsterman's fear was not of his Catholic neighbour but of the distant foreign power, the Vatican, that power which historically had transcended even the divine right of kings. Not the Pope's religious convictions but his dominance over prelate and priest and through them of an entire population was the Ulster Protestant's apprehension. He had to go back no more than two or three centuries for evidence that his fears were justified, and anyway there was a suspiciously large number of priests in Ireland. Let a parliament be set up in Dublin and its ministers would be mere puppets of the Pope. Home Rule would be Rome Rule, he did not doubt.

If that were not enough to deter any good Ulster Protestant from breaking the Union bond, there was the economic factor. It was Ulster, or at any rate Belfast, that had industry and relative prosperity. The rest of the country was primitively rural and the poor were everywhere. Obviously the burden of taxation would fall upon Ulster. Ulster's industry would have to subsidise the indigent rural communities.

When he addressed the great assembly in the grounds of Craigavon, Carson hit the right note. His was a performance of great histrionic ability with dramatic silences and then intimate, conspiratorial words. He cheerfully accepted the grave responsibility his audience were putting upon him. "I now enter into a compact with you and every one of you," he told them, and brought God in on their side. Together they would defeat "the most nefarious conspiracy that has ever been hatched against a free people". He gave them the course they must follow. They had to be prepared, not merely to reject Home Rule, but "to become responsible for the government of the Protestant Province of Ulster".

Carson's thinking was, therefore, five years in advance of Pearse,

Clarke and their friends in Dublin. A small committee, the Commission of Five, comprising Craig and four others, was appointed to work out with Carson the constitution for a provisional government which was to have "due regard for the interests of Loyalists in other parts of Ireland". This came as something of a shock to the Liberal Government but Churchill made light of it. "I dare say when the worst comes to the worst we shall find that civil war evaporates in uncivil words," he declared in a speech at Dundee and promised a Home Rule Bill almost at once. But he was jolted out of his insouciance when in February 1912 he arrived in Belfast to address a meeting arranged by the Ulster Liberal Association. He was given a hostile reception by the Protestants, a genial one by the Roman Catholics who, later, with less justification than they believed, reviled him. The meeting, at Celtic Park football ground, was a washout both metaphorically and in fact.

2

AT WESTMINSTER, as the introduction of the Home Rule Bill was awaited, political tempers began to rise and the Conservatives, angered by the means used to force through the reform of the Lords, resentful of the purchase of Irish Nationalist votes and having an affinity with the land-owning Irish Loyalists, supported their Unionist colleagues to the point of treason. At Easter, Bonar Law, the Conservative leader whose own roots were in Ulster, spoke at another huge meeting in Belfast. He hinted then what he was to put in plain terms a few months later, that even force was permissible if the Liberals forced Home Rule through. If Bonar Law was throwing democracy to the winds it was only because the Conservatives thought the Liberal ploys smacked of chicanery rather than democracy.

To Craig the idea of hiving off Ireland—although when it came the Home Rule Bill was little more than a Local Government Bill—was the first step in the disintegration of the Empire. In a pamphlet, *The Lesson of Craigavon*, published by the Ulster Unionist Council, he advocated less drastic changes.

"If necessary tear out Dublin Castle. If necessary, sweep away the Viceregal Court—at present partisan—and let us have what is really wanted in Ireland, a Chief Secretary having the courage of his convictions and with a continuity of policy, the completion of the Land Purchase scheme, further provision for the housing of the labouring classes, technical education and the Department of Agriculture." But justice, the police force and taxation must remain in Imperial hands. "Why," he asked, "should Ulster be asked to place in jeopardy the position she has manfully won for herself by industry and enterprise, by patience and perserverance?"

St John Ervine holds that this policy remained the lodestar of Craig's political career. He was highly critical of the Roman Catholic Church, not from any innate hostility but because he firmly believed that, by actively discouraging Catholics to mingle with Protestants from the cradle to the grave, they inhibited integration. Especially he deplored the cherished separateness of their schools, a condition existing today for reasons which seem excellent to the Catholic bishops but which inevitably perpetuate inimical barriers.

Demonstrations continued in Ulster and Craig made numerous speeches in England in an effort to rouse the people to fend off the Liberal blow to the Empire. They remained apathetic. By June 1912 the Bill had reached the Committee stage and it was then that Agar-Robartes, a Cornish Liberal, proposed as an amendment the exclusion of the four counties in which the Protestant Unionists had large majorities, Antrim, Armagh, Down and Londonderry. The Unionists had been resisting Home Rule for Ireland as a whole, although there were vague thoughts of partition in some minds. Doubtfully they decided to support the amendment but its rejection saved them some embarrassment. Nevertheless, minds began to turn upon the idea of giving both sides what they wanted—by separating them. Half a province could not impose a permanent veto on the nation, said Churchill. "Do they ask for a parliament of their own, or do they wish to remain here?" he questioned. Asquith derided the idea of splitting Ireland into parts but later talked ambiguously of not allowing "a permanent and insuperable bar to Irish unity". To Redmond, any idea of a divided Ireland was "an abomination and a blasphemy".

In Belfast there were clashes between Protestants and Catholics, and Catholic workmen were hounded from the shipyards. Sectarian strife threatened to flare dangerously and Carson was anxious to divert energies and emotions away from the merely religious plane. He needed a symbol and found it in the Covenant, a solemn pledge on the model of the old Scottish Covenant. Craig was in his organisational element. Bands and torchlight processions whipped up enthusiasm. There was a great rally in Belfast's Ulster Hall on the eve of the great day and the climax was reached on

Ulster Day, September 28th 1912, when, after services in the Protestant churches of a muted Belfast, Sir Edward Carson signed the Covenant at the City Hall. Thousands of men added their signatures beneath his, pledging themselves "throughout this time of threatened calamity to stand by one another in defending for ourselves and our children our cherished position of equal citizenship in the United Kingdom, and in using all means which may be found necessary to defeat the present conspiracy to set up a Home Rule Parliament in Ireland". They further pledged to refuse to recognise the authority of any such parliament. The women, who were not quite such equal citizens, signed a declaration in support of their men. In every town and village in the province of Ulster signing ceremonies took place. Altogether nearly half a million people signed either the Covenant or the Women's Declaration. Asquith's Government at last realised that the Ulster Unionists were not bluffing.

In the Commons on November 13th Craig assailed the Government. They were to be regarded not as a government but as a caucus led by rebels. He warned them sombrely, "Although you may do your worst here in this House, thank God the North of Ireland will be more than a match for you." On New Year's Day 1913, with the approval of his friends in Belfast, Carson moved unavailingly that Ulster be excluded from the scope of the measure. Despite scenes of indignation and disorder in the House of Commons, the Home Rule Bill was finally passed, by means of the guillotine, later in January. Much of the Bill was never debated. The Lords predictably threw it out.

On January 31st 1913 a carefully detailed draft plan for a provisional government was submitted by the special committee appointed by the Ulster Unionist Council. It even provided for a separate judiciary. Here was an exquisite paradox indeed: in order to protect their cherished Act of Union, the Ulster Unionists were prepared to establish their own rebel administration. They also set up their own army, the Ulster Volunteer Force, amalgamating into one organisation innumerable groups of volunteers from Orange Lodges all over the province who had been drilling and training ever since the big demonstration at Craigavon in

September 1911. Such "unofficial" military activity was quite lawful; any two Justices of the Peace could sanction it in their area provided that the object was to maintain the Constitution of the United Kingdom and to protect the rights and liberties of its citizens. There was no denying that the aim of the Volunteers was to do exactly these things as the Justices of the Peace, Unionists almost to a man, were delighted to recognise.

Rifle clubs provided a splendid cover for training in the use of firearms, and rifles in ever increasing numbers began to be imported into Ulster. The British Government looked upon the Ulster Volunteer Force as something of a joke, but the Ulstermen were well organised and, with plenty of ex-army officers and NCOs to help, drilled assiduously and with determination. In July, recommended by no less a person than Lord Roberts, Sir George Richardson was appointed Commander-in-Chief.

No one admired the canniness of the Ulstermen more than their adversaries in the South, who quickly recognised that the Government could hardly quibble if they also set up a volunteer force. In November the Irish Volunteers came into being.

Craig meanwhile had been exceedingly active, stumping the country, soliciting support, but he still found time to organise yet another massive demonstration at Craigavon at which the formation of the UVF was officially announced. This followed the seizure of consignments of rifles which could have been imported legally but were smuggled in order to preserve secrecy. By now the Government saw rather less humour in the situation. In a letter to *The Times*, Lord Loreburn, former Lord Chancellor, who had earlier rejected any suggestion that part of Ireland should be excluded from the provision of a Home Rule Bill, pleaded for a conference at which a settlement could be negotiated. The alternative, as he saw it, was civil war. Overtures were made by several Liberal leaders but the Unionists would not countenance any proposal which would involved any form of rule from Dublin.

There seemed no way out. Asquith needed Redmond's support, while Redmond was well aware that if he weakened it would be the end of the Irish Parliamentary Party.

At an Ulster Unionist Council meeting on September 23rd the establishment of a provisional government in the event of Home Rule was approved and the following day a fund was started to take care of Volunteers or their dependants if casualties resulted. Within a few months over a million pounds was raised. There were splendid parades of Volunteers and hints from Carson that certain high-ranking army officers would throw in their lot with the Ulstermen if coercion were attempted.

This was one of many factors worrying King George V who, reluctant though he was to overstep the bounds of constitutional monarchy, was impelled to put his views to Asquith. He felt that a general election should decide the Home Rule issue. On his part, Asquith was trying not to involve the King. He played down the danger and urged the King not to contemplate forcing a dissolution. Still apprehensive, the King pointed out that soldiers were also citizens and that "by birth, religion and environment they might have strong feelings on the Irish question".[3] He wanted to know how Asquith intended to use the army. Again he pleaded for agreement by consent.

As always, Asquith was looking for the line of least resistance but no crack showed in the adamantine façades of either the Ulster Unionists or Redmond's Nationalists. A partition arrangement looked more and more tempting but he did not dare advocate it.

On March 9th 1914 he introduced an amendment to the Home Rule Bill, conceived by Lloyd George. This was an attempt to buy time. Each of the Ulster counties was to be permitted to exclude itself from the operation of the Home Rule Bill for six years at the end of which it would be brought in unless Parliament had decided otherwise in the meantime. Asquith had in mind that a general election would intervene "so that the electors of the United Kingdom can determine whether or not and to what extent the exclusion should be further continued or other provision made".[4] Had this amendment been accepted it would certainly have made an impact on the events of the next few years. Only four of the nine counties would certainly have opted out. Tyrone and Fermanagh would have gone to the South and the position would have been exactly that which, Lloyd George suggested to the Irish plenipotentiaries in December 1921, would be produced by the Boundary Commission.

Dubiously Redmond gave the proposal his blessing. "All that we can be expected to do is to give our acquiescence to the solution as the price of peace,"[5] Redmond wrote to Asquith. But the Unionists vehemently opposed it. Carson's witty "We do not want a sentence of death with a stay of execution for six years" summed up their feelings.

At this juncture the Liberal Government began to take a much harder line. Asquith told the King[6] that police reports suggested the "possibility of attempts on the part of the 'Volunteers' to seize by *coups de main* police and military barracks and depots of arms and ammunition". Alarmed, the Cabinet had appointed a small committee, whose members were Lord Crewe, Birrell, Churchill, Seely and Sir John Simon, "to look at all aspects and report". Asquith was also apprehensive that the House of Lords might bring in limiting amendments to the Army Annual Bill, "such as prohibition of the employment of regular troops in Ulster". In a speech at Bradford on March 14th, Churchill charged the self-elected Provisional Government of Ulster with engaging in a treasonable conspiracy and warned there were "worse things than bloodshed even on an extended scale", a precept which Eamon de Valera with rather more justification was to follow in days to come.

Sir Arthur Paget, Commander-in-Chief of the Forces in Ireland, received orders to reinforce guards on arms and stores depots at Carrickfergus, Enniskillen, Armagh and Omagh which were considered vulnerable, and was summoned to London. Paget was reluctant to provoke trouble by the movement of troops, of which there were 23,000 in Ireland, 9,000 of them in Ulster. Disregarding Paget's advice and that of Sir John French, Chief of the Imperial General Staff, the Cabinet sub-committee appointed Sir Nevil Macready, who enjoyed a reputation as a trouble-shooter, to command the Belfast district and gave him authority over the police who were scattered in small detachments over the countryside. Orders were given to move troops from the South into the province and, on March 17th, the First Lord of the Admiralty told the Cabinet[7] that "the forthcoming practice of the 1st Battle

Squadron would take place at Lamlash". Two days later the squadron was ordered from Spanish waters to Lamlash, Isle of Arran, intimidatingly close to Belfast. More ships were made available to protect coastguard stations and to transport troops if required. A cruiser was to be stationed at Carrickfergus and two or three destroyers were to be sent to the south of Ireland.

These moves were seen as provocative, as evidence of the Government's intention to compel Home Rule upon Ulster, by force of arms if necessary, and the Ulster Volunteer Force was prepared to fight. The UVF had been on a war footing for some time and had imported a number of Army Reserve officers to take direct charge of units. A detailed plan of action had been prepared. Civil war seemed perilously near and there was no certainty that it would be confined to Ireland.

A vote of censure on the Government was moved by Bonar Law on March 19th. Carson, well-briefed by Sir Henry Wilson, castigated the Government Front Bench. "Let the Government come and try conclusions with us in Ulster," he challenged. "Ulster is on the best of terms with the Army." And, indeed, Paget's main fear was that some of his officers would refuse to move against Ulster. He was able to secure permission to exempt from duty those officers whose homes were in Ulster. Any other officers who objected to their orders could resign. Their resignations would not be accepted and they would be dismissed. This was not quite what Paget had been told—which was that objectors would not be allowed to resign but would be dismissed if they disobeyed orders. Paget also talked in terms of a military operation, although only precautionary measures had been decided upon. The plan was to take possession of public buildings in Belfast but not to use force unless the Ulstermen did so first.

Brigadier Hubert Gough and a number of other officers exercised the right of choice given them by Paget and tendered their resignations, anticipating subsequent dismissal. There were likely to be many more of them. They were suspended and haled to the War Office where there appeared to be as much confusion as in Ireland. When it was realised that the officers had not "mutinied" but had been given a choice, the whole thing was smoothed over, but Gough, with great canniness and persistence, extracted from Sir John French and Colonel Seely, Secretary of State for War, a document which not only authorised Gough to inform the officers concerned that the Army Council were satisfied the incident had been a misunderstanding, but gave an assurance that although the Government retained the right to use the forces of the Crown to maintain law and order, they had "no intention whatever of taking advantage of this right to crush political opposition to the policy or principles of the Home Rule Bill".

This seemed ambiguous to Gough and, after consultation with other officers, including Sir Henry Wilson, he added a paragraph, which French initialled, interpreting the statement to mean that the officers "would not be asked to proceed against the Ulster loyalists to enforce the Home Rule Bill upon them in the event of its becoming law and the Ulster people resisting its application". Gough and his friends, fully reinstated, happily returned to the Curragh but in London a row blew up over the episode. Seely, French and Sir Spencer Ewart, the Adjutant-General, who had also had a hand in the document, resigned.

Carson returned to Belfast immediately after his speech in the censure debate had ended in uproar in the Commons. Craig had gone on before. Both felt they had to take seriously rumours, openly bruited by the Press, that warrants were being prepared for the arrest of a number of Ulster Unionist leaders. Craigavon was turned into a near-fortress.

The plan unfolded by Paget to his officers envisaged a dawn "invasion" of Belfast on Saturday, March 21st. Although they had no knowledge of it, the UVF leaders realised from the various activities of the army and police that something was in the wind. Throughout the Friday night the tension was almost tangible. News of the Curragh "mutiny" reached Craig and Carson on that evening, before even the War Office received it. In London the situation might have been contrived by W. S. Gilbert. Asquith was not aware of military and naval movements ordered by his Ministers, but the news of the wholesale resignations at the Curragh could not be kept from him. He cancelled the whole operation and at the King's instigation issued a statement to the Press in which he claimed that troop movements had been precautionary only and denied any intention to arrest Unionist leaders. Neither the Press nor Parliament were satisfied with the explanation and alleged a plot against peaceful Ulster. Churchill and Seely were said to be the culpable ones, but the resignations of Seely, French and Ewart suggested, to Bonar Law at least, that the Government was responsible. "What they are concealing we do not know, but we do know they are ashamed of it," he declared. For weeks to come the affair rumbled like thunder at the horizon's edge and, on April 17th, the Unionists published their own indictment of the Government.

Inevitably, this was somewhat tongue-in-cheek because the Unionists were awaiting a large consignment of arms purchased in Germany by a spectacular character, Major F. H. Crawford, who had studied the international arms market for several years. The import of arms had finally been proclaimed in December 1913, and the Government's edict was believed by the newly-formed Irish Volunteers in the South to be directed against them. They thought that the Unionists were well supplied with arms already. They were wrong on both counts. The UVF were nowhere near fully armed and it was their repeated efforts to smuggle in guns which had led to the prohibition. At this time it was the UVF which posed a threat to the Government. On the night of April 24th/25th some twenty-five thousand rifles and a large quantity of ammunition were landed at Larne, Bangor and Donaghadie.

The landing of the guns was meticulously organised by Craig, who himself supervised the unloading at Donaghadie. Asquith, after his first furious reaction, played down the episode. To have arrested the Ulster leaders in all probability would have brought down the Government. "The Attorney General for Ireland was instructed to prepare Informations in the High Court against the leaders of the various parties concerned," Asquith told the King,[8] "but on a general review of the political conditions the Cabinet on Thursday doubted the wisdom of instituting criminal proceedings and so far the Informations have not been filed."

In July the Irish Volunteers emulated the UVF coup, with

Erskine Childers playing Crawford's part as the gun-runner in chief. Both made dramatic voyages with perilous transhipments at sea. In each case the authorities were brilliantly hoodwinked but in the North there was some connivance by police, Customs men and coastguards, whereas the Howth landing ended in a clash with the army in Dublin, a "lamentable incident", Asquith told the King. It seemed to the Irish Volunteers that there was one law for the North and another for the South, but the law favoured neither, nor did the British Government. What had been made obvious was that the British Government could not depend on the army, the police or any other of the officers of the Crown in Ulster to enforce regulations which would curb the Unionists.

Yet, immediately after the gun-running, Carson made a propitiatory speech in the Commons. He hoped that if Home Rule were to pass, much as he detested it, "the Government of Ireland for the South and West would prove and might prove such a success in the future, notwithstanding all our anticipations, that it might be even for the interests of Ulster itself to move towards that Government, and come in under it and form one unit in relation to Ireland." Looking even further ahead, through Churchill's spectacles, he envisaged a stronger Ireland "as an integral unit in a federal scheme". But, he insisted, this depended on goodwill and could never be brought about by force.

Carson spoke as if the exclusion of Ulster or part of Ulster was cut and dried and Redmond remained unresponsive. The Unionist leader could afford to be a little patronising. The Bill went to the House of Lords accompanied on this occasion by an Amending Bill which embodied Asquith's early proposal of options for individual counties. On July 2nd the Lords extended the Bill so that the whole of Ulster was excluded. This the Commons were not likely to accept, but the King now took a hand to try to break the deadlock and Asquith dropped the Amending Bill for the time being. George V proposed a conference of all the interested parties at Buckingham Palace. This began on July 21st with an address (approved by the Prime Minister) of welcome and exhortation. "We have in the past endeavoured to act as a civilising example to the world," said the King, "and to me it is unthinkable, as it must be to you, that we should be brought to the brink of fratricidal war upon issues apparently so capable of adjustment as those you are now asked to consider, if handled in a spirit of generous compromise."9

For four days Asquith, Lloyd George, Bonar Law, Lord Lansdowne, Dillon, Redmond, Carson and Craig tried to reach agreement and failed. Afterwards the King talked to each of the conference members in turn. His anxiety and sympathy impressed them all but no one yielded any ground. Ervine tells us that Craig suggested a general election to the King as the wisest course but, if that were not possible, then, as a constitutional monarch, the King should sign the Home Rule Bill. Craig warned him that he would resist it. All hope now was gone and the Ulster Volunteers awaited word from Carson, who was advised by Craig that all was ready. Plans had even been made for the evacuation of refugees.

3

SUDDENLY, BUT not unexpectedly, the world changed. Europe went to war and the old order was never restored.

Beside this cataclysm the threatened *coup d'état* in Belfast seemed insignificant. The House of Commons were relieved when Sir Edward Grey told them that they could count on Ireland's support and rose emotionally to Redmond's offer of the Irish Volunteers to serve as a home-guard force in Ireland—Craig had already telegraphed Carson suggesting that the Home Rule question be postponed and that the officers and men of the Ulster Volunteer Force be offered for service anywhere. He was able to persuade Kitchener to allow the formation of an Ulster Division and, now aged forty-three, himself joined the army. Kitchener, however, stupidly baulked at the idea of an Irish Division from the South, a piece of discrimination which roused much resentment.

Bonar Law and Carson persuaded Asquith to abandon the Amending Bill debate altogether because of the international situation and Asquith announced this intention to the Commons on July 31st. They expected him to let the Home Rule Bill drop too and were shocked when they found it was to go to the King for assent. Nevertheless, at a meeting of the Ulster Unionist Council, Carson declared: "However we are treated, and however others act, let us act rightly. We do not seek to purchase terms by selling our patriotism."[10] The Government of Ireland Bill became law on September 18th 1914, but it was accompanied by a Bill which postponed its operation until the end of the war, a matter of months it was thought. An Amending Bill to deal with the un-settled Ulster problem was to be introduced at a later date. It is probable that, but for the need to impress the United States of America, the legislation would have been dropped altogether. With this in mind, Sir Edward Grey stressed the necessity to get the measure through at the earliest possible date.[11]

When it finally reached the Statute Book the Home Rule Bill pleased neither North nor South. All the Ulster Unionists had was a vague promise of future consideration of their case. As it stood, the Act went too far for them. For the IRB and the Irish Volunteers in the South it did not go nearly far enough. The Home Rule measure had been too long in the pipeline and had gone sour. The Easter Rising of 1916 flared and was doused effectively, but pitilessly, by Sir John Maxwell.

Asquith himself went to Dublin on May 12th, the day that the last two of the sixteen executions ordered by Maxwell were carried out. In six days he learned a great deal and returned to admit to the House of Commons that the existing machinery of government had broken down. He had come to the conclusion that it was a mistake after all to put the Government of Ireland Act in cold storage. He had given Lloyd George the task of beginning further discussions with the Nationalist and Unionist leaders. If the Act was to be brought into operation then the Ulster problem had to be reconsidered. Lloyd George worked it out to his own satisfaction. Ireland was to be divided into a Home Rule area of twenty-six counties and an excluded area of six counties. Three of the Ulster counties, Donegal, Cavan, and Monaghan, which were predominantly Catholic-Nationalist, were detached from the province. Unionist disappointment at the loss was compensated for by Lloyd George's assurance to Carson that the arrangement would be permanent. "Sir E. Carson's claim for the definitive exclusion of Ulster could not be resisted," the Cabinet decided.[12] The Nationalists were also disgruntled, since their majority in Fermanagh and Tyrone justified a claim for those counties. But they, too, were mollified, Lloyd George giving them to understand that the exclusion of the Ulster counties was not permanent. When Redmond realised what had happened, he declined to co-operate further and Asquith informed the King that for the immediate future of Ireland "the simplest and least objectionable plan would be to revert for the time being to the old system of a Lord Lieutenant and a Chief Secretary".[13]

The episode was disastrous for Redmond's Irish Parliamentary Party. Once again they had failed. In October, the Chief Secretary "drew a gloomy picture of the prevalent state of feeling, estimating that some three-quarters of the population are more or less sore and embittered that they have been 'cheated out of Home Rule.'"[14] The Cabinet were worried about the depletion of Irish divisions in France and by the resentment in Great Britain at the "slackness of Irish recruiting", but Asquith, with prescience, "deprecated any resort to compulsion". Two months later, on December 6th 1916, Asquith lost the Premiership to Lloyd George.

Carson, who not so long ago had planned a rebel government in Belfast, now became First Lord of the Admiralty and Craig was given a minor appointment. At the outbreak of war Craig had become a lieutenant-colonel in the Ulster Division, but a few months later he fell gravely ill. In August 1915 the Division went to France and won renown at great cost. Despondently, Craig remained behind. Continued efforts to pass a Medical Board failed and, in April 1916, he resigned his commission.

In May 1917, partly to impress America, who had entered the war the previous month, partly to counteract the growth of Sinn Fein, Lloyd George wrote with a new Home Rule plan to Redmond and to Sir John Lonsdale, the new leader of the Ulster Unionists. This provided for the six and the twenty-six counties as before, but this time the position of the six counties was to be reviewed after five years. A new proposal was a Council of Ireland with equal membership from both sections. At the same time Lloyd George offered his alternative, the Irish Convention. The first suggestion attracted neither the Nationalists nor the Unionists, but both agreed to the alternative, the Unionists rather doubtfully and on condition that no scheme was foisted upon them for which their representatives had not voted.

Lloyd George put his faith in the success of the Convention and promised Sir Horace Plunkett, its Chairman, a Home Rule Bill modelled on its recommendations. This was no ploy of Lloyd George's to gain time while he busied himself with the war. The military position early in 1918 was critical, with Russia out of the fight and the Americans still flexing their tyro muscles, yet a good deal of the War Cabinet's time was spent in discussing the Convention and the possibility of yet another Home Rule Bill. When the Cabinet considered their explosive conscription measure, Lloyd George was fearful that it would disrupt the Convention and even deferred introducing the Bill until the Convention's report was received. Henry Duke, now Chief Secretary for Ireland, warned that if the Conventioned failed the Government would be compelled to rule by force.

After eight months the Convention produced a majority report, but it was not very helpful. Too much had been expected of it. Among the delegates were men of great wisdom and ability but they had to chart a course to a misty destination. The crew had very different ideas about navigation and the Sinn Fein element had never boarded the ship at all.

Ulster Unionists dissented from the Report but Lloyd George clung to the hope that they could be persuaded to join the majority if proper safeguards were guaranteed. Walter Long was given the task of preparing a Bill but it was apparent now that Sinn Fein would stand out against any legislation deemed adequate by the British Government. The promised Bill was forgotten.

Craig had declined to participate in the Convention but had continued his assiduous political life and was rewarded by a baronetcy in the 1918 New Year Honours. Shortly afterwards, Carson and he both resigned from the Government. Action on the Convention Report had been promised and they were likely to be embarrassed if they remained.

From the back benches, during a debate in June, Craig bluntly put the Irish situation, as he saw it: "Where are you to find men, outside Ulster, who would be really fit to govern Ireland?" he asked. If there were an election in Ireland, Sinn Fein would win it, he said, and pointed out that de Valera and his colleagues, at present in English prisons, would have to be released before a constitution could be set up and an executive formed. This was farcical. He asked that six of the nine counties be excluded altogether from the 1914 Act, that they should remain irrevocably part of the United Kingdom with the same rights and the same responsibilities as the rest of the country. For a start, the six counties would accept their fair share of conscription, something the rest of Ireland would never do.

Conscription was never applied in Ireland. The Allies survived the military crisis, began to hit back and the Germans cracked. In December 1918 Lloyd George's Coalition Government was swept back into power and in the racing tide the Liberal Party all but disappeared. The Coalition Liberals exultantly skimmed the waves, leaving their boat to go on the rocks. Redmond had not lived to see the Irish Parliamentary Party crushed. Sinn Fein, no longer interested in Home Rule, took the country with them—except for the obstinate North-east—and ignored Westminster to set up the First Dail.

Colonel Sir James Craig was returned with a devastating victory over a Sinn Fein opponent who, being in prison, was unable to take part in the campaign. Both Lloyd George and Craig appeared to think that the danger of embarrassment was past, as Craig now became Parliamentary Secretary to the Ministry of Pensions under Sir Laming Worthington-Evans, later to become one of the British signatories of the Treaty.

Lloyd George's Government was faced with a colossal task. The terms of the Peace had to be settled, the country reorganised and revitalised. England had impoverished herself; her debts were enormous and there was little chance of recouping from Germany. Her people were down at heel, hungry and in mourning for a lost generation. Thousands of servicemen had to be slotted back into the civil machine. Industrial unrest vitiated the endeavour to rebuild and refurbish the country. It was little wonder that Churchill epitomised the realisation that the Irish Question was still unanswered by his famous allusion to the dreary steeples of Fermanagh and Tyrone reappearing as the floodwaters receded.

By the end of 1919 Sinn Fein had set up in the South an administration in opposition to Dublin Castle, and it was working. Vast sums of money had been raised by way of a National Loan both in Ireland and America. The Dail, though proscribed in September, was meeting in secret. De Valera was in America trying to gain

American support. Michael Collins's network in Dublin and guer-
rilla groups in the country had claimed a score of victims and on
December 19th the Lord Lieutenant, Lord French, had been
ambushed, though he had escaped. The separatist movement in the
South was gaining momentum and somehow had to be stopped.
In July, Carson had threatened to bring out the Ulster Volunteers
if there were any attempt to dilute the rights Ulstermen enjoyed as
British citizens.

On December 22nd Lloyd George announced the Government's intention to introduce a new Bill which differed con-
siderably from the 1914 Act. A Cabinet Committee had been
appointed to deal with the Irish situation and their first scheme met
with criticism in the Cabinet.[15] For one thing, it gave to the three
southern provinces "rather less than they would obtain under the
Home Rule Act and is therefore not likely to be acceptable to
them". Inevitably, their first action would be to declare themselves
an independent republic—"unless this was provided against in
some way in the Bill". This would mean hardship for Loyalists in
the South. Again, Ulster Unionists insisted that they should be on
exactly the same footing as citizens of Great Britain; under the Bill
this would not be the case.

The Cabinet felt that whatever scheme they adopted would be
wrong. A tricky aspect was the effect that any decision would have
on relations with the Dominions and the United States of America.
The mere repeal or postponement of the Home Rule Bill was out
of the question "in view of specific pledges given to Lord Grey on
his appointment as Ambassador in Washington", and this course
would probably not be acceptable to Parliament anyway. It
was suggested that, after a certain date, the three southern provinces
should be cut off by Act of Parliament from the United Kingdom
unless before that date the people decided by plebiscite that they
were in favour of the Union. This alternative was quickly dropped
on the grounds that if the South were able to remain neutral in
time of war, because of Ireland's geographical position and thus its
importance to naval defence, there would be a danger to the
Empire.

It is a pity, perhaps, that more thought was not given to this plan because in its broad outline it would appear to offer more freedom than the Treaty conferred two years later. The Irish were not oblivious to Britain's defence requirements, and the 1921 pleni- potentiaries took a very realistic line. An agreement on defence safeguards reached in 1919 might well have lasted as that under the Treaty did not. The real value of the scheme was that, except for defence facilities, it gave the Irish people the opportunity to vote themselves out of the United Kingdom or to remain within it if they wished. There might have been a real hope for de Valera's external association plan if it had been conceived at that time.

Later in the day, H. A. L. Fisher, Minister of Education, in- formed Craig of the Cabinet's intention to introduce a new Bill. Craig asked permission to consult Dawson Bates, Secretary to the Ulster Unionist Council, "who knew the mind of Ulster better than almost anyone else". Fisher referred the request to a Con- ference of Ministers and Walter Long, himself once the leader of the Unionists in the House of Commons, with fine impartiality declared that "there would be a strong temptation to anyone interested, as Mr Bates was, in the affairs of Ulster to engineer an agitation in order to influence the Government".[16]

By December 3rd the shape of the new Government of Ireland Bill was beginning to emerge. Ireland was to have two parliaments, one for Ulster, one for the three southern provinces. They would enjoy all the powers of government except those reserved to the Imperial Parliament, namely foreign affairs, defence and trade. Control of the magistracy and police would also be reserved until an all-Ireland Parliament was established and it was hoped this would provide an incentive.[17] Meanwhile there was to be a Council of Ireland comprising an equal number of members from Northern and Southern Ireland (the Cabinet deliberately used these names "to escape from terms associated with old and pro- tracted controversies") which would have powers of Private Bill legislation.[18]

The Bill was to become known pejoratively as the "Partition Bill" and it lies at the heart of the perennial Irish problem. Ironically, although it was seen as the only possible compromise, the Bill was drafted on the assumption that ultimately there would be a united Ireland with a single parliament. The two legislatures were to have large constitutional powers so that by simultaneous legislation they could confer on the Council of Ireland any power not reserved to the Imperial Parliament and could, if they wished, without reference to the Imperial Parliament convert themselves into a joint parliament.

It was hoped that in the fifteen months before the partition of Ireland would actually take place both North and South would have time to consider the disadvantages of a division of Irish services, and to make arrangements for the operation of common services.[19]

A week later, on December 10th, the Cabinet considered their policy in depth.[20] They were reminded that a principal aim was "to produce a good effect in the Dominions and in the United States of America and other foreign countries. This could not be achieved by anything short of a measure which paved the way for a single parliament if and when it was wanted." The Bill also "possessed the advantage of fitting into any scheme for the establishment of a federal system in the United Kingdom should such a scheme ever be adopted".

Because Westminister was to retain powers which affected Ireland, there would still be Irish representatives at Westminster. The question concerning the Cabinet was how many. They did not want the position to arise where the Irish could exercise a decisive vote in Great Britain's domestic affairs. The difficulty was that Ulster would claim to be still an integral part of the United Kingdom. In the end, the number was put at twenty-four.

Thus far the intention was to include the whole of Ulster in the Northern Parliament, but at this point the Unionist leaders took fright at the prospect of having a too large proportion of Catholic-Nationalists within their jurisdiction and intimated to the British Government that they could not effectively govern three counties with a Nationalist majority. They preferred that the scheme applied only to the "six Protestant counties".[21] The count suggests that the number of apostates in Fermanagh and Tyrone had been grossly over-estimated. What the Unionist leaders really meant was that they could count on an overall majority in six counties but not in nine.

Interestingly, the idea of a Boundary Commission, which persuaded the Irish plenipotentiaries to accept the Treaty in December 1921, was first suggested by Sir James Craig in a private conversation with Sir Laming Worthington-Evans two years earlier. The Commission would examine the distribution of population and "take a vote in those districts on either side and immediately adjoining the boundary in which there was a doubt as to whether they would prefer to be included in the Northern or the Southern Parliamentary area". The Cabinet thought this "in consonance with the principles and practice adopted at the Peace Conference", although patently it would be impossible to avoid isolated minorities.[22] A suggestion that a Boundary Commission be appointed at once was dropped in case it led to unrest,[23] but it was referred to the Cabinet Committee presided over by Walter Long, and it was no doubt the origin of the Boundary Commission arrangement provided for under the Treaty.

In the Cabinet it was strongly urged that "if the ultimate aim of the Government's policy was a united Ireland, it would be better that the jurisdiction of the Northern Parliament should extend over the whole of Ulster, which included both Roman Catholics and Protestants, both urban and rural districts, and by its size was more suited to possess a separate Parliament".[24] But Craig insisted on a "six-county" area and the Cabinet decided that although their plan for the whole of Ulster was more logical, "even the eventual unity of Ireland would be better assured by a scheme which was acceptable to those who had to work it".

A great deal more in like vein is to be found in British Cabinet records but enough has been set down here to show that the mutilation of Ireland was not a wicked British plot but a weary compromise tinged with optimism.

The emphasis was on winning over the Northern Irish. Craig had a long conference with Lloyd George before the Cabinet meeting and was insistent not only on restricting the scheme to six counties but on the Boundary Commission plan, by which no doubt he hoped to secure a larger but more homogeneous area.

The Cabinet agreed that "a scheme which was advocated both by Sir James Craig, a representative Ulsterman, and Sir J. O'Connor, who could speak for the Irish hierarchy, would be likely to meet with a better reception than one which they both condemned".

It never occurred to the Government at this point that there was any possibility of negotiating with the leaders of Southern Ireland. They were trying to do their best for the people of Ireland but were not yet convinced that the people, in spite of their vote for Sinn Fein, were behind men like de Valera and Griffith. Instead they were considering legislation against the attempt by Sinn Feiners to terrorise Ireland by murder and assassination. A conference of Ministers decided that "the best way to stop murder was to convict and hang some murderers".[25] A telegram to de Valera in America inviting him to discuss the proposed legislation might have been rebuffed but it was worth a try. If de Valera had accepted he would have seen that Britain had no wish to foist permanent partition on Ireland, that the provision of a Northern Parliament, which the Unionists did not want, instead of an arrangement whereby the Six Counties opted out, was expressly designed to lead towards a single parliament for the whole of Ireland.

The Bill was formally introduced in the House of Commons in February 1920. Even then, the loss of three counties rankled with some Ulster Unionists at a meeting of the Council on March 6th. "But," writes St John Ervine, "Carson and Craig repeated the arguments they had used four years earlier when their exclusion had been agreed upon, and they were accepted again, although there was bitterness about them."

Craig was in a curious position. Deeply involved in Ulster, he was also a member of the Government and, indeed, in April was promoted Financial Secretary to the Admiralty, where his old chief, Walter Long, was First Lord.

In the South violence was intensifying like monsoon rains, and in June 1920 the storm swept into the North. Rioting began in Derry and spread to Belfast. July 12th, the day of the Orange processions with their insistent drums and fifes which excite fervour and pride on the one hand and loathing on the other, was tense in Belfast. Carson lambasted Sinn Fein which he claimed masked its true identity behind both the Roman Catholic Church and Labour. "We in Ulster will tolerate no Sinn Fein—no Sinn Fein organisation, no Sinn Fein methods," he declaimed.

On July 21st began three days of bloodshed and destruction. Nearly a score of people were killed. Protestant workmen in the shipyards drove out their Catholic fellows, demanded their repudiation of Sinn Fein, beat them up, burned their homes. As always, religion was petrol on the fire but the fire had been smouldering since the war, during which Catholics from the South had gone north to find employment in the shipyards and had not yielded their jobs to returning servicemen. In Bangor, Lisburn, and other towns the same pattern of violence occurred. There was provocation on both sides but the aggression was primarily on the Protestant side, stemming largely from the fear that the terror tactics of Sinn Fein against the British, of which British propaganda made the most, would spread into Ulster, from apprehension that the new Bill was the first step towards Dublin rule and Papal dominance and jobs going to the Catholics. Police and troops who tried to quell the riots found themselves the targets of both sides. By the end of September, over eighty people had been killed and thousands of Roman Catholics had lost their jobs. As a protest, in August the Dail introduced the Belfast Boycott which Boycott patrols soon made effective, though it hurt Dublin shopkeepers as much as it did Belfast wholesalers.

4

THE GOVERNMENT of Ireland Bill became law in December 1920, the same month in which the Clune negotiations fell through because of the British Government's insistence that the IRA surrender arms. The elections for the two new parliaments were to take place in May 1921. Craig was asked to undertake the Premiership of the unhappy Six Counties and out of a strong sense of duty accepted, though he had seemed marked out for a notable career at Westminster.

On May 5th, shortly before the election, Craig was persuaded by Alfred Cope to meet de Valera in Dublin. Cope, ever seeking a way to achieve peace, was anxious to bring the two men together. Craig expected to meet the Sinn Fein leader at the house of Sir James O'Connor, a Lord Justice of Appeal, but arriving there found that he was to be escorted to a secret destination. De Valera was, in fact, safe from arrest but he did not know that. "Three of the worst looking toughs I have ever seen" drove Craig by a roundabout route to a house in Clontarf. One of those toughs was Emmet Dalton, a debonair young Irishman who not long since had been a major in the British Army and had won a Military Cross. Today, Dalton still has the greatest admiration for the courage of Sir James Craig.

The meeting achieved nothing. Craig's account of it, given by his biographer, suggests that de Valera spent almost the whole time "harping on grievances of Ireland for the past 700 years instead of coming down to practical present-day discussion", but de Valera's biographers claim that this is "hardly fair", that de Valera talked mainly of the Act of Union. Craig seemed to the President "anxious and ill at ease".[26] The impression Craig had of de Valera was that he had "very much the look of a hunted man".[27] Probably both were right.

The election in the North took place on May 24th and the Unionists won forty of the fifty-two seats, with the Nationalists and Sinn Fein, neither of whom intended to take their seats, winning six each. Craig formed his Government and thirteen members were elected to the Council of Ireland, which never met.

It was at the opening of the new Parliament on June 22nd that King George V, prompted by Field Marshal Smuts, made the very moving speech which led swiftly to the Truce in the South. Prior to the King's arrival, there was more trouble in Belfast, probably instigated by the IRA to prevent his coming. Two days after the opening they also blew up a troop train carrying cavalry who had escorted the King. Four men were killed. In spite of the break in the clouds, the sky still looked ominous.

When de Valera received an invitation to meet Lloyd George in London, Craig was also invited. Almost immediately de Valera asked him to Dublin. Craig declined on the grounds that he had already agreed to go to London. De Valera represented himself as spokesman for the whole Irish nation properly sounding out the views of the minority leaders of whom he regarded Craig as one. This Craig considered insolence. He was the Prime Minister of Northern Ireland, a State constitutionally established by Act of Parliament.

There was logic in the views of both men. The argument turned upon whether or not the British Parliament had the right to dictate the manner of government of Ireland or of any part of it. De Valera contended that an ancient conquest and the subjection of centuries conferred no right upon the British Parliament to divide Ireland, nor to deny self determination to her people, that the rights of minorities should be respected but only in so far as they were consonant with the will of the majority.

An Irish Parliament voted Ireland into the United Kingdom, ran the counter argument, and the Act of Union must stand at the very least for that part of Ireland which wished it so. The Ulster Scots had lived in Ireland for centuries and time had made it as much their home as it was the home of those who thought of themselves as the native Irish. But they could claim more than that; they sprang from Irish stock rather than Scottish, from ancestors who had crossed the narrow sea to Scotland and from a later generation which had returned.

On July 6th Craig crossed to London and was assured by Lloyd George that there would be no violation of the new Northern Parliament. He returned home but, on July 14th, after Lloyd George and de Valera had met for the first time, Lloyd George sent for him once more. Belfast was in disarray but Craig went, determined to preserve what the Act of 1920 had given. Several times he had talks with Lloyd George. When again he set out for home he left a statement with the Press in which he declared that it was up to de Valera and the British Government to come to terms on the question of self determination for the twenty-six counties. Northern Ireland had already determined its own future. He promised co-operation on equal terms with the South "in any matters affecting our common interests".

Incensed, de Valera issued a statement in contradiction. "The Ulster Cabinet represents a very small minority of the Irish people," he said, "and we claim that that small minority has been systematically, wilfully and fundamentally misled by a foreign power."

In an indignant letter to Lloyd George, de Valera declared that he had a mandate from the Irish people as a whole and denied Craig's claim that "six counties of Ulster, arbitrarily selected and containing a minority of one fifth of our people, who oppose the national demand are, and must permanently remain, a separate political unit with a right to self determination . . ." He, and the Irish people, recognised the special position of the minority in North-east Ulster and were "willing to sanction any measure of local autonomy which they might desire, provided that it were just and were consistent with the unity and integrity of all Ireland".

He demanded from Lloyd George a statement as to whether Craig had the support of the British Government and hinted at an end to negotiations. Lloyd George merely shrugged off responsibility for either Craig's statement or de Valera's. It was not the end of the road.

The proposals that de Valera finally took with him, though he

7

nearly didn't bother, were rejected in Dublin. Offering dominion status with certain limitations, they did not mention the Six Counties. Smuts talked separately to de Valera and Craig and found them equally immovable on Ulster. In a letter from the Savoy Hotel dated August 4th 1921 Smuts told de Valera that he could not help any more and was going home. "My conviction is that for the present no solution based on Ulster coming into the Irish State will succeed."[28] He believed that over the years Ulster would find community interests so compelling that she would come in voluntarily.

"My strong advice to you is to leave Ulster alone for the present, as the only line along which a solution is practicable; concentrate on a free constitution for the remaining twenty-six counties, and, through a successful running of the Irish State and the pull of economic and other peaceful forces, eventually to bring Ulster in to that State." Smuts realised that this course was repugnant to Irish patriots but counselled, "A humble acceptance of the facts is often the only way of finally overcoming them."

It was not until October 11th, after much preliminary skirmishing between Lloyd George and de Valera, that negotiations between the representatives of Great Britain and Ireland began. Craig held quite aloof. His part of Ireland had been settled and he had Lloyd George's assurance that there would be no encroachment. What the British Government and the Irish representatives agreed between them was not his concern, although clearly the future of Northern Ireland would be affected by the outcome.

Lloyd George took much the same line as Smuts when the Ulster question came up on October 14th.[29] Union was bound to come but it would never be brought about by the use of force. The stubborn Griffith produced a map showing the distribution of Catholics and Protestants in Ulster. "If it is admissible to rule off a section of Ireland, Tyrone and Fermanagh should, on the same principle, be ruled off from Ulster," he maintained. He asked Britain to stand aside and allow the Dail Government to put proposals to Northern Ireland. Lloyd George answered that the Ulster problem had not been created by the British. The British Government would approve any persuasion short of force by the

South. Britain regarded the border "as a compromise which had been reached as the result of negotiations with previous representatives of Southern Ireland".

Conferring privately on October 24th, the British representatives heard Lloyd George suggest that the only way to reconcile Ireland to the Crown was to secure Irish unity. He did not consider this denied autonomy to Ulster—presumably since the Irish plenipotentiaries were offering to allow the Northern Parliament to continue, though subordinate to Dublin instead of Westminster.

On the following day, Chamberlain and Hewart met Griffith and Collins and satisfied themselves that under such an arrangement minority rights would be safeguarded. The Irishmen had been adamant that homogeneous Catholic areas could not be left in Ulster. This was taken to mean that their offer of autonomy "applied to a reduced area of some kind". Churchill had made it plain that the British Government were not free agents and could not simply abandon the 1920 Act, but they would do their best to recommend the inclusion of the Six Counties in a larger parliament, with autonomy held from Dublin.

The British representatives decided among themselves that if the Irish agreed on all other points then an approach to Craig would be possible. On October 30th Lloyd George, hoping to be able to report that he had made headway in the negotiations when he faced a censure motion in the Commons next day, confirmed to Griffith and Collins that he would try for the autonomy from Dublin arrangement or, alternatively, for a new boundary or even a plebiscite in the Six Counties.

Arriving in London on November 5th, Craig was shocked to find that his Northern Parliament was not so securely anchored to Westminster as he had been led to believe. He flatly refused to have anything to do with the proposal to tie the Northern Parliament to Dublin and sought the transfer to the Six Counties of those services, such as the postal service, which Westminster was retaining pending the setting up of the Council for Ireland.

At a second meeting with the Prime Minister he was told that if he did not accept the plan Lloyd George and his Government would be in the unhappy position of having broken faith with the plenipotentiaries. A disillusioned Craig saw that the Six Counties had been used as a bargain counter. He was not going to submit to political blackmail of this kind and insisted that if the Six Counties ever united with the Twenty-six it would be their own decision. Lloyd George sighed regretfully that he might be compelled to resign. The same ploy he tried more successfully on the plenipotentiaries from the South, pointing out to them the possibility of the much less sympathetic Bonar Law succeeding him. He had a touching faith in the reluctance of others to do anything to unseat him. It was true, however, that the Prime Minister himself saw Bonar Law as a threat. He did not know whether Bonar Law merely saw an opportunity to become Prime Minister, or whether he was "solely activated by a conscientious desire to champion the cause of Ulster". He told Lord Riddell, "I am not going to continue the Irish war if a settlement is possible. I shall resign and the King will have to send for someone else."[30]

Between November 10th and 18th Lloyd George and Craig exchanged a series of lengthy letters in which Lloyd George sought to induce Northern Ireland into unity with the South and Craig with consummate skill fended him off. The preliminary drafts reveal more of the British Government's reasoning than the letters themselves.[31] For the first letter, dated November 10th, two drafts, surprisingly emotional in phrasing, were prepared by Sir Edward Grigg and Thomas Jones. The final letter was written by Chamberlain and Churchill.

It was suggested that formal consultation between the two Governments was now necessary for further progress of the Irish negotiations. The settlement towards which the British Government were working was based on the proposals of July 20th. "Ireland would give her allegiance to the Throne and would take her place in the partnership of Free States comprised in the British Empire. Provision would be made for those naval securities which His Majesty's Government deem indispensable for Great Britain and her overseas communications." So far Craig could have had no quarrel, but then came the kernel of the nut: "The Government of Northern Ireland would retain all the powers conferred upon her by the Government of Ireland Act. The Unity of Ireland would be recognised by the establishment of an all-Ireland Parliament, upon which would be devolved the further powers necessary to form the self-governing Irish State."

In July, Lloyd George had promised Craig that the powers of the Northern Parliament would not be meddled with. He was sticking to his promise to the letter. But Craig had assumed that the powers reserved to the Imperial Parliament would remain there. Now the proposal was to hand them over, not even to a Council for Ireland as provided under the Act of 1920, but to an all-Ireland Parliament.

Cleverly Lloyd George anticipated the possible objections, that appointments to common services such as Customs and Excise might not be made without some discrimination on religious and other grounds, that although the Northern Ireland Parliament would control education in the Six Counties, the purse strings would be held in Dublin, that control of exports and imports by an all-Ireland Parliament might imperil Ulster's industries. These were matters which Lloyd George wanted to discuss. In draft form the letter had promised safeguards of a "most stringent kind".

There was the hint of a threat in the passage: "The question of the area within the special jurisdiction of the Northern Parliament we have reserved for discussion with you. The creation of an all-Ireland Parliament would clearly further an amicable settlement of the problem."

That bland statement, coming after nine years of resistance and near civil war, must have seemed rather on the naïve side to Sir James Craig. Lloyd George sought to overcome his objections in advance by listing the disadvantages of remaining aloof from an all-Ireland Parliament. There were, for example, the Customs barriers that would have to be set up "over a jagged line of frontier"—an adroit choice of words. There would be the "large elements of the population on both sides whose sympathies would be across the border".

Then a financial carrot was dangled. As part of a dominion any contribution towards Imperial charges was voluntary. But, as part of the United Kingdom, "Northern Ireland would have to bear their proportional share of all Imperial burdens . . ." Finally there was Britain's noble example. She was prepared to let Northern Ireland go and, single-handed, to assume responsibility for Imperial defence except for any voluntary contribution from the dominions.

In his reply of November 11th[32] Craig carefully misunderstood Lloyd George's allusion to allegiance to the Throne. It "did not arise in the case of the people of Ulster, as they have always been amongst His Majesty's most loyal and devoted servants". To ram the point home, Craig added, "It has always been the desire of Northern Ireland to remain in the closest possible union with Great Britain and the Empire, which Ulstermen have helped to build up, and to which they are proud to belong." Craig was surprised that the British Government were discussing the tie with Crown and Empire since they had earlier made it clear that these two fundamentals were not open for discussion. It was a question for the British Government, though naturally the Northern Government hoped for the permanent allegiance of the people of Southern Ireland and their enduring participation in the British Empire.

The Government of Ireland Act of 1920 had been accepted by Northern Ireland "as a final settlement and supreme sacrifice in the interests of peace". It alarmed Craig and his Cabinet colleagues that there was any question of a revision of boundaries. Craig pointed out that the area was defined in the Act and was an essential part of it.

An all-Ireland Parliament was not acceptable. The possible unity of the country was already anticipated by the provision made under the Act for a Council of Ireland. Far from being weakened, the determination of the Six Counties to avoid coming into an all-Ireland Parliament had been strengthened by recent events. Dismissing "paper safeguards", Craig insisted that no Government representing the loyal population of Ulster could even agree to discussion of a single parliament. He pointed to an alternative course. If the difficulties of transferring the reserve powers to part of Ireland were so great, they could be given to the governments of both Northern and Southern Ireland "within the areas of their respective jurisdictions". If this involved loss of representation at Westminster, this was still preferable to a central parliament in Dublin. Thus he was suggesting that Northern Ireland should also become a dominion.

In a reproachful answer, dated November 14th,[33] Lloyd George scorned the idea of two dominions in Ireland. In essence, his argument was that the whole of Ireland was a natural unit of self-government; the Six Counties was not. "All experience proves, moreover, that so complete a partition of Ireland as you propose must militate with increasing force against their ultimate unity which you yourself hope will one day be possible," he wrote, and added, "when once such frontiers are established they harden into permanence." An earlier draft read, more succinctly perhaps, "We should also greatly deprecate the establishment of an international frontier across Ireland as an obstacle to that ultimate unity which you yourself agree to be desirable."[34] The Prime Minister insisted that an interchange of ideas was essential and hoped Craig would not "persist in making preliminary conditions upon matters which can only be properly explored in conference".

In his reply,[35] dated November 17th, Craig said it would be dishonest to enter a conference to discuss Ulster's permanent subordination to Sinn Fein since it was totally unacceptable. He denied that he had submitted counter proposals and summed up his arguments by saying simply, "If you force Ulster to leave the United Kingdom against the wishes of her people, she desires to be left in a position to make her own fiscal and international policy conform as nearly as possible with the policy of the Mother Country, and to retain British traditions, British currency, British ideals and the British language, and in this way render the disadvantages entailed by her separation from Great Britain as slight as possible."

At this point influenza struck down Northern Ireland's Prime Minister and the British Cabinet decided not to trouble him further but simply to send him a "get-well" message. On November 20th, Craig wrote that he had recovered and was returning home as the Northern Parliament was to assemble on the 29th. He was anxious to publish the correspondence which showed that the North had not refused to take part in the Conference but had been prevented by the Sinn Fein delegates' insistence that they should do so in a subordinate rôle.

Wrote Craig, "I should also have to let our Parliament be informed whether Sinn Fein was prepared to give allegiance to the Crown without reservation, which was one of the conditions of your invitation, or whether their consent to do so is still withheld and made dependent on your first having procured the consent of Ulster to an all-Ireland Parliament."

As always, Lloyd George had played an ambiguous part, but it must be remembered that he was punctilious in consulting his Cabinet, and documents signed by him had generally been mulled over very thoroughly by his colleagues. His was a coalition government, some of whose members were inherently opposed to Home Rule, some whose links with the Ulster Unionists were close. On balance, it does seem that Lloyd George really was anxious to settle the Irish problem by establishing a senior parliament in Dublin and he took as hard a line with Craig as he dared. He had sworn not to coerce Ulster and he did not want civil war. Neither did he wish to provoke dissension in his Cabinet.

In a draft memorandum[36] Lloyd George recognised that attempts to settle with a constitutional party in Ireland had always failed "because behind that party were elements who believed only in physical force and were prepared to accept no settlement short of a republic". He was elated because, for the first time, a British Government was dealing direct with the physical force movement and seemed likely to achieve a settlement short of a republic. To release Ireland from the Empire was unthinkable, to forgo the use of Irish ports and leave Britain's back door unguarded was to court disaster, but apart from this aspect Ireland was to have the same rights and privileges as any dominion. Devious though he was, Lloyd George was a stickler for the rules of the Empire. The powers he intended the Six Counties to have would be secured "as firmly as the powers of Quebec are reserved to that province under the terms of the Canadian Constitution".

Craig won the points from his correspondence with Lloyd George but his was the easier task. Lloyd George had to attempt to persuade Northern Ireland to accept a course they had resisted for years while Craig, though he put his arguments skilfully, basically had only to say no. In the end, Craig was the unseen dominating force in the Treaty negotiation. To the last, Collins and Griffith pressed Lloyd George to get from him a definite answer on whether or not Northern Ireland would accept unity. But it was Craig who, for some reason, had to know the answer at once. Which letter was to go to him, the one telling him that the negotiations had failed, the other that agreement had been reached? If Craig were not informed by December 6th, the British Government could not wait any longer before visiting war again on Ireland. A destroyer waited for the bearer of the letter.

5

THE PLENIPOTENTIARIES signed and Geoffrey Shakespeare hurried to Belfast with the letter enclosing the Articles of Agreement, the Treaty. He would observe, Lloyd George told Craig, "that there are two alternatives between which the Government of Northern Ireland is invited to choose. Under the first, retaining all her existing powers, she will enter the Irish Free State with such additional guarantees as may be arranged in conference. Under the second alternative she will retain her present powers, but in respect of all matters not already delegated to her will share the rights and obligations of Great Britain. In the latter case, however, we should feel unable to defend the existing boundary, which must be subject to revision on one side and the other by a Boundary Commission under the terms of the Instrument."

Hastening to London, Craig met Lloyd George on December 9th and told him that the Six Counties Government would give up none of their territory. He also demanded revision of the financial arrangements as they affected his Government. The British Prime Minister reassured him on the boundary question. It was merely a matter of tidying up—a bit of give and take right along the line. Yet the key to the acceptance of the Treaty terms by the plenipotentiaries was Lloyd George's expressed conviction that Fermanagh and Tyrone would undoubtedly go to the South, leaving the rump of the Northern Parliament area economically unworkable. When Craig and Collins compared notes during their talks in January, the deception was plain to them both.

In a letter dated December 14th Craig expressed with bitter dignity the feelings of his Cabinet about the Articles of Agreement, some idea of which he had already communicated informally to the British Prime Minister. He charged that, as late as November 25th, he had had a written assurance that "the rights of Ulster will be in no way sacrificed or compromised until new proposals had been placed before the Cabinet of Northern Ireland". Yet the Agreement, "which materially involved Ulster's interests", had been signed without consultation.

The Boundary Commission provision was, he declared, a breach of the 1920 Act and he reserved to his Government the right of dissenting from any boundary commission. In placing Northern Ireland automatically within the Irish Free State, even though allowing for her to contract out, Great Britain had reversed her well-publicised policy "that Ulster should remain out until she chose of her own free will to enter an all-Ireland Parliament". There had been "neither explanation nor justification for this astounding change". The principle of the Government of Ireland Act, which was to give equal rights and privileges to North and South, had been violated. Moreover, the Free State was to have financial advantages which the North could only enjoy if she agreed to become subordinate to Sinn Fein Ireland.

Remarking the abandonment of the requirement that there were to be "no protective duties or other restrictions upon the flow of trade and commerce between all parts of these islands", Craig foresaw friction and tariff wars. (Events justified his apprehension, though the trade war of the 1930s had a quite different origin.)

Again prophetically, Craig wrote: "We feel that in years to come the British nation will realise the advantages in having in Northern Ireland a population which is determined to remain loyal to British traditions and citizenship . . ." (Having restored the Treaty ports to the Irish Free State shortly before the Second World War, gambling on the gesture winning her support, Britain found herself in dire trouble when she was denied the use of the ports by Eire's neutrality. If the Six Counties had been part of that neutral state, the shipping losses would have been even more devastating. But then, a united Ireland might well have thrown in her wartime lot with Britain.)

Craig's letter clearly spelled out complete rejection of a united

Ireland and, as turbulent Belfast saw out 1921 in a fume of violence, all the omens for persisting hatred were there. The beginning of 1922 was no better. It was impossible to pin down the instigators of violence. IRA units were active but as to whether they began the trouble or merely sought to defend their co-religionists opinions differed. Figures showed that more Catholics than Protestants died in those grim days.

Collins and Craig were both concerned for their own people and met in London on January 21st. The outcome was the first of two agreements. Craig gave an assurance that he would take steps to prevent the persecution of Catholics in the Six Counties and, in particular, to try to have Catholic workmen reinstated in employment from which they had been driven by their Protestant fellows. Collins promised in turn to end the Belfast Boycott. They agreed, further, to revise the Boundary Commission formula. Each Government would appoint a representative for preliminary talks though the final arrangement would be entered into by Craig and Collins. In his public speeches, however, Craig reiterated the intention of his Government to resist any allocation of Six Counties territory to the South. In signing such an agreement Collins was recognising the right of the Northern Parliament to its own existence, but he had every reason to believe that there would be a transfer of territory and that this would leave the North-east as an expensive pendant round Brittania's neck.

The British Government were already looking askance at Craig's claims for £6 million to finance the Northern Government, but had no hesitation in financing the Special Constabulary to the tune of £625,000 up to March 1922 and a further £850,000 for the next year. The expense was justified on the grounds that it meant a saving of British troops but the payments were to be included in a general grant "for unemployment and other services, so as to avoid, if possible, raising a controversy in Parliament with regard to this force". The Specials were detested by the South and were blamed by them for murder and violence in Belfast: that the British Government financed them made Collins exceedingly bitter.

Craig and Collins met again in Dublin to discuss points which the agreement had left open. Craig had promising news about the likely re-employment of the Catholic workers who, it was claimed, had fallen foul of their fellows not because they were Catholics but because they were Sinn Fein supporters. But Craig's obstinacy on the boundary question prevented any real *rapprochement*. The two men had little in common apart from a formidable stature and a stubborn belief in the rightness of their respective causes, but they got on well enough, though their public utterances were laced with accusation. Writing to his fiancée, Collins revealed that he was afraid of war on a north–south axis: "The Craig business is serious and if we don't find some way of dealing with it all the bravos will get a great chance of distinguishing themselves once more."[37]

A hint of what might happen was given by the IRA, who on February 11th attacked a carriage containing eighteen Specials when their train stopped at Clones just inside Free State territory. Several were killed, the rest taken prisoner.

In these early months of 1922 Craig made frequent trips across the Irish Sea to confer with Lloyd George, Churchill and other British Ministers. He was careful to say nothing that Lloyd George could twist. His duplicity had left Craig disillusioned and, as Churchill reported to the Cabinet, Craig was depressed with his reception at the Treasury. He also refused to see Collins again until the Clones prisoners had been released and Churchill did not attempt to press him while civil war in the South was threatened at Limerick. Churchill told him he proposed to address a formal letter inviting Northern Ireland to enter into negotiations with the South. He would "not be disposed to accept a simple refusal from the Northern Government, in view of the heavy obligations in regard to troops and Special Constabulary which we were incurring on their behalf".[38]

Churchill's idea, resisted by Sir Henry Wilson, lately Chief of the Imperial General Staff, was to station troops at critical points on the border—if both Irish Governments agreed. He intended then to bring Craig and Collins together and to obtain from Collins a "repudiation of the revolts on the part of the Irish Republican Army". Collins, perturbed by the fate of so many

Catholics in the North, was himself secretly involved in the IRA's operations.

Sir Henry Wilson was appointed adviser to the Northern Government on March 17th. Craig hoped he might put down the persistent rioting but the engagement of Wilson, a brilliant but meddlesome man who made no secret of his dislike for the Southern Irish, was seen as a provocative move against the Twenty-six Counties. As there were 48,000 Specials and nineteen British battalions in the North, armed by courtesy of the British Government, apprehension in the South was scarcely remarkable.

In spite of the bristling atmosphere, Craig and Collins met on March 28th and again the next day. Collins complained that Craig had done nothing to alleviate unemployment among Catholics but Craig had no easy task. There simply were not enough jobs to go round. The Dail had ended the Belfast Boycott but it was reimposed by the Executive forces and it is doubtful that Collins discouraged them.

On March 30th Craig and Collins, with several colleagues, signed a second agreement which began: "Peace is today declared . . ." Declared it might have been but peace went no further than the paper on which the agreement was signed. An attempt was to be made to find a way to Irish unity or, failing that, to adjust the prickly boundary. Craig himself was not prepared to stand for unity, Churchill told the Cabinet, but he would resign rather than stand in its way. It has often been contended that any kind of unity was no more than a pipe-dream, but even Carson talked of the possibility and Craig himself did not deny that it might come in time.

Despite the agreement, Craig and Collins continued to squabble, and when Collins signed the Pact with de Valera in May, Craig gave up any idea of further transactions with him. He was taking strong measures to remove troublemakers from the scene but Collins could not believe in his impartiality. "I can't leave these people unprotected with 48,000 Specials out against them," he told Lloyd George.

And the Collins–de Valera Pact was soon broken. Once the British Government rejected the draft Constitution, submitted to them by Griffith and Collins, which might have allowed de Valera to take his seat in the Dail without rupturing his principles, the Pact was no longer viable. Civil war flared in the South and Craig could only be thankful that the Six Counties were not embroiled.

Griffith died, then Collins. It was with the much milder William T. Cosgrave that Craig next treated. The two men met in London on November 10th 1922. Their only agreement was to battle against each other on the boundary question and each knew that the other would play the game fairly. By this time Craig, given a respite, was able to begin to build up the new State. He was coming round to the idea that, after all, it was better for Northern Ireland to have its own parliament, its own government. Lloyd George had shown him into what danger a British government could thrust the Six Counties. Craig was not likely to forget that behind his back the British representatives had negotiated with the plenipotentiaries from Dublin about the future of his territory, that they had been ready to throw aside assurances in order to seek the easy way out, that even their own Act of Parliament, twelve months old, meant no more than a sack of potatoes in the market-place.

Lloyd George and his uncomfortable coalition had gone in October 1922. For a few months the ailing Bonar Law was Prime Minister, and Baldwin succeeded him in May 1923. The return to power of the Conservative Party should have allayed Craig's fears but, now that he was cut off from the arena at Westminster, he saw it with a more dispassionate eye and was not impressed. The electoral defeat had broken the back of the Liberal Party and in the wings were a new and motley crew, the Labour Party, whose thoughts might well turn to ending Partition for the sake of democracy.

The first Labour Government, led by Ramsay MacDonald, took office in January 1924, and in Cabinet records names like Arthur Henderson, Home Secretary, and J. H. Thomas, Secretary of State for the Colonies, suddenly appear for the first time.

In April 1924, Craig and Cosgrave attended a conference in London to discuss the setting up of the Boundary Commission. According to Article 12 of the Treaty, "a commission consisting of the three persons, one to be appointed by the Government of the

Irish Free State, one to be appointed by the Government of Northern Ireland, and one who shall be Chairman to be appointed by the British Government, shall determine in accordance with the wishes of the inhabitants, so far as they may be compatible with economic and geographic conditions, the boundaries between Northern Ireland and the rest of Ireland, and for the purposes of the Government of Ireland Act, 1920, and of this instrument, the boundary of Northern Ireland shall be such as may be determined by such Commission".

Craig was adamant that his Government would refuse to nominate a representative and, on his return to Belfast, repeated in Parliament that the North would not budge. He contended that their territory had been delineated, their Parliament established by the Government of Ireland Act of 1920 and that a Treaty signed by two other governments and ratified in their respective parliaments had no legality so far as Northern Ireland was concerned. A little nip and tuck along the border was as much as they would countenance.

Even the wily Thomas Jones failed in extra-mural attempts at persuasion. In his valuable diaries, Jones recalls that during a conversation on April 24th, at the home of J. H. Thomas, "Cope ventured to suggest that Craig might be placated with a peerage." Thomas inimitably replied, "He can have a bloody dukedom if it will do the trick; I made a peer and two knights yesterday . . ."[39]

Jones's diary entry on May 8th is also illuminating: "Impressed on Henderson—as I also have on Hankey*—the importance of the P.M., J. H. Thomas and Henderson seeing Asquith, L.G. and Baldwin with a view to their advancing together on this question. Once Craig can be made to realise that he could not split the parties on the issue here, it would make an immense difference. Henderson said it was very unlikely that J.H.T. would be willing to join in any step which took away his own importance in the matter."

Professor Eoin MacNeill had been named the Free State Commissioner and Great Britain appointed as Chairman Mr Justice Richard Feetham of South Africa.

Feelings ran high in both Northern Ireland and the Free State.

* Sir Maurice Hankey, Secretary to the Cabinet

Cosgrave's Government intended to claim large concessions of territory and made no secret of it. British politicians who visited Belfast to confer with Craig were met by crowds of Unionists chanting, "Not an inch!"

The British Government wondered whether the Commission could function without a representative from Northern Ireland or whether the King's Representative in Northern Ireland, or the King himself, or anybody else, could appoint one over the heads of Craig's Government.

Mr Justice Feetham added to the confusion by asking whether a majority decision of the Commission would be valid. No one seemed to have thought of that when Article 12 was drafted.

In a memorandum dated July 17th 1924[40] Henderson and Thomas put the Government's quandary. No Commission, they decided, could be unanimous upon every point along a boundary. If unanimity was required then the scheme was unworkable, "and the view will be taken in the Free State that Article 12 was a mere pretence". They felt sure that the framers of the Treaty must have intended a majority decision to be valid. This question, together with the problem of the absence of a Commissioner from Northern Ireland, would be put to the Judicial Committee of the Privy Council.

It was to be made clear to the Free State that the question was put at the request of the Chairman-Designate, not of the Government, to avoid political consequences "of the gravest kind".

The Judicial Committee, which reported on July 31st, ruled that a majority vote was valid. To the question as to whether, without a Commissioner for Northern Ireland, the Commission would be competent, the answer was that the tribunal must correspond with the words of Article 12. The Governor of Northern Ireland could not appoint one, nor could the Crown, and there was no constitutional method under existing statute law to bring the Commission into being.[41] Sir James Craig had maintained from the beginning that that was the answer.

On August 4th Ramsay MacDonald and W. T. Cosgrave signed an agreement to amend the Treaty so that power of appointment of a Northern Commissioner passed to the British

Government. The Irish Free State (Confirmation of Agreement) Act, 1924, was then hurried through and Joseph R. Fisher, a distinguished Ulsterman, was appointed, a choice of which Craig approved.

Anxious about the situation, the King instructed his secretary, Lord Stamfordham, to write to Craig. The King felt "that the solution of the problem is only to be found by agreement between you and Cosgrave. He earnestly trusts that you will continue to work to this end, for he knows that as a great Irishman you believe as he does, that such a consummation would be for the lasting peace, happiness and prosperity of Ulster itself, Ireland as a whole, and of the British Empire generally."[42]

Nevertheless, Craig told the Northern Parliament in October that, if the Boundary Commission wrested territory from the Six Counties, he would resign as Prime Minister and himself lead the defence of the threatened area. In the meantime, he got on with parliamentary business, but believing that a demonstration of the electorate's opposition to any tinkering with the boundary might exert a useful influence on the Commission, who were now amassing vast quantities of documents and maps as they made their way through the border areas, Craig called an election in April 1925.

His official Unionist Party won thirty-two of the fifty-two seats and four independent Unionists also were returned. Sinn Fein won only two seats, the Nationalists ten, and Craig was delighted when the mercurial Joe Devlin, opponent and friend of many years, forswore the Nationalist abstention policy and took his seat. A few months earlier, in October 1924, the Ramsay MacDonald Government, after a brief term in office, had found themselves on the Opposition benches. They had done well and the Liberals upon whose support they depended saw their success as a danger to themselves. Baldwin was returned with a good majority. Unionist gains were made, in most timely fashion for Craig, in Tyrone and Fermanagh, the two counties to which the Free State made such vigorous claim. Sinn Fein and the Nationalists split the vote.

6

SMALL INDICATIONS of the Boundary Commission's findings appeared in the *Morning Post* of November 7th 1925, evidently from an inspired "leak". Small areas of Armagh and Fermanagh were to be transferred to the Irish Free State and a piece of Donegal was to be included in the Six County area. Belatedly, Eoin MacNeill resigned from the Commission on November 21st. Five days later, Craig and Cosgrave met in London. Both preferred the existing boundary to that proposed by the Commission whose report, therefore, was never published.

Free State representatives, led by Kevin O'Higgins, met Craig and his colleagues at Chequers on November 29th, then Cosgrave returned to London and, on December 3rd, a tripartite agreement was signed.

The proviso (quoted earlier) in Article 12 of the Treaty document was scrapped and the boundary fixed by the 1920 Government of Ireland Act was upheld. The Irish Free State was released from liability for the service of a proportion of the National Debt of the United Kingdom and for War Pensions but in return assumed liability, retrospective to January 21st 1919 when the First Dail assembled, for various compensatory payments for which the British Government had undertaken responsibility.

Finally, Northern Ireland received powers which, under the 1920 Act, were reserved for the Council of Ireland and had been held since by the British Government. The agreement was signed by Baldwin, Churchill, Joynson-Hicks, Birkenhead and L. S. Amery for the British Government, by Cosgrave, O'Higgins and Ernest Blythe for the Free State and by Craig and Charles Blackmore for the North.

By stubbornness, courage, not a little acumen and inviolable honesty, Craig had at last won his struggle to resist inclusion in a sovereign state ruled from Dublin. The Six Counties could go their own way and the Government of the Irish Free State had recognised their right to do so. Sir James Craig had done well for his tribe and the Viscountcy he received in the New Year's Honours of 1926 was a well-earned reward. He took the title of Lord Craigavon of Stormont.

It was a victory for a hardy minority and in half a century no part of that victory has been whittled away. The border stands as a memorial to Lord Craigavon. "Not an inch" was the slogan during his election campaign of 1925, and not an inch of territory has been yielded. Yet, so long as that border remains, there will be trouble in Ireland, but it cannot now, any more than it could fifty years ago, be scratched out by force and it is unimaginable that the leaders of the Republic of Ireland today would wish the Six Counties restored while they remain in a state of virulent inflammation.

Even at the time Cosgrave did not seem distressed by the arrangement. In answer to Christmas greetings from Craig, the Free State leader wrote, "You will be interested to know that the Agreement was, and is, regarded by a very large number of people here, including the professions and business classes, as the best contribution so far made by its signatories and their Governments."[43] In the same letter he reciprocated the hope expressed by Craig that they might "get into closer touch in future for the common good".

Unhappily, the two men did not meet again, perhaps unable to withstand the pressures applied by Orange extremists, whose only wish was that the Twenty-six Counties could be set adrift in the Atlantic, and by the Republicans in the South who were never prepared to accept the establishment of the Northern State. Furthermore, the murder of Kevin O'Higgins in July 1927 seemed to point to a brittleness in the Free State which deterred any overtures from moderates in the North.

Craigavon only casually noted Cosgrave's fall from power in February 1932, and so secure did the border now seem to him that he scarcely glanced across it at the tall glinty-eyed de Valera brooding upon the demolition of the Treaty, border and all. The trade war which developed between Great Britain and the Irish Free State over disputed payments obtruded into Craigavon's pre-occupation with domestic affairs, not the least of which was the opening of the proud new Parliament building at Stormont in November 1932. Both parts of Ireland as well as Britain were hurt by the retaliatory dues at a time when the great Depression befogged the globe and the dole queue became an unspeakable indignity.

It came as no surprise to Craigavon when de Valera took advantage of the abdication of Edward VIII to legislate the Crown out of the Constitution of the Irish Free State. As he passed through London after a cruise he was shown the letter which the British Government delivered to the Irish High Commissioner in London on April 3rd 1937. Not without reproach, the British Government accepted the measure and set out the position with regard to Commonwealth and Crown as they now saw it. The Taoiseach's reply, which was considered unsatisfactory, included the sentence, "It would be impossible for any Government in Saorstat Eireann to express an unqualified desire to remain a Member of the British Commonwealth of Nations whilst Ireland remains a partitioned nation."[44] Craigavon's reaction to the British note had been to regret the British Government's expressed desire to co-operate with the Irish Free State. He saw it only as an indication that Britain would make further concessions if pressed.

Shortly afterwards, de Valera produced his new Constitution which was essentially republican in character and provided for its ultimate application to the whole of Ireland. It clearly stated that the national territory consisted of the whole of the island of Ireland, its islands and territorial seas. To Craigavon this was brazen impertinence. Even the name of the new state, Eire or Ireland, was provocative and there was a suggestion that Northern Ireland retaliate by renaming itself Ulster. Without the three excluded counties this was a misnomer calculated to infuriate the South.

The suggestion was dropped but shortly before the new Constitution became effective—on December 29th 1937—

Craigavon's deputy, J. M. Andrews, had discussions with the British Home Secretary and insisted that the British Government issue a categorical statement that they would accept no interference with the jurisdiction of the Government of Northern Ireland without their express approval. Earlier, Craigavon had discussed the Constitution with the Prime Minister and two other Ministers and intimated that, while he considered it objectionable, he was in favour of reducing controversy to the minimum and would not make a fuss. In answer to a parliamentary Question at Stormont, he stated that the Government of Ireland Act of 1920 and other measures protected Northern Ireland's constitutional position and no special steps were required to safeguard it.

In January 1938 Lord Craigavon learned that after the years of economic warfare which had damaged both parts of Ireland as well as Great Britain, an attempt was to be made to reach agreement. De Valera, it appeared, was hoping as part of the bargain to secure the end of Partition.

Craigavon was disconcerted by this challenge, having been confident that the whole issue had been settled with the Cosgrave Government. At once he decided to call a general election to demonstrate that Unionist solidarity was as strong as ever. He was sixty-seven and ailing and he had enjoyed seventeen years of uninterrupted power. Yet his party won thirty-nine of the fifty-two seats and a breakaway Unionist group calling themselves Progressives, which had caused him some apprehension, failed to win a seat.

He made his point and the British refused to deal with de Valera on Partition. De Valera saw that he could make no headway and turned the British refusal to advantage by using it as a lever to gain every other point.

Craigavon was vitally interested in the negotiations, for the British Government were insisting on free trade across the border. De Valera would agree to no more than a system of reciprocal preferences. With J. M. Andrews, his eventual successor, Craigavon discussed the problem with Sir Samuel Hoare, then Home Secretary, who reported them depressed and in fear of a serious upheaval in Northern Ireland if the negotiations continued their present trend.

However, by April 13th, Hoare was able to report that Craigavon was reluctant to upset the prospect of an agreement and would accept a solution which he could defend in his own Parliament. As Eire would make no concession and Craigavon could not accept the position and hope to stay in office, Britain had to make the concessions to Northern Ireland herself. The Chancellor of the Exchequer agreed to certain subsidies and to guarantees of unemployment pay. To alleviate unemployment, the manufacture of arms in Northern Ireland was mooted. Within days the agreement between Great Britain and Ireland on trade, finance and defence was signed. To Craigavon's dismay, Britain handed back the Treaty ports in the South.

It had been hoped that Eire would make the ports available to Britain in time of war but de Valera opted firmly for neutrality. In June 1940 the British Government tried to persuade the Eire leader to allow the use of the ports and to enter the war on Britain's side, offering as bait intercession with Northern Ireland to end Partition. Chamberlain wrote to Craigavon to inform him of the offer and received a blistering reply in which Britain was accused of trading behind Ulster's back. Chamberlain answered by telegram regretting that Craigavon had made such an unfair charge. Craigavon had surely not appreciated that his position was entirely protected. If any decision had to be made, Craigavon would be given every opportunity to put his views. Tartly, he concluded, "Meanwhile please remember the serious nature of the situation which requires that every effort be made to meet it."

Poor Craigavon must have felt he ill deserved the rebuke. From the outbreak of war, and even before, he had done his utmost to throw all of Northern Ireland's resources behind the Imperial Government. On May 2nd 1939 he had travelled to London especially to ask Chamberlain to include Northern Ireland in the Government's Conscription Bill. The offer was declined. Lady Craigavon confided her views to her diary: "The British Government were frightened of the issue being complicated by de Valera kicking up a dust, though Ulster affairs are *nothing* to do with him." She mentioned other factors—American opinion, the danger of rioting in Northern Ireland if Nationalists were conscripted and disaffection in the army.

In May 1940 Craigavon tried to persuade Churchill to extend conscription to Northern Ireland but the reply was in the same vein as Chamberlain's had been twelve months earlier.

In his last decade, his sixties, Craigavon suffered a good deal of illness and aged prematurely. He left Northern Ireland for long periods while he went on recuperative sea voyages. Retirement he did not consider very seriously. He would have welcomed it himself but the Party regarded him as indispensable. In five elections, from 1921 to 1938, his Unionist Party had won 33 to 40 seats of the 52.

He was deeply affected by the death in 1934 of the irrepressible Joseph Devlin, founder of the Ancient Order of Hibernians (the Molly Maguires) and lifelong Nationalist. Bitter political opponents, outside Parliament they were staunch friends. Lord Carson's death in the following year was another blow. For a quarter of a century, they had fought together to resist the merger of Northern Ireland in a single Irish State.

Almost pityingly, Craigavon warned British statesmen that the concessions they made to de Valera one after another would bring no return from him. In this he saw further than they for all their attempts to win a wintry smile from de Valera failed. They failed because de Valera did not consider that to extract a right from those who withheld that right demanded any benefaction from him. With each move that de Valera made to dismantle the Treaty, to extirpate British influence, to disassociate the Irish Free State from the Commonwealth, to draw nearer the goal of the cherished republic, he hardened the line of the border. Whether a less rigid leader might have arranged an accommodation with the North is open to question, but with de Valera in power the chances were nil.

Despite ill-health, Lord Craigavon made unflagging attempts to meet his people. From time to time there were rumours of IRA plots against his life but he scorned armed guards. He was often to be seen on the streets of Belfast talking to whomever was passing, tilting his large frame back on his heels, his inevitable watch chain resting upon his well-filled waistcoat. Genial he was always, but paternal rather than matey. His pipe seemed a deliberate symbol of informality, ameliorating the stern face with its sharp hook of a nose over a white military moustache. Each year he toured the Six Counties meeting as many people as he could, lingering in the border areas. He did not differentiate between Catholic and Protestant, only asked that they were loyal to their country, to the United Kingdom and the Commonwealth, especially the Commonwealth.

The loyalty of the Northern Irish is not to England and they feel no propinquity with the English people. They share allegiance to the Crown and a belief in the Commonwealth concept, that is all. With good reason the Northern Irish have very often suspected that there is less idealism than practical advantage in England's Commonwealth connection and they are determined to keep British traditions alive even if the English themselves forsake them. That the British should ever use Northern Ireland in their bargaining with the South, as they did at the time of the Treaty and again during the Second World War, to Craigavon and his people was almost unbelievable. Yet always they had looked across the water with some scepticism.

Craigavon was a good man who dealt honestly with everyone, even those who were devious with him. As obstinate in his political convictions as de Valera, he was a warmer, less inflexible man, able at least to recognise that others had a right to a belief which conflicted with his own. Like de Valera he was the product of his land, moulded by his upbringing in the shadow of traditions that had endured for centuries. Leader of a party which contained many militants and a few bigots, he did not succeed in preventing, and was probably not really aware of, discrimination in some areas of social and political life.

On occasion, he appointed Catholics to high position but, in general in the country, Protestant employed Protestant in both the private and public sectors. By the same token, Catholic favoured Catholic. The best jobs went to Protestants as a rule, but this was partly because Protestant children were better educated. They were so because the State-financed schools had far more resources, better facilities and less overcrowding. That was not Craig's fault for he deplored sectarian education and would have wished all the children to have equal opportunity.

Gerrymandering in the electoral field, particularly in local government, drove Catholic disadvantage deep into the fabric of the State. The electoral system was complex. The local government structure dated back to the nineteenth century and creaked at the joints. Boundaries of constituencies and wards favoured Protestants and ensured that their representation was, on the basis of population, disproportionately high. There was privilege voting. Queen's University sent members to Parliament and business men, mostly Protestant, had additional votes. Again, in local government elections business men and companies had extra votes. Moreover, only the occupier of a house and his wife had the right to vote; adult children living with parents and parents living with married children were disenfranchised. Generally it was the Catholics who were affected, partly because their families were larger and closer knit, partly because in housing, too, they were at a disadvantage.

The blame was not all on the Protestant side. The Catholics were unwilling citizens of a State they believed had no right to exist. Their eyes gazed longingly across the border and they declined to participate in the life of the State or to contribute to its development. Protestants feared that the growth of the Catholic population would outstrip their own and that they would then expunge the border and subordinate Belfast to Dublin. So they protected themselves by denying Catholics their rights and consoled their consciences by pointing to the fact that the Catholics did not seek to use their rights anyway.

Fundamentally, Craigavon was a conformist and could not go against the grain of his Unionist breeding. He was proud of his Protestant Parliament and his Protestant people but Protestant meant for him not so much a difference in religious belief as faith in the Empire, allegiance to the Crown and adherence to the Act of Union. The Catholic who believed in these things was no less Craigavon's friend than any Protestant. Of England he had become a little sceptical. The Baldwin and Chamberlain Governments he saw as disciples of appeasement and he was dismayed when even Churchill seemed ready to trade the autonomy of the Six Counties for the Treaty ports which his predecessor had weakly given away.

He was intensely suspicious of de Valera and in a speech on June 29th 1940, after he had received Chamberlain's reproachful telegram, accused him of "once again blackmailing the British Government to end Partition, and this at the very moment when the enemy is at our gates". But he was willing to co-operate with him on matters of defence provided he took his stand at Britain's side, threw out the Axis diplomats and refrained from raising constitutional issues.

In a newspaper interview just before his death, Lord Craigavon said that Ulster would never divorce herself from the Union Jack. "We will not accept any status that takes us outside the British Empire. Ulster will stay where she is."

He died on November 24th 1940, content that he had done his duty as an Ulsterman.

EAMON
DE VALERA

I

FOLLOWING HIS fall from power in 1969 General Charles de Gaulle arrived unexpectedly in Ireland. His choice of a haven was, one could see at once, strikingly appropriate. Misunderstood as he believed himself to be, it was natural perhaps that he should seek the shelter of a man with whom he enjoyed a strange propinquity. The former President of France and the President of Ireland had much in common. There was that same unshakeable single-minded purpose, the inflexible holding to a principle to the point where others thought them pig-headed, the uncompromising belief in the glory of their respective countries, and their utter faith in themselves as leaders. Each had built up his country after a devastating occupation and in face of civil strife with courage, tenacity and a degree of ruthlessness, and each had a devouring ambition which somehow was selfless. They were physically alike, tall, aloof, seemingly arrogant, and each had enjoyed making the life of Winston Churchill a misery. Like Churchill, they were larger-than-life characters and in this century few statesmen have more illustrious names.

Today, the name of de Valera has as Irish a sound as O'Reilly, but it struck an odd note in the ambience of those revolutionary days when he first came into prominence. Born in New York in October 1882, Eamon de Valera was the child of the marriage of Spanish-born Vivion Juan de Valera and Catherine Coll, an immigrant Irish daughter of a farm labourer. Vivion de Valera died when his son was three years old and his widow, who had to go out to work to keep herself and the boy, agreed with her family that he should be brought up by his grandmother in Ireland.

At the age of six he began school in Bruree, County Limerick, walking from his home at Knockmore a mile or so distant. His uncle, Pat Coll, was politically active and the boy was soon aware of Ireland's land problems. His grandmother died when Eamon de Valera was thirteen and the boy found his duties in the house multiplied. He also helped his uncle with farm tasks. It was a hard, simple, warm life and one that helped him, as he was to claim one day, to know what was in the people's hearts. In 1896, when he was fourteen, he almost returned to America, but instead persuaded his uncle to allow him to attend the Christian Brothers College in Charleville. Often he walked the seven miles to school. Two years later, he won an exhibition which took him as a boarder to Blackrock College in Dublin. There he became interested in mathematics but he did well in all his subjects and went on to University College. Again he distinguished himself and at the age of twenty-one received his first teaching appointment, at Rockwell College near Cashel in County Tipperary.

He was not at this time a political animal, though he took an enthusiastic part in debating. Poverty in the country was familiar to him; his own life had been circumscribed and conditioned by it. But poverty did not rob a countryman of his dignity. The poor of the Dublin slums whom he visited as a voluntary worker of the St Vincent de Paul Society were very different and his experiences cut deep. Deeply religious and half inclined towards the priesthood, he might easily have embarked upon a missionary career. Mathematics won out and after two years at Rockwell he sat his university examinations and obtained a pass degree, a result which disappointed him.

At this time Michael Collins was still a schoolboy and Arthur Griffith had already published *The Resurrection of Hungary* in the *United Irishman*. De Valera was normally preoccupied with advancement in his profession and devoted most of his leisure to rugby. He was a tall, ascetic looking youngster and had recently taken to spectacles which, set on his beaky nose, have always given him the look of a wise bird. In the next few years he held a succession of posts as teacher, lecturer and examiner, and pursued his own mathematical studies with characteristic determination. There was one other interest which stemmed from his boyhood and has excited him ever since—the Irish language. In 1908 he joined the Gaelic League, the gateway of so many young Irishmen to the independence movement. One of his Gaelic teachers was Sinéad Flanagan and early in 1910 they were married.

At first he was active in helping develop the educational side of the Gaelic League and his interest in Irish history was aroused. He became aware of the emergence of Irish nationalism but his interest in politics was not fired until the Home Rule Bill of 1912. Collins had had a grounding in politics since boyhood and entered the independence movement by way of the secret Irish Republican Brotherhood; Arthur Griffith had from apprenticeship days steadily progressed from debating societies and discussion groups to the founding of the Sinn Fein Party; de Valera's preparation for what was to come had been a much less conscious one, but in its way no less thorough.

The fanatical resistance of the Northern Unionists to the very moderate Home Rule measures proposed and the support of the English Conservatives—to the point of treason—brought home to him that the alien "Ascendancy" had every intention of clinging to their power, their possessions and their colonialist philosophy. The good of Ireland was not their concern; their own well-being gained at the expense of the indigenous Irish, was. "Home Rule is Rome Rule!" they trumpeted, but they did not really fear political intervention by the Pope, although they genuinely detested and mistrusted Roman Catholicism. What they were afraid of was democracy in Ireland, rule by the majority—who happened to be Catholics—and the attenuation of the link with the Crown, symbol of the authority which had given and now sustained their position as a privileged class. Religion, then as now, was a potent additive, an emotive catalyst of indignation and passion, but it was, and is, as much a uniform which distinguishes friend from foe as it is the cause of their enmity.

De Valera saw that the Ascendancy were not to be grubbed out of their entrenched positions by a Parliament in which the powerful opposition party supported them and the Government saw Home Rule as no more than a price to be paid for the division-winning votes of the Irish Parliamentary Party. The constitutional line of

8

the Irish Parliamentary Party, which until now de Valera had supported, he now realised was bound to fail, and when the Irish Volunteers came into being at a meeting in the Rotunda in Dublin on November 25th 1913 de Valera joined. Their object was "to secure and maintain the rights and liberties common to all the people of Ireland", and Eamon de Valera, still unknown, was convinced that freedom could be won only by force of arms. Involvement was a big risk for a man with three young children but, having made his decision, he set about making himself proficient with a meticulous attention to detail which soon won him promotion and came to be recognised as his stock in trade.

"To secure and maintain the rights and liberties common to all the people in Ireland" was an ideal which attracted men of many shades of opinion, providing a focus for the numerous movements stemming from pride in being Irish which until now had not been cohesive. The Volunteers encompassed the moderate Gaelic Leaguer, the follower of Sinn Fein, the member of the Gaelic Athletic Association, the middle of the road supporter of the Irish Parliamentary Party, and the Irish Republican Brotherhood extremist. From the beginning, the influence of the IRB permeated the Volunteers, unobtrusively but potently, unknown even to Eoin MacNeill, their founder and nominal head. Members of the IRB were to be found in all the nationalist organisations. There was, in any case, much overlapping of membership.

Pearse, Clarke and their colleagues in the IRB were already determined upon insurrection, but they were not alone in scorning Redmond's helpful attitude towards Britain. The Government of Ireland Act for which he was so grateful was a short-weight measure and even that was to be brushed conveniently under Britain's wartime counter. The Volunteers had been divided and weakened by Redmond's offer to use them as a Home Guard in Ireland and by enlistment in the British armed services. Among those who remained to reconstitute the movement was Eamon de Valera, who had not yet become a member of the Irish Republican Brotherhood.

When, in co-operation with Connolly's Irish Citizen Army, the Volunteers embarked upon the Easter Rising, de Valera was commandant of a battalion. By that time he had, with reluctance, taken the IRB oath. Although he frowned on secret societies, de Valera found that men under his command knew more about the planned Rising than he. With MacNeill at their head, the Volunteers were committed to take up arms only if England introduced measures, such as the enforcement of conscription, which were inimical to the ideals or interests of the Irish. Only by joining the IRB could de Valera receive the confidences of the leaders for whom preservation of the *status quo* held little attraction.

When the Rising came, Commandant de Valera took possession of Boland's Mill. He had had no military experience but he had studied military theory with a mathematician's acumen. Of all the commandants he was the only one who did not simply take up a defensive position and fight gallantly to hold it. The trap he set for British reinforcements at Mount Street Bridge accounted for nearly half the British casualties of the Rising.

The Volunteer garrisons knew that they could not win their freedom by their insurrection, that the majority of the Irish people were not ready for the drastic action they had taken, but they believed they were right. In a way, the Rising was bungled, and it was bungled because the ostensible authority, MacNeill, did not know how the hidden power of the IRB was working. Had there been no division at the top, Britain would have been faced with a much more widespread rebellion. As it was, Britain's predictable policy of retribution converted the Irish failure into success. Pearse and Connolly had been convinced that only their blood would win freedom for Ireland, and so it proved.

Sentenced to death but reprieved, Eamon de Valera, one of the last commandants to accept Pearse's surrender instructions, was sent to Dartmoor. When MacNeill, upon whom many of the Volunteers unjustly placed the blame for the apparent failure of the Rising, joined them, de Valera improvised a ceremonial parade and saluted him. It was less a magnanimous gesture than recognition of what was just. It was also a demonstration of the innate authority that this gaunt, unostentatious man possessed. At Dartmoor and later at Lewes, though they were treated as felons, under de Valera's guidance the Irish conducted themselves as prisoners of war. De Valera, like any prison-camp leader in enemy hands, sought to make difficulties for the detaining power and, at the same time, to avoid needless hardships for his men.

Often punitive measures were taken against them, when, for the sake of a principle, they resisted discipline, but de Valera discouraged hunger strikes because the death of any of them would not significantly help the Irish cause at this time. This kind of sacrifice demands the right time and the right setting, as Terence MacSwiney knew when he fasted to death in 1920. His long agony in Brixton caught the imagination of the world and helped swing public opinion in Great Britain against the continued suppression of Ireland.

De Valera's active mind ranged far beyond the walls of the prison but news of what was happening in his own land came sparsely and ambiguously in letters from home. Nevertheless, he was able to arrange for occasional smuggled messages. In a letter to his friend Simon Donnelly[1] he wrote: "We regard ourselves as at present, in a very special way, identified with the cause, the ideals and aspirations for which our comrades died last Easter." He urged that the Volunteers "must not be allowed to disappear" but he was less certain of the advisability of contesting elections against the Irish Parliamentary Party. Of Sinn Fein's objectives he was none too certain. He knew little of Arthur Griffith and was not very much in sympathy with his dual monarchy proposals. The idea of submitting Ireland's case to the Peace Conference when it came did appeal to him, especially after America's entry into the war, and he insisted, "If delegates are sent and are admitted they should be given no powers of agreeing to anything less [than absolute independence]."[2] This precept was still in his mind when he dispatched the Irish delegation to the conference table in London more than four years later and it was a precept he never relinquished.

In May 1917 de Valera organised strike action in the prison to try to gain official recognition of the prisoner of war status of the Irish prisoners. He was moved to Maidstone and released from there less than three weeks later. The Frongoch internees had been released for Christmas 1916, and Michael Collins and others were already working to reconstitute the Irish Republican Brotherhood. This was the one section of the independence movement de Valera would have preferred not to revive. He and the other sentenced prisoners of the Rising were released as a goodwill gesture by Lloyd George, who had succeeded Asquith as Prime Minister, partly to impress the Americans but also because he was anxious to shake off the political Old Man of the Sea that Ireland seemed to him to be. Lloyd George offered Redmond immediate Home Rule, with Ulster excluded from its operation for five years. At the same time he satisfied Carson that the division would be permanent. Redmond declined but agreed to an alternative, a great Convention to which representatives from all aspects of Irish life would come and whose conclusions were to form the basis for fresh legislation.

Sinn Fein stood aloof from the Convention and held its own Ard Fheis in October 1917. This marked de Valera's political coming of age. From the moment of his return to Ireland, when he received a vehement welcome from a people who had witnessed his departure for English prisons with scant sympathy, Eamon de Valera had been recognised as a leader. He quickly accepted the rôle and one of his first actions had been to address to the President and Congress of America, in the name of the Provisional Government of Ireland, a declaration of Ireland's right to independence. He saw that if he could only enlist the formidable support of America Britain would be unable to deny that right.

2

ELECTED MEMBER of East Clare within a month of his return, de Valera followed the Griffith line of abstaining from an appearance at Westminster. At the Sinn Fein Ard Fheis he succeeded Griffith as leader and a day later, on October 27th 1917, was also elected President of the Volunteers. The two movements had become linked to pursue the campaign for independence. Until now there had been no liaison between Sinn Fein, the political movement whose aims were most in tune with the aspirations of the separatists, and the Volunteers—and through them the IRB— who saw physical force as the only way of compelling England to accept Ireland as an independent small nation.

Already the name of Sinn Fein was becoming a blanket title for the various separatist groups, whether or not they belonged to the movement. Broadened in this way, and deepened to tap the springs of physical force, Sinn Fein became something quite different from the party Arthur Griffith had founded and he recognised that he was not the person to lead it. In de Valera he saw the man he could follow, in a sense as the successor to William Rooney. They talked together before the Ard Fheis. De Valera was confident that he would be elected president of what was virtually a new organisation which, however, still had Sinn Fein at the heart of it. Satisfied that de Valera was the man of the new hour, Griffith decided not to contest the election—and Count Plunkett who had also been nominated withdrew as well.

On much Griffith and de Valera were agreed. Both were intensely interested in the revival of the national language and both believed that the Ulster Unionists, led now by James Craig, who constituted a minority in the whole country, should not be allowed to arrange the exclusion of part of the country from an independent Ireland—if independence could be won. The presentation of Ireland's case to the Peace Conference, preferably with the support of the United States, also was common ground. President Woodrow Wilson had clearly indicated his sympathy with small nations and his belief in their right to rule themselves.

But whereas de Valera had set his sights on a republic, Griffith, though not unsympathetic to the ideal, was still, as he would sometimes confess, a King, lords and commons man. He was convinced the Unionist minority would never accept a republic but could, in all justice, be required to bow to a majority decision which allowed them to preserve some link with Britain. De Valera was not willing to make this concession; equally, he was determined that, provided they were loyal to Ireland, there should be no discrimination, no inequality.

The new Sinn Fein was a federation of interests which included men of moderate views and moderate ambitions and those whose opinions were more stringent. It was an alliance of the flexible and the implacable and a formula was needed which would give them a common ideal. It was de Valera who devised one: "Sinn Fein aims at securing the international recognition of Ireland as an independent Irish Republic. Having achieved that status the Irish people may by referendum freely choose their own form of Government."

Ardent Republicans like Brugha were satisfied by the stated objective and Griffith's followers and other moderate groups appreciated the less doctrinaire note of the second part of the formula. But the time was to come when the formula would fall into two pieces, when the republicans insisted that the first objective had not been won and that therefore the second part was not relevant, while the moderates maintained that the Republic was not possible, that it had been primarily a symbol for independence and that the wishes of the Irish people must be the first consideration. If the first sentence had read simply: "Sinn Fein aims at securing the international recognition of Ireland as an independent nation", there would have been no paradox, no room for misunderstanding, but it would not have satisfied those who had accepted the Proclamation of 1916 as an irrevocable creed.

A modest salary went with the presidency of Sinn Fein and this enabled de Valera to give all his time and his whole stringy energy to the work of securing Ireland's independence. For this he campaigned with unflagging zeal, making speech after speech with calculated militancy and engendering in the eager young men and women of Ireland a devotion, and in the older people a faith, which united and sustained the whole independence movement.

Lloyd George, already anxious to staunch the blood of the Irish Parliamentary Party, watched de Valera's rise to power with wary admiration. He did not under-rate this new force stirring Ireland. Of de Valera's speeches Lloyd George said, "They are not excited, and so far as the language is concerned they are not violent. They are plain, deliberate and, I might almost say, cold-blooded incitement to rebellion." Somehow the new Irish leader escaped arrest, although the British were busy rounding up those who preached sedition. Thomas Ashe, arrested in August 1917, died the following month in Mountjoy prison from ill-treatment and neglect after being forcibly fed for a week. His death caused a great surge of sympathy and anger in Ireland and provoked the British Government into employing the "Cat and Mouse" Act to combat the hunger-strike weapon. Irish martyrs always succeeded in making a telling point.

Subversive speeches, the drilling of the Volunteers and conflicts between Sinn Fein and the police impelled Duke, Chief Secretary for Ireland, to obtain the Cabinet's sanction to proclaim Sinn Fein a dangerous association in some areas and to arrest, and deport if necessary, any Sinn Fein leaders "whose speech or action was dangerous to the public interest". Internment of the intractable Irish leaders was contemplated by the British Cabinet but, ironically, it was recognised that this could not be done because they were British subjects. It was necessary to prove legally hostile association.[3] This became an important consideration when the Cabinet proposed to extend conscription to Ireland.

Assessments of the consequences of conscription in Ireland varied but the concensus was that it could be done though it was inadvisable. Cabinet discussions were long and analytical, reflecting desperation and doubt. There was on the one hand that reservoir of fresh manpower, on the other fear that Ireland would again erupt into armed rebellion. There was also British public opinion to be reckoned with. Lloyd George proposed a new Home Rule Bill, not as a bribe but to redeem his pledge to the Convention. A decision on conscription in Ireland was deferred, despite the exasperated protests of the Generals, until the Report of the Convention was received.

On April 10th, the day that the new Military Service Bill was introduced in the Commons, Duke warned the Government that de Valera was out to cause trouble. Old Irish leaders and new met on the platform of an anti-conscription meeting at the Mansion House in Dublin and Dillon, Tim Healy and William O'Brien were impressed by the younger men, especially de Valera whom they studied with great interest. Their own day was nearly done, they knew, and with them on the platform were the new generation of patriots, men whose plans for Ireland were far more ambitious than they had ever envisaged.

The meeting produced a declaration, drafted by de Valera, that Britain's conscription plan "must be regarded as a declaration of war against the Irish nation"; the people should "resist it by the most effective means at their disposal". The Catholic hierarchy, until now critical of the independence movement and scornful of the republican ideal, came out strongly against conscription. On May 6th Lloyd George received a deputation of Belfast trade unionists[4] to whom he had pointed out that "it was impossible to enforce conscription in Ireland without some reasonable measure of Home Rule". Playing on their Protestant earnestness, he had also "shown them how the supremacy of Parliament had been challenged by the action of the Catholic hierarchy". Seeking to enlist their support to "defeat this challenge", he asked them for practical suggestions for a Home Rule Bill.

The Military Service Bill was not to apply to Ireland immediately but the provision was to be invoked by Order in Council when required. Duke had warned that conscription might well result in the loss of Ireland[5] and he reported also that de Valera was urging "that it would be better for their policy if conscription came, when they could undertake systematic and violent opposition to its enforcement".[6] It would be advisable, Duke thought, to arrest all known dissidents. General Byrne, head of the Royal Irish Constabulary, advised that the situation in Ireland was grave; the people were united against conscription. He intimated also that he had learned of "movements in force which implied that assistance could be expected from German sources".[7]

Rather primly anxious to observe the letter of the law and at the same time to get rid of the Irish troublemakers, the Cabinet became more and more interested in the possibilities of "hostile association". Rumours reached the War Cabinet that de Valera had been discovered to be in communication with the enemy but they had to admit that there was no evidence of this.[8] Even Lord French wrote from Ireland that opposition to conscription was passive rather than active, but he harped on German intrigues. He informed the Cabinet that he intended to issue a proclamation and to arrest any "against whom evidence of intriguing was produced". He intended also to deal with seditious speeches but was advised that "to hold a meeting to organise resistance to a prospective law was not treason".[9] Privately Lloyd George informed him that if there were to be any shooting he wanted the Irish to start it.

French took up his appointment on May 11th and, on the 17th de Valera, Griffith, Count Plunkett, Countess Markievicz, Cosgrave and other leading lights in the Sinn Fein movement were arrested, seventy-three altogether. Like the others, de Valera had disregarded Collins's advance warning. De Valera did not court arrest but felt he could accomplish little if he went "on the run".

In recent months Sinn Fein had failed in by-elections but now Arthur Griffith was nominated for East Cavan in Ulster. It was probable that Griffith would swing support irrevocably away from the crumbling Irish Parliamentary Party. Already the public had begun to see that, although they preached the same gospel on the conscription issue, the Parliamentary Party were followers rather than leaders, and de Valera had already resisted a bid by Dillon to win Sinn Fein's support for the Parliamentary Party's candidate for the Cavan by-election. The party's acknowledgment of Sinn Fein, implied in the offer of co-operation, was in itself a cachet which encouraged moderate voters hitherto doubtful of

Sinn Fein. That it was far more likely to achieve independence for Ireland was already apparent.

The "German Plot", usually written off as a fabrication, had very little substance, but some British Ministers were afraid that a German-assisted rising in Ireland was possible. Others were anxious that the evidence should be put to Judges and that justice should be seen to be done. A public statement had to be prepared.

In de Valera's attaché case a number of documents were found. They included a history of Sinn Fein in French, a draft statement of Ireland's case to be put to the Peace Conference and a carefully prepared plan for the defence of Ireland after independence. Not much to link him with Germany, but Lloyd George was satisfied that de Valera's own speeches "identified him with the German Sinn Fein plans".[10] Absent in Paris, the British Prime Minister telephoned plaintively that he wished "to insert some words which would connect with the German designs in Ireland persons who had been detained other than de Valera". His Cabinet colleagues could find nothing helpful. A rather spurious mélange of 1916 transactions with Germany and ambiguous allegations of more recent negotiations was put out by the British Cabinet.

De Valera went first to Gloucester then to Lincoln prisons. The war ended but still he and his friends were held. Lloyd George's pious intention to bring in Home Rule had gone by the board. Walter Long had prepared a draft bill and had warned percipiently that if the six Ulster counties were excluded it would be "the worst settlement of all". In Ireland Lord French was busy trying to suppress Sinn Fein and other Nationalist organisations under the Defence of the Realm Act, the accommodating "Dora", but raids and arrests made little impression. Collins, Brugha and Mulcahy reorganised the Volunteers, who trained determinedly and Collins steadily built up his Intelligence system.

In December came the general election and Sinn Fein's success in 73 of 105 seats in the whole of Ireland. The threat of conscription had proved to be Britain's biggest blunder, more calamitous for her perhaps than Maxwell's Easter execution programme. Yet it had been a calculated risk taken by a desperate Cabinet faced with the overwhelming defeat of an empire. Sinn Fein's electoral victory meant that the House of Commons would be missing seventy-three Members who instead set up their own parliament in Dublin, the first Dail. From his early days Arthur Griffith had advocated the withdrawal of Irish Members from Westminster and the establishment of an Irish parliament. The new-look Sinn Fein clung to his precept but it is possible to wonder what those seventy-three Sinn Fein members might have achieved if they had taken their seats. Certainly they could have made parliamentary life a nightmare.

Confident in the knowledge that the Irish people were behind them, twenty-seven elected members of the first Dail Eireann met in Dublin and ratified the establishment of a republic. Forty-three members were still imprisoned and two others, Collins and Harry Boland, were in England trying to arrange the escape of Eamon de Valera. Patiently and with great ingenuity de Valera had smuggled out instructions and now had a master key made in the prison from a blank brought in concealed in a cake. Collins and Boland were waiting when in the evening of February 3rd 1919 de Valera, Sean McGarry and Sean Milroy slipped out. The escape route had been thoroughly organised and within five hours of escaping the men were in Manchester. As he had intended, de Valera's escape gave the Irish independence movement some excellent publicity, while psychologically it was splendid for the Irish and traumatic for the British.

For several weeks before the escape, Shortt, now Chief Secretary for Ireland, and Barnes had urged the release of the Sinn Fein prisoners and, immediately after the Lincoln Prison break, French suddenly swung round from opposing liberation to vehemently advocating it. The Cabinet were doubtful, less because of the trouble in Ireland than because of conditions of acute industrial unrest and fear of communist activities in England. The Government felt that it needed to show that it took a tough line with would-be revolutionaries.

De Valera returned quietly to Ireland on February 20th, then, having had a meeting with Ministers of the new Dail Cabinet and set in train arrangements to travel to America, crossed to Liverpool. He was still in hiding when on March 4th the British Government finally decided to release the Sinn Fein prisoners. Assured that he could return safely to Ireland, he crossed to Dublin but the British Government proclaimed the reception organised for him. On April 1st he was elected President of the Dail, in which position Brugha had been acting in his absence.

Brugha became Minister of Defence in de Valera's Cabinet. Arthur Griffith was in charge of Home Affairs and W. T. Cosgrave of Local Government. Count Plunkett was Minister of Foreign Affairs, Countess Mackievicz Minister of Labour and Michael Collins Minister of Finance.

The Peace Conference was very much in the minds of all of them. If the sovereignty of the Irish Republic were to be recognised by an international assembly, especially with American support—and they counted a great deal on Wilson's declared sympathy with small countries compelled to some procrustean pattern by more powerful nations—then they would cut the ground from beneath Britain's imperial boots. The Dail had already nominated de Valera, Griffith and Count Plunkett as delegates to the Peace Conference but how they were to be got there was another matter. Three Irish-American delegates called at Dublin on their way to Paris to advocate Ireland's case, and their visit greatly heartened the independence movement, but the great powers were already drawing arbitrary boundary lines on the map of Europe, Wilson was not so strong as he had seemed and Ireland's case was refused a hearing. De Valera had faith in American public opinion and was convinced that Ireland must utilise it. He believed, too, that he himself could best perform the task of mobilising the moral forces of America.

First he set the pattern for Ireland. At every opportunity her people should make it clear to the world that their country was occupied by alien forces. On April 10th he put a resolution to the Dail, which was passed, ostracising the Royal Irish Constabulary whose history he saw as "a continuity of brutal treason against their own people". This was a harsh judgment. It was true that Dublin Castle relied on the reports of RIC men to keep them informed of all that was happening in the country, and certainly they reported on the subversive activities of certain young men in their area, but

the country had changed quickly and it was difficult for many of
the friendly, unimaginative constables to accept that what had been
for long years their duty suddenly had become treachery towards
their own kin. For a family man a secure job and a pension at the
end of it was not easy to throw up for the sake of an untried ideal
and a group of mostly young men who would not even take their
seats in the House of Commons but set up their own parliament.
The move to ostracise the RIC was a clever one, however. Sinn
Fein could not afford to allow this vast Intelligence network to
remain in existence and, anxious to avoid trouble, the constables
tended to be less zealous. As time went on many of them defected
to Sinn Fein.

3

DE VALERA appointed Arthur Griffith as acting President, insisting that Griffith take the Presidential salary, and stowed away on an American-bound boat. He saw no incongruity in this. While still in prison he had half decided to go to America, and when after his escape the Dail Cabinet heard of his intention from Collins, they were not very happy about it. Cathal Brugha travelled to Liverpool to dissuade him but succeeded only in getting his assurance that he would spend some time in Ireland before his departure.

Not without misgivings, the Dail Cabinet allowed themselves to be persuaded that de Valera was needed in America. It was not easy to reconcile themselves to the loss of their leader on the eve of revolution, but at that point he did not intend to absent himself for long. What his colleagues most feared was that the inspiration the whole independence movement, which encompassed the great majority of the Irish people, gained from him would dry up without the immediate impact of his personality. They were wrong, for that personality exerted its magnetism across the Atlantic and held together the variegated segments of the revolutionary movement. Griffith's solid reliability and the dash of Collins held a compensatory reassurance and stimulus.

De Valera undertook three main tasks. Despite the lack of encouragement in Paris, international recognition was still the first priority and he was to try to get that recognition in America. His second task derived from Article 10 of the new League of Nations Covenant by which existing territorial boundaries of member nations were to be sacrosanct. This came as a shock to the Irish who realised the danger that the American Government would accept Britain's claim that the Irish coast was a territorial boundary. De Valera wanted to demonstrate the injustice of this to the American people and through them to put pressure on their Government. Finally, in order to finance the establishment of the Republic and the inevitable struggle with Britain, de Valera was to float a loan in America. In Ireland the launching of the loan was in the safe hands of Michael Collins.

There is not the slightest doubt that in his own mind de Valera was sure he could fulfil a more valuable function in the United States than he could in Ireland, but it is arguable that the place of the leader in troublous times with his own people, that a lesser man could have undertaken the work in America. Any man faced with complex alternatives can only do what in his judgment seems right at the time. One would have been less inclined to suspect de Valera's judgment on this occasion had it not been the first part of a curious pattern, for on two more big occasions he saw as his prime responsibility what appeared to others to be the lesser one.

Remaining in America from June 1919 to December 1920, de Valera missed all but the last few months of Ireland's determined fight to rid herself of British overlordship. It was a conflict which led a war-hardened British Government to conduct a campaign of terror, engendering a hatred which to this day lingers in the embittered streets of Belfast. It was a war of horrible retaliation which might conceivably have developed on quite different lines had de Valera been able to lead Ireland through it. As it was, he could only agonise from afar and when he did return was out of touch with the realities.

De Valera was not alone in the United States. Harry Boland had preceded him and Liam Mellows and Dr Patrick MacCartan had been there for some time. The alleged activities of these two played a small part in the putative German Plot. Americans everywhere welcomed de Valera as the President of Ireland, yet the only title he laid claim to was President of the Dail. No doubt his enthusiastic reception was satisfying, though he took it as recognition of his courageous country rather than as a personal tribute, but his American road was stony in many ways. Within Irish-American circles there was friction and Boland had already run into trouble with the Loan. The Friends of Irish Freedom had established their own Irish Victory Fund but it was proposed to spend most of the money on propaganda in America. The Irish-Americans did not understand the nature of the system of government the Dail proposed to establish in opposition to the existing departments of Dublin Castle and were suspicious of the need for good American dollars to be sent to Ireland.

Despite opposition from the two most influential Irish-American leaders, John Devoy and Judge Cohalan, de Valera pressed on with the flotation of the Irish bonds and finally was able to borrow initial finance from the Victory Fund. The Irish National Loan (External) was an immediate success and altogether some five million dollars were raised. Much of the donkey work was taken over by James O'Mara who arrived from Ireland in November, and this allowed Eamon de Valera to give more time to political matters.

But his sojourn in America was, on the whole, neither very happy nor very successful. There was a vivid clash of personalities between him and Devoy and Cohalan. Groping for an analogy during a newspaper interview, he suggested that Britain could adopt the Cuban solution to settle the Irish problem. He had not thought the parallel through and was assailed in the *Gaelic American* for daring to suggest that Britain should have rights in Ireland similar to those enjoyed by the United States in Cuba. In vain he protested that he had not intended that at all. He suspected a plot against himself and his mission, prompted, he told Griffith in a letter, by "some devilish cause". Dr MacCartan was sent home to explain his difficulties. Later Boland returned on a similar mission.

Shortly afterwards he sent to Collins and Griffith copies of a dignified but rancorous exchange of letters with Cohalan, in which he had put himself at a disadvantage, and attached a long and acrimonious memorandum about it. In reply Griffith assured de Valera of the steadfast support of the Cabinet. Then O'Mara resigned, apparently also over differences with de Valera, and despairingly Collins wrote to Boland, "There always seems to be something depressing coming from the U.S.A. I cannot tell you how despondent this particular incident had made me."[11]

In June 1920 de Valera went to Chicago for the Republican Convention, hoping to have the recognition of the Irish Republic included in the election platform of the Presidential candidate. He was frustrated, he believed because of Cohalan's machinations, and at the Democratic Convention in San Francisco shortly afterwards a similar proposal was voted out. A letter to President Wilson went unanswered. These were disappointments to which perhaps he contributed by pitching his demand too high and refusing to compromise, but the wall was not entirely impenetrable. A few days before his arrival in America the Senate had adopted a resolution of "sympathy with the expectations of the Irish people for a government of their own choice", and when on March 18th they ratified the Peace Treaty the Senate declared its adherence to the principle of self determination and to that resolution. This was heartening to de Valera who, on the following day at a meeting at a New York hotel, routed his opponents who were not expecting him and had hoped to have him recalled to Dublin.

Disillusioned with the leaders of Friends of Irish Freedom, de Valera founded his own organisation, "The American Association for the Recognition of the Irish Republic". The name was clumsy but it left no doubt as to what its members were undertaking. It flourished at once.

When de Valera departed for home following the arrest of Griffith after Bloody Sunday, he left the Irish-Americans in a state of disarray. Whether that was his fault or theirs is difficult to determine, but it does seem that he counted too much upon the Irishness of the American Irish. Cohalan put his own position cogently in his letter to de Valera: "What I have done for the cause of the Irish people, recently and for many years past, I have done as an American, whose only allegiance is to America, and as one to whom the interest and security of my country are ever to be preferred to those of any and all other lands." He accused de Valera of interference. Yet, in the same letter, referring to American sympathisers, he wrote, "Those millions do not desire to see a return of the conditions which, under the late Mr Redmond, made political activities in Ireland a football in English party politics."

One suspects from his tone that he was more concerned with spiking England's guns than promoting Ireland's cause for its own sake.

De Valera acknowledged that the first loyalty of Irish-Americans was to America but never seemed quite able to believe it. If he was sometimes confused it was not altogether surprising. Obstinately he pursued his aim to secure recognition of the Republic and in the pursuit he trampled on political toes. Ironically, at the end of it all, he declared that only if the United States and England went to war—relations between the two powers were certainly at breaking point—would the United States be likely to recognise the Republic of Ireland. "If I were President of the United States," he told the Dail, "I could not, and I would not, recognise Ireland as a Republic." He seemed satisfied that he had put the case.

Although his wife joined him in America for a short time, he saw little of her and was glad when the long break from family life was at an end. His stint in America had endured for much longer than he had intended. This was partly because the Dail Cabinet felt that he was on the edge of success and urged him to stay, though afterwards Collins at least began to doubt that they had been as well informed as they believed.

His biographers state that Sir John Wheeler-Bennett's suggestion that de Valera returned to Dublin "with the connivance of the British Authorities"[12] was disproved by the minutes of the British Cabinet, that it was only after his return that they decided not to arrest him, "supposing he could be found". But Sir John was right. The decision (reversing an earlier one) to allow de Valera to land without hindrance was made on December 20th. No action was to be taken until there had been further consideration.[13] On January 14th the Cabinet confirmed their decision not to arrest him unless "some new, definite criminal charge" could be brought against him. Griffith was in prison and Collins had been branded a murderer, so de Valera was thought to be the one man with whom the British Government could negotiate. As undisputed leader he was in any case the right man.

He had returned to a new and totally unfamiliar situation and to subordinates hardened by experience such as he had never known and grown accustomed to larger responsibilities. In his absence they had been devoted to him and it says much for him that he lost none of their loyalty now that he was back with them, no longer a distant deity but a leader out of touch with what was happening.

Cautiously he began to pick up the threads and, appropriately enough, first examined the lapsed negotiations which Archbishop Clune had conducted with Collins, Griffith and MacNeill. He was resolved that any further negotiations must be on the initiative of the British and in the open. He had little taste for undercover methods in anything. However, the Dail was compelled to meet clandestinely and de Valera himself had to live in hiding. He had no reason to suspect that he would not be arrested on sight and, even if he had known, he would not have wished to serve as bait to catch badly wanted men like Collins, Brugha, Mulcahy or O'Malley. It was at this point, actually on January 18th, that de Valera wrote proposing that Collins should go to America, a plan which showed that de Valera had not yet understood how vital Collins was to the revolution. There were a number of tasks he wanted Collins to undertake but the programme has a concocted look about it and his real motive was probably that "we will not have here, so to speak, 'all our eggs in one basket', and that whatever coup the English may attempt, the line of succession is safe, and the future provided for".[14] De Valera might also have had it in mind to relieve the tension between Brugha and Collins by separating them and to lift the struggle in Dublin out of its secret gang warfare pattern. Collins strongly opposed the plan and, partly because of the swift run of events, de Valera dropped it.

4

THE FRESH, cool mind of the returned leader brought a new cohesion to the weary but indefatigable forces, political and military, ranged against Britain. All the members of the Dail Cabinet were men on the run, hunted and harassed. With incredible success they had set up and were running their own Government departments. These were not paper bureaux but effective organs of government working in rivalry with their British-run counterparts. These same men were conducting a revolutionary war against bitter and unscrupulous opponents who insisted that they were dealing not with soldiers but with criminals, who hanged idealistic youngsters like Kevin Barry and would have hanged the chivalrous Sean McEoin if first his wounds and then the peace had not prevented it. Collins himself had a price of £10,000 on his head.

Little wonder, then, that there were tensions among these men, particularly between Austin Stack and Cathal Brugha on the one hand and Collins on the other. De Valera contained these tensions, exercised his authority over the various departments and concentrated on building up the strength and the authority of Dail Eireann, determined that it should be recognised all over the world as the properly elected, constitutional Parliament of Ireland. He was at pains to convince the Irish bishops of this but most of them were not impressed. Publicly he stated that the IRA, whose members had pledged their loyalty to the Dail, was "a regular State force, under the civil control of the elected representatives", and that the Government was responsible for the actions of its army.[15] He introduced new blood, the young Kevin O'Higgins to assist Cosgrave who was Minister for Local Government and, to replace the gaoled Desmond Fitzgerald, Erskine Childers as Director of Publicity, a "civil service" appointment.

Childers was a curious but brilliant choice, not wholeheartedly approved by the Cabinet. Until his death in the Civil War, he was distrusted by many who thought of him as an English turncoat. Childers had seen British imperialism at close quarters and had been disillusioned by it. An orphan, he had been brought up with his cousin, Robert Barton, in County Wicklow and educated at Haileybury and Trinity College, Cambridge. In the next few years he was a clerk in the House of Commons, fought with the Honourable Artillery Company in the Boer War, wrote of his experiences in *In the Ranks of the C.I.V.*, sailed to the West Indies in a tramp steamer and roamed the North Sea in *Vixen*, his 7-ton yacht; from his observations of German naval activity he wrote his prophetic thriller *The Riddle of the Sands*.

Physically he did not seem made of the stuff of adventure. Thin but wiry, he suffered from sciatica and limped. He was pinched, pallid and intellectual looking, full of energy and a passionate believer in justice. In 1908 he became a convert to Home Rule and, thorough as he always was, made himself an expert on the subject. His carefully thought-out *The Framework of Home Rule*, published in 1911, made him a reputation, and English as well as Irish statesmen consulted him during the tortuous discussions on the Home Rule Bill of the following year.

His wife, formerly Mary Osgood of Boston, though partially crippled, shared in all his activities, even the expeditions in *Asgard*, the yacht given to them as a wedding present by her parents. A woman of acute intelligence and high principles, Mrs Childers disliked British imperialism and perhaps influenced her husband, but Childers was never anti-British, hostile only towards the colonial system.

When it seemed in 1914 that Carson, Craig and their Ulster Volunteers would stop at nothing to defeat Home Rule, and in April landed a huge consignment of arms, Childers realised that the southern counties were almost defenceless. With a powerful London Committee behind him, he took part in a dramatic gun-running adventure in *Asgard*. The arms were landed at Howth and

Eamon de Valera, then an unknown Volunteer, was among those who collected them.

During the First World War Childers flew as an observer in naval aircraft in the North Sea and Mediterranean areas and later joined the Royal Flying Corps. He saw nothing paradoxical in fighting for Britain after running guns to Ireland. The arms, so far as he knew, were never intended for use against Britain but for the defence of Southern Ireland against the intransigent North. But as the news of events in Ireland reached him, his disillusionment with the British imperial pattern was heightened. After the Easter Rising he wrote, "There is no moment in Irish history that I know of when it would not have been best both for England and Ireland that Ireland should govern herself."[16] He was convinced that had the Government of Ireland Act been implemented, despite the War, there would have been no Easter Rising. But Childers set too much store by Home Rule when already Irish claims had run far ahead of it.

Appointed secretary of the Irish Convention of 1917, he thought there was a hope that the many Irish interests would co-operate to produce a solution. But it all ended in compromise, which he detested, and because of the independent line taken by Sinn Fein and the growing support they were attracting, he began to realise that if Ireland were ever to achieve self-government it would be Sinn Fein which brought it about.

When, in 1922, he faced the military tribunal which condemned him he explained, "The collapse of the whole Convention and the attempt to force conscription convinced me that Home Rule was dead, and that a revolution, founded on the Rising of 1916, was inevitable and necessary, and I only waited till the end of the War, when I had faithfully fulfilled my contract with the British, to join in the movement myself. With the formal establishment of the Republic in 1919, it became necessary for people like myself, of mixed birth, to choose our citizenship once and for all. I chose that of the Irish Republican Army ... I threw myself into the work of the Republican movement, and after a year took up my permanent residence ..."

These words, and the sympathy he expressed for the uneasy

firing squad who executed him, reveal a remarkable man. It was Michael Collins who introduced him to de Valera and that shrewd judge of character was quick to place his confidence in him. "He said much later," de Valera's biographers tell us, "that if he could choose a person along whose lines of character he would like to have modelled himself, that person would have been Childers."[17] While Griffith disliked and distrusted Childers as a "disgruntled Englishman", de Valera leaned on his loyalty and experience, Childers helping him in a significant way to formulate his ideas.

Although he justified the ambush as a fair means of fighting in the circumstances, de Valera was very concerned with the reprisals visited upon the Irish people. To ease their suffering and to improve the "image" of the IRA he advocated not a reduction of military effort but a concentration on raids on selected targets carried out by larger groups. But he listened to Mulcahy and other military leaders and did not disturb their strategy.

The last months were among the most bitter of the war with a large part of the country under martial law and a policy of "official reprisals" being carried out by the British. The killings and burnings continued but in the Cabinet in London earnest discussions about peace proposals were going on. Several British Ministers, including Churchill, opposed the insistence on a surrender of arms by the Irish, the stumbling block to peace during the Clune negotiations, but the majority were adamant. Lloyd George was suspicious of the Irish leaders, especially de Valera, though in January, having apparently received a letter from him, he was keen to meet him and rather carried away by a rosy vision of what a settlement in Ireland might bring about, not least a favourable arrangement concerning Britain's war debt to America. On this occasion Thomas Jones urged that the Cabinet recognise the idealism of the Irish nationalist spirit.[18]

It was decided by the British Government that no offer of a truce would be made until after the May elections to be held under the Government of Ireland Act of December, 1920.

It was convenient for Sinn Fein to use the British election machinery to elect a new Dail and, refusing to accept Partition, Sinn Fein presented candidates in Six Counties constituencies. Six were successful, including Collins, de Valera and Griffith. Like the six Nationalists who also won seats, the Sinn Fein men had no intention of taking their seats in the Northern Ireland Parliament. In the South, a few days later, the election was a formality. Sinn Fein were unopposed in all constituencies except for Trinity College which provided a quota of four Unionists.

So the North had a parliament they did not really want but which, today, they are determined to cling to. And in the South members had been elected ostensibly for a parliament which never met, although the gathering which ratified the Treaty in 1922 bore some resemblance to it. The British Cabinet did not expect the Southern Parliament to meet and had intended, after July 12th, to impose Crown Colony government and to extend martial law instead, but they were hopeful now of a truce.

In April Lord Derby had sounded out de Valera informally but received no encouragement. A fortnight later Sir James Craig visited him, but little came of their meeting, which had been arranged by Sir Alfred Cope, the one man in Dublin Castle who seemed to have some understanding of the Irish problem. Cope had contrived to give each the impression that the other had taken the initiative. They did not get far beyond the Act of Union of 1800, which Craig held to be morally binding and which de Valera dismissed as a piece of skulduggery.

When the British Government were informed that Craig and de Valera were likely to meet they hastened to brief Sir James "to avoid the risk of placing the British Government in the invidious position of possibly having to reject joint proposals made by the leaders of the two parts of Ireland".[19]

An end to the fighting was becoming more and more vital to the British Government. Committed to Crown Colony rule and extended martial law in Ireland, they were also faced with a turbulent industrial scene at home. Some of the militant workers were almost as difficult as the Irish. Mines were flooded and volunteers were attacked when they tried to pump the water out. It was no time to have to find the reinforcements promised to Macready.

A further worry was the swing of public feeling in England

against the methods of the Black and Tans. The *Guardian* was implacably opposed to the policy of the Lloyd George Government and even *The Times* was fulminating against them. Even now, by a majority decision the Cabinet would not take the initiative. Lloyd George advocated propaganda. He wanted to show how generous were the powers conferred by the Government of Ireland Act, how cantankerous were Sinn Fein in rejecting them and how vicious in murdering civilians merely because they were Protestants or ex-servicemen.

But a fortnight later, on June 2nd, the Cabinet decided to notify General Sir Nevil Macready "that reprisals which have already practically ceased outside the martial law area, must also cease within that area and that aggressive action must in every case be based on strictly military ground, defined by military orders".[20]

In Belfast, on June 22nd, the King, who had for years been critical of his Government's handling of the Irish crisis, made his appeal for "forbearance and conciliation". Lloyd George suggested to his Cabinet that this should be followed up. Rather embarrassingly, de Valera had been arrested on the night of June 22nd and hurriedly released the following day. Within a few days, Griffith, MacNeill, Barton, Duggan and several others were released from prison and executions were suspended.

At first de Valera was bewildered by his release, which seemed designed merely to humiliate him, but the invitation from Lloyd George received two days later made the reason plain. It signalled a dramatic change in British policy. De Valera did not jump at the invitation, which expressed "a fervent desire to end the ruinous conflict which has for centuries divided Ireland and embittered the relations of the peoples of these two islands . . ."

"We most earnestly desire to help in bringing about a lasting peace between the people of these two islands," replied de Valera, "but see no avenue by which it can be reached if you deny Ireland's essential unity and set aside the principle of self-determination." Those two points were to him as irrefutable as a proven mathematical formula and he was never persuaded from them.

Craig, who was also to meet Lloyd George, refused to visit Dublin first. Like de Valera, who had described him as merely a "representative of the politcal minority in this country", Craig was jockeying for position.

On July 5th, Field Marshal Smuts arrived incognito in Dublin, his visit having been arranged at de Valera's request by Tom Casement, Sir Roger's brother. The South African leader met de Valera, Griffith and others and extolled dominion status. "Make no mistake about it; you have more privilege, more power, more peace, more security in such a sisterhood of equal nations than in a small, nervous republic having all the time to rely on goodwill and perhaps the assistance of foreigners," he told them.[21] Smuts earned the respect of the Irish leaders but did not divert them from their republican ambitions.

On Lord Midleton's representations Lloyd George agreed to a truce. This was confirmed when Macready attended a meeting in Dublin on July 8th and it came into force on the 11th.

5

Three days later, de Valera led a delegation to London. Lloyd George put proposals which de Valera thought scarcely worth taking back to Dublin. At this stage, with the prospect of Conservative opposition even within his own coalition Government, Lloyd George was afraid to offer any real concessions. What he suggested was a watered-down form of dominion status. An independent Ireland could mean an open back door to Britain and this defence aspect alone meant that the British Government were not ready to concede the same degree of freedom that Canada and Australia enjoyed. They were reluctant, too, to encourage dissidents in India by appearing to show weakness in dealing with Ireland. An independent India was unthinkable.

Sir James Craig had put his own case to Lloyd George and was every bit as obstinate as de Valera. If the South were entitled to self-determination then so were the Six Counties, he claimed. Angrily de Valera made it clear to Lloyd George that if his Government supported an attempt by an Irish minority to treat separately, there was no point in continuing to negotiate.

It had become "increasingly clear that Ulster was the real difficulty", Lloyd George told his Cabinet on July 20th.[22] Sir James Craig had been adamant that under no circumstances would he accept a single parliament. The South would be able to impose and collect taxes and to "pack the fiscal administration with Sinn Feiners and Roman Catholics".

The Prime Minister had pointed out to de Valera that if there were to be a single parliament Southern Ireland might find herself in much the same position as Britain faced now. Civil war might result and lead to trouble throughout the Empire. Again it was

India he had in mind. "Mr de Valera stated Southern Ireland would never allow itself to be implicated in civil war," Lloyd George went on. They would rather leave the North alone. To this he had rejoined, "Why don't you leave Ulster alone now?"

Lloyd George had stretched to the full his highly professional craft in his three meetings at which, upon de Valera's insistence, they talked alone. He began by trying to impress the young and inexperienced Irish politician and then to establish between them the cameraderie of the Celt. Finally he had thrown out that "a great military concentration would take place in Ireland with a view to the suppression of the rebellion and the restoration of order". The cool de Valera was not impressed, recognised no affinity with the little Welshman and was not alarmed by threats. The Prime Minister ended the talks both chagrined and admiring.

Chamberlain and Balfour assisted him to draw up the formal draft of the proposals which the Dail President reluctantly took back to Dublin. As de Valera expected, the Dail Cabinet felt the same way as he.

With Childers's help, de Valera drafted a letter which did not give too much away, but he had already convinced his Cabinet that his alternative to dominion status was workable. "External association"—the name he gave it—was a brilliant formula to bring in the North, with their strong attachment to Union and the Monarchy, and to satisfy at the same time his friends who, as Liam Lynch was to put it, had declared for a republic and would not live under any other law. What de Valera suggested was a paradox, a republic connected with an empire at the head of which was a monarch. It was a new concept and patently ridiculous, yet it was to become the solution for the largest of Britain's imperial problems in the course of time.

The second Dail met on August 16th 1921, and when the old administration had given an account of its stewardship they resigned. Eamon de Valera was now elected President, not just of the Dail this time but of the Republic of Ireland. In this capacity he exchanged a long, sometimes farcical, sometimes solemn and always adroit series of letters with Lloyd George. His aim was to induce Lloyd George to accept, if only by implication, that he was dealing with the elected President of a constitutional republic. At the back of Irish minds, too, was the idea that if the Truce were to break down it would be better that this could be avoided until the longer nights and the mists of autumn gave an advantage to the IRA's flying columns. When, on August 26th, Robert Barton and Art O'Brien took delivery of a letter from Lloyd George, they asked him point blank what notice could be expected if the British decided to terminate the Truce. "One week by proclamation," they were told.

But the long Truce also told against the IRA, for although Macready reported[23] that IRA activity was intensifying everywhere and that the smuggling of arms had been stepped up, he also noticed a weakening of discipline, a running down of momentum. It would not be easy, as the Irish leaders recognised, to gear up their men to fresh endeavour and to expect the public, already settling into peaceful ways, to accept the almost intolerable burden of the British reprisals campaign yet again.

A loss of momentum on the British side offset this disadvantage to some extent. Sir Henry Wilson, Chief of the Imperial General Staff, deplored that the forces in Ireland were being run down to "ration strength" and urged the recruiting of 40,000 trained men to ensure the success of a winter campaign. Whether the British public would have accepted the necessity for this is doubtful.

Other reports reaching the British Cabinet put it that "the whole crux of the matter is Ulster".[24] Lloyd George had offered the Irish something they did not want, "and the one thing they do want—unity with Ulster—he had no power to give them". This was a shrewd assessment of the situation for it was to prove that it was indeed beyond the power of the British Government—if they were to cling to office—to restore unity to Ireland.

On September 7th Lloyd George extended a definite invitation to a conference on September 20th. He felt the correspondence had gone on long enough. Although opinions differed in the Cabinet, it was finally decided that allegiance to the Crown should not be made a prior condition. In accepting the invitation, however, de Valera did not drop his own condition. "Our nation has formally declared its independence and recognises itself as a sovereign state," he wrote. As the whole object of a conference was, in the eyes of the British Government, to persuade the Irish to accept a much more limited form of freedom, they were hardly likely to concede the Irish case before the conference began. Telegrams went from one leader to the other and, on September 21st, Lloyd George told the Gairloch Conference of Ministers[25] that his latest message "had produced for the first time quite a different tone of answer from the Sinn Fein leader and it would appear that de Valera was losing his public and dividing his followers". It was a comforting assumption by the British Prime Minister, but not very accurate.

He told his Ministers that "on de Valera's present claim it was impossible to proceed without grave danger. It was stated by some that de Valera had got himself into a tangle by inserting in his reply the unwise paragraph about a sovereign and independent state, and that he should be helped out of his position." But, he went on, "if the sovereign and independent state claim was a reality it was better to fight the matter out now".

A fresh invitation was sent which neither laid down any prior condition nor accepted any stated position, which virtually disregarded all that had gone before, and de Valera accepted. Both sides had gained their point, but perhaps the British had slightly won the advantage. Certainly they had not insisted that the Irish discard their republic before a conference took place, but the Irish delegates were to come simply as "spokesmen of the people whom you represent", which gave them no official standing at all. Moreover, in accepting this position it did appear that de Valera must be ready to make concessions. As Longford and O'Neill show, "By hiding his hand from Lloyd George, he had also hidden it from the public."

Nevertheless, de Valera had done well. By standing up to Lloyd George who not only led a mighty nation but was one of the shrewdest political operators in that nation's history, he had won a position of equality at the negotiating table and stultified the attitude of benevolent dominance taken up by the Prime Minister at their July meetings. He had held the Dail and the Dail Cabinet together, despite frictions and despite the genuine differences in viewpoint which were coming to the surface again. The old Sinn Fein formula, though it threatened to fall back into the two parts which constituted it, still worked. Above all, Eamon de Valera had produced an entirely new concept in his "externally associated" republic. As with all new ideas, people backed away from it, lacking the imagination of the inventor. Although it succeeded in satisfying both the moderate and the extreme factions of his own Cabinet, and it must be remembered that they were an unusually inspired group, although it offered an answer to every interest—to the southern Irish a republic, to the British continued association with the Commonwealth, to the northern Unionists the maintenance of a link with Britain—ironically, the people who were one day to prosper from it most, because it held their Commonwealth together when its anachronism threatened to break it up, failed to perceive its potential benefit.

Inexplicably de Valera left it to others to try to persuade the British to recognise the merit in his radical scheme. He chose to remain in Dublin during the negotiations, which began on October 11th 1921. His reasons for doing so were perfectly logical, and much could be said for them, but the bigger task surely was in London. The parallel between this course of action and his long stay in America during the struggle with the British is most marked. It is impossible to say in either case that his decision was the wrong one but, on the face of it, in each case he accepted for himself the lesser, though demonstrably important, rôle.

In the Cabinet de Valera's own vote decided the matter, but in the Dail, which subsequently discussed the composition of the delegation, his judgment was accepted without much ado. His official biographers carefully explain his reasons and all their points are valid: as President he was the symbol of the Republic and could not risk tarnishing that symbol if it were necessary to "finesse" a little; detached from the conference table he was better placed to recognise any trickiness from Lloyd George, and the delegation themselves would be afforded the safety net of his vigilance from afar; he was in a better position to keep a rein on the uncompromising republicans and to sustain their adherence to his external association plan if the British accepted it; he could the better maintain the strength of the nation and demonstrate the unity of their resolve; and, if the negotiations fell through, the moderate Griffith was less likely to be accused of intransigence than he.

None of this is completely convincing. On the other hand, it is difficult to see who could have acted for de Valera in his absence. Griffith certainly could have done, but he was needed in London almost as much as de Valera himself. Collins might have done, but the ill feeling between him and Brugha and Stack might have led to trouble, and de Valera, justifiably or not, was afraid of Collins's ambition. Probably Cosgrave would have been the best choice but, much though his work was valued and his influence felt, he had not yet emerged as a leader. Most of the delegates were able to return to Dublin at weekends and de Valera, too, could have travelled between the two capitals, taking part in the negotiations at certain vital stages and leaving his colleagues to carry on with more routine argument. He expected too much of Griffith and Collins to put over his new concept when the one was not very interested and the other did not really believe in it, though both argued it well enough.

In the event, the arrangements made did not work out very happily. Ambiguity concerning the powers of the delegation, appointed plenipotentiaries by the Dail but restricted by secret instructions from de Valera, confused them and perhaps the British negotiators. The antipathy Griffith felt towards Childers, the principal secretary, soured and divided the delegation and the British negotiators were well aware of the rift.

Direction from Dublin was something of an irritant, for whereas the plenipotentiaries would have been happy to have de Valera leading them in London, they tended to resent his "interference" from a distance. The first upset occurred when de Valera sent his famous telegram to the Pope to ensure that he was not misled by "ambiguities" in George V's message to him. It angered Lloyd George and, though Griffith defended his leader, privately he felt that his action had raised unnecessary difficulties.

In retrospect, de Valera's strategy, though carefully thought through, gave Britain an initial advantage. After hammering it home in his correspondence that Ireland was a republic, he did not

9

immediately attack on that point but instructed Griffith to probe the British mind first, to find out what they were prepared to offer. This allowed the British to propound the doctrine of dominionism, and it persuaded them, perhaps, that the Republic was less vital to the Irish than they had believed.

There was a good reason for the Irish to play down the republic-versus-dominion argument. If the Conference were to end in stalemate, it was important that the break were made on the Ulster issue, when the fault would lie with the intractability of the Northern Irish rather than with the British or the plenipotentiaries from the South: the English would hardly think it was playing the game to make war again on the South. Conversely, the British were determined to force the issue of sovereignty so that the break, if it came, should be due to the obstinate desire of the South to sever the tie with Great Britain.

Briefed by de Valera, Griffith urged that England stand aloof from the Ulster problem. He said that in the Six Counties there were 800,000 Protestants and 400,000 Roman Catholics. In the nine counties of Ulster lived 850,000 Protestants and 750,000 Catholics. Cogently he put it that "if it were admissible to rule off a section of Ireland, Tyrone and Fermanagh should, on the same principle, be ruled off fromUlster".

To this Lloyd George replied that the British Government were not refusing to allow them to unite with the rest of Ireland but, on the contrary, would be very glad to see them do so of their own free will.

Pressed to accept the Crown if agreement were reached on other points, Griffith told Lloyd George, "If we came to agreement on other points I could recommend some form of association with the Crown." The British Prime Minister was convinced that the Irish could be persuaded to accept dominion status provided Ulster were included. Chamberlain was more pessimistic. He thought the real difficulty would be the Crown. He was right. Receiving Griffith's report, de Valera smelled danger. "Some form of association with the Crown" might mean external association but it was an ambiguous phrase too easily misconstrued. It hinted of concession and he would brook no concession in the matter of allegiance to a British monarch. "If war is the only alternative we can only face it, and I think that the sooner the other side is made to realise that the better," he wrote.

It was then that the plenipotentiaries shot back to Dublin their angry protest against this curb on their powers to engage in full discussion. A startled de Valera reassured the delegation that he was not seeking to shackle them but only to keep them informed of the views of the Cabinet in Dublin.

At this point he would have been wise to hasten to London. His message to the delegation had been quite clear: even for the sake of a united Ireland the Republic was not to be diminished in any way. He did not seem able to see that he was, whatever he thought, fencing in the delegation so that they had practically no room to manœuvre at all. To tell them then that the fences were not there, that he was merely keeping them informed, was to delude them. The real difficulty arose because he had no inkling of the atmosphere of the negotiations, because he could be given only summaries of long discussions in which every single phrase, however incautiously uttered, was pregnant, because he could not see the expressions on faces or hear the nuances given to words. Much misunderstanding could have been obviated if he had taken over the leadership of the delegation then.

Embroiled in the argument, able to sense the atmosphere, to assess the significance of words, face to face with Lloyd George, Chamberlain, Churchill, Birkenhead, he would have been able to decide whether or not to end the Conference and risk almost certain war, or whether to accept, as ultimately the plenipotentiaries did, a compromise. It is unlikely that he would have let Craig dictate to the British Cabinet as he did and he might even have forced the break on Ulster. What is certain is that with de Valera as leader the delegation would have been a united group. Renewed war with the British might have followed but there would have been no Civil War.

By November 3rd it seemed to Griffith that the British Government were committed to put pressure on the North to enter a united Ireland, even if they had some form of autonomy, and to resign if they failed. He also saw some hope of devising a formula which would enable Ireland to remain outside the Commonwealth while yet being linked to it. But there was never the remotest chance of the British Government accepting de Valera's scheme. Shrewd, experienced statesmen though they were, they were rooted in the imperial tradition. Self-government was doled out little by little to the colonies as the mother power recognised their impatience and their readiness for responsibility. But cut the umbilical cord?—never!

Gradually the British Ministers strengthened their grip, twisted a little this way or that, like a wrestler trying to get a better purchase. Craig was unyielding, so the Ulster solution had to be got by manœuvring the South. Lloyd George's promised resignation would not help because he would be succeeded by the unfriendly Bonar Law. There was still the Boundary Commission alternative with its promise of the transfer of areas where Catholics predominated, with its hint of a northern enclave so wasted it could not exist alone.

On November 16th, the British presented a rough draft of the terms they were now ready to offer. Ireland was to have "the status of a self-governing dominion". No direct reference to the Crown was made and the plenipotentiaries thought there was still hope for association "for the purposes of common concern". They formalised this in a *Memorandum by the Irish Representatives*, and proposed to recognise the Crown "as the symbol and accepted head of the Association", a conciliatory formula devised by John Chartres, one of the secretaries to the delegation.

Alarmed to find they had made little headway towards securing Irish acceptance of allegiance, the British negotiators sent Tom Jones to persuade the Irish to moderate their language. Lloyd George was ready to break off negotiations, but Tom Jones and Arthur Griffith together kept them alive. There were further meetings. On November 24th the Irish agreed to set down a formula explaining the "limited sense in which they were prepared to recognise the Crown". The next day, the plenipotentiaries took their formula with them to Dublin to put it before the Dail Cabinet. It was approved.

Back in London, neither the formula nor a well-reasoned note from Griffith pleased Lloyd George and his colleagues. Griffith had argued that Ireland was not being offered a status truly similar to that of Canada and was invited to include any phrase he chose which overcame Ireland's fears on this score. Lloyd George offered, too, a modified Oath.

By now de Valera could see no future for the negotiations, but Griffith had been yielding. If the Crown Representative in Ireland could be elected, "it would greatly facilitate things for us", he said, hoping that to his Irish friends there would be a flavour of republicanism about an elected Governor-General. His suggestion was not accepted but, in effect, he had already yielded the Republic.

On December 3rd, the Dail Cabinet met to consider the Articles of Agreement delivered to the plenipotentiaries late on November 30th but modified a little during the next two days. Griffith showed the proposals to de Valera on December 2nd and at once he declared he could not accept them. He left further argument until the Cabinet meeting next day. According to his biographers, "He always reproached himself for having missed his most favourable chance of persuading Griffith of the consequences of acceptance." It is anyway doubtful that he would have prevailed on Griffith, who thought the bargain driven by the English was ungenerous but not unfair. Allegiance to the Crown had never held the horror for him that it had for de Valera. For Griffith the consequences of refusal were grimmer by far than those of acceptance. De Valera saw that acceptance would split the country.

The Cabinet meeting was bitter. De Valera considered crossing to London himself but decided against it for fear the British might interpret the visit as anxiety to get a settlement. He might still have gone had not Griffith "given an *express undertaking* that he would not sign a document accepting allegiance but would bring it back and refer the matter to Dail Eireann".[26]

Instructions to the plenipotentiaries were that they were to inform the British that the terms, in particular the Oath of Allegiance, were not acceptable and that, if no amendment were forthcoming, Ireland was prepared to break off the negotiations whatever the consequences. The plenipotentiaries were given the almost impossible task of forcing the break on Ulster.

De Valera can be pardoned for feeling disappointment and anger when, disregarding his instructions, the plenipotentiaries signed the Treaty. Even though they had obtained further concessions, in particular the offer of full fiscal powers, the plenipotentiaries achieved no amendment of the fundamental point. But they, as well as de Valera and the rest of the Cabinet, knew they would not. In effect, their mission now was simply to break off negotiations but at the same time to try to force the break on Ulster.

De Valera's insistence on the document being brought back *unsigned* for presentation to the Dail seems unnecessary, since even a signed agreement required ratification by the Dail and, in the end, received it. He may have feared that a signed instrument, while not a *fait accompli*, would have a cachet which might influence middle-of-the-road Dail Deputies. It is worth noting, too, that in his letter to McGarrity[27] de Valera described the British proposals as "Dominion status nominally ... inclusion in the Empire, the British King as King in Ireland, Chief executive of the Irish state, and the source from which all authority in Ireland must be derived".

These were anathema to de Valera, running counter to his deep-seated ideal of Irish sovereignty. But on a practical plane he underrated the powers Ireland was offered. He was not offered dominion status *nominally*—unless the status of Canada also was nominal. Though Ireland's history gave him the right to be sceptical of Britain's intentions, in fact British Governments have stuck to the code devised to cover their relations with former colonies as meticulously as a fussy solicitor holds to the ethics of his profession. During the history of the Irish Free State, with all the quarrels and contumely, Britain never gainsaid the Dominion's powers, though de Valera systematically obliterated the Treaty clause by clause. In British eyes it was unsporting of him to break their rules, but they did not interfere. And to describe the King as the source from which all authority must be derived was hyperbolic, surely. In symbolistic terms it was true, and, in these terms, repugnant to Eamon de Valera. Practically it was irrelevant. Power in any democracy derives from the people whether their head of state is elected or hereditary.

6

For the plenipotentiaties December 5th was a day of drama, tension and the agony of a vast responsibility. Like a conductor goading his orchestra to a grand climax, taking the tempo ever faster, building up to one crescendo after another, Lloyd George played out the last hours of the Conference. Almost dazed by his pyrotechnics, benumbed by their own searing dispute, the plenipotentiaries signed and returned, like men lost, to their own country.

Until this point de Valera had right on his side, though his judgment was questionable, and his readiness to risk the lives of the Irish people and to jeopardise their freedom for years to come for the sake of a greater freedom, which he himself demonstrated could be won peacefully in the end, may be deplored. But, while one cannot but admire a man who will not bend from an ideal, de Valera owed faith also to the canon of democracy, and in the next months he gave democracy no more than an occasional and casual salute.

On December 7th de Valera called together those members of the Cabinet who were available—Brugha, Stack, Cosgrave and O'Higgins (who had no vote). He intended, he told them, to ask for the resignations of Griffith, Collins and Barton. Cosgrave asked that first they be allowed to state their case. De Valera agreed and the full Cabinet met the following day. In an acrimonious atmosphere Cosgrave voted with the three returned delegates, which meant that de Valera, Stack and Brugha were outvoted.

With the agreement of the Cabinet de Valera that night prepared a statement for the Press in which he took the extraordinary step of publicising the split. Forthrightly, he declared, "The terms of the agreement are in violent conflict with the wishes of the majority of the Nation as expressed freely in successive elections during the last three years." He went on to say that he could not recommend the Treaty either to the Dail or the people and that he had the support of the Ministers of Home Affairs and Defence. He asked the people to face their greatest test "worthily without bitterness, and above all, without recriminations". There was, he told them "a definite constitutional way of resolving our political differences—let us not depart from it, and let the Cabinet in this matter be an example to the whole nation".

Unusual though his proclamation was, it had the virtue of putting the dilemma clearly to the people and it suggested that in resolving it the rules of democracy would be impeccably observed. This was of comfort to the majority, who felt that they had emerged from a dank cellar into air full of sunshine and birdsong. To have said that the Agreement was in violent conflict with the wishes of the Nation was to fail to recognise that a cross on a ballot paper scarcely epitomised a whole complex of emotions and convictions. The people had voted for Sinn Fein because Sinn Fein was the one party determined to wrest freedom for Ireland. The Republic was the symbol of that freedom and the majority would have wished to see the symbol become the reality, but freedom came first. When the people's vote destroyed the old and ineffective political institutions and replaced them with freedom fighters, the choice had been to continue in subjugation or to fight for freedom. The alternatives were very different now. They were to enjoy freedom in peace or to plunge back, through the maelstrom of war, to a condition of subjugation.

That Eamon de Valera and his friends should believe passionately that they had not yet reached their goal and that they must devote their futures to attaining it is both understandable and laudable. That the people had approved that objective was undeniable. But they owed it to the people to consult them now and to accept their verdict. They were supposed to be fighting, not for themselves, but for the people, and the fight could go on only with the support of the people and through their suffering. To have examined their wishes was surely not weakness nor mere expediency. Ireland was in the position of a family promised rescue from a slum, who had dreamed of a detached house on a hill but found they could have only a semi-detached in a suburban street. They were happy to take the semi-detached and to save up for the house on the hill.

De Valera believed that he had only to consult his own heart to know the wishes of the people. It was a fine sentiment but he forgot he had outgrown his humble beginnings. And can the heart of any one man serve as a barometer for the surging emotions of a whole nation?

In the long Treaty Debate in the Dail, de Valera forgot his exhortation to put aside bitterness and recrimination. The sight and sound of the men he believed had been faithless, their words of self-justification and continued denial of their wrong exacerbated his hurt and aroused the indignation he had been able to control in the peace of the night, with a blank sheet of paper in front of him. He gave them little credit for their sincerity, little recognition of the success they had won from experienced, adamantine negotiators.

For the Debate he prepared a document in which he endeavoured to set down his externally associated republic model clothed as nearly as possible in the phraseology of the Treaty. He intended to show how narrow—but how deep—was the gap between the Treaty and what was acceptable to those who refused to depart from the ideal of the Republic. In a way he was too convincing. He had had the time and the opportunity to illuminate his new concept for his close associates in the Cabinet, but it baffled many of the Dail Deputies who saw only how narrow the gap was and did not see how deep was the chasm. They were not sophisticated enough or subtle enough to recognise the difference on fundamentals. To them the de Valera proposal was a compromise little different from the compromise reflected in the Treaty.

The Treaty comprised eighteen Articles and an annex in which the specific defence facilities required by Britain were set out. De Valera's alternative, which came to be known as Document No. 2, had twenty-three Articles and the same annex. Of the eighteen Articles of the Treaty nine were reproduced word for word in Document No. 2. These covered a share of the Public Debt and of war pension payments, ports, compensation to public servants and officials discharged or retired by the new Government, religious freedom and relations with the North. Three more Articles, on defence, differed only in minor details and were more lucid in de Valera's wording. The final Article in each case required ratification of the instrument by the Parliaments of both sides but the two were subtly different in wording. The Treaty required that the instrument be submitted by His Majesty's Government for the approval of Parliament and by the Irish signatories to the members "elected to sit in the House of Commons of Southern Ireland". De Valera did not miss a trick. His Document No. 2 provided that the instrument should be submitted by His Britannic Majesty's Government for the approval of the *Parliament at Westminster* and by the *Cabinet of Dail Eireann* to members "*elected for the constituencies in Ireland set forth in the British Government of Ireland Act, 1920*".

He thus made it clear that any document signed by the Irish would not hold the cosy implication that His Majesty had dominion over Ireland or that the Southern Parliament was mutually recognised. The Treaty was to be an agreement between sovereign nations, not submitted by mere spokesmen to an assembly set up by an Act of the British Parliament but by the Cabinet of Dail Eireann to an assembly whose members represented constituencies which happened to have been set out in that Act. Similarly, where Article 17 of the Treaty provided that the British Government would transfer to a Provisional Government the "powers and machinery requisite for the discharge of its duties", Document No. 2 named the British Government *and* Dail Eireann as the transferors.

To de Valera the differences were vital and accorded with the wording of Document No. 2 where it departed absolutely from the Treaty. How did it differ? The Treaty conferred upon Ireland the same constitutional status as that of Canada and the other dominions and named her the Irish Free State; a Crown Representative would be appointed in the same way as a Governor-General in Canada; members of the Parliament of the Irish Free State would be required to take an Oath of allegiance to the Crown. De Valera dropped the Oath and the Crown Representative altogether: "The legislative, executive and judicial authority of Ireland shall be derived solely from the people of Ireland." There, in essence, was the Republic.

Then, "for purposes of common concern, Ireland shall be associated with the States of the British Commonwealth" and "when acting as associate the rights, status and privileges" were to be "in no respect less than those enjoyed by any of the component States of the British Commonwealth". Those purposes of common concern were to include Defence, Peace and War, Political Treaties, "and all matters now treated as of common concern amongst the States of the British Commonwealth". Irish citizens were to enjoy, and offered in return, the same privileges as citizens of Commonwealth states enjoyed in each other's countries. Finally, for purposes of the Association, Ireland would recognise the King as its head.

The Ireland de Valera envisaged would claim the same rights and accept the same responsibilities as any member state of the Commonwealth. Her domestic government would operate exactly as theirs did. The only difference would be that the titular Head of State would not be the King, nor would the King's Representative act for him in Ireland; instead, there would be an elected Head of State. It was, one can see now, a practicable and workable arrangement and there was no reason why Great Britain should insist on one symbol, which even Lloyd George admitted to his Cabinet the Irish had no reason to love, when the Irish wanted another. Eamon de Valera's whole idea in narrowing the quarrel to a matter of symbols, without making too much of what the symbols stood for, was to demonstrate the absurdity of England's going to war on so flimsy an issue, but to many Dail Deputies who listened to him expound the scheme in secret session, the converse also was true. Except for the right to call themselves a republic, they were in practice accepting the whole arrangement set out in the Treaty, and it would be absurd to risk war for the margin. Moderates favoured the Treaty, extreme republicans rejected both Treaty and Document No. 2, and de Valera was left with a handful who supported the cause he advocated—to go back to the British Government and plead for sweet reason.

Failing to get the support he sought in the quarrelsome secret session, de Valera now declared his proposal withdrawn. Without nearly unanimous approval it ceased to be of value. In public session he went back to arguing against the Treaty as it stood. It rankled with Griffith and Collins that he was not prepared to publish for the people to see for themselves how close to the Treaty was his solution, for the people to know that the signatories were being abused, even traduced as traitors, when the alternative offered gave them no more than did the Treaty—except a symbol. On his side, de Valera maintained that "a war-weary people will take things which are not in accordance with their aspirations". Later they would regret it.

For days the waves of words descended upon the Dail, one wave after another, one wave like another, and the winds of anger raged. Sometimes there was a lull when wisdom and dignity held sway, but there was much snarling repetition, much inarticulate passion and the air was turgid with the ectoplasm of martyrs. It was throughout a battle of one oath against the other. And yet, as Collins pointed out, "if we all stood on the recognition of the Irish Republic as a prelude to any conference we could very easily have said so, and there would be no conference". In essence, "it was the acceptance of the invitation that formed the compromise".

Collins was not yielding the Republic for ever. He wanted to accept the Treaty, use its power to the full, build up a healthy State then take the next step to the "ultimate freedom that all nations desire and develop to . . ." It was exactly the course which, in time, de Valera was to take. He has lived for a quarter of a century since that "ultimate freedom" was achieved. The Irish Free State's existence was but a comma in history.

In their preoccupation with the quarrel over the Crown and the Republic, few Deputies made more than passing reference to the unity of Ireland. It was on this point that Great Britain's case was weakest and if the plenipotentiaries, or even the Dail, had accepted the status of dominion but only on condition that it included all thirty-two counties, if that had been made the point upon which they declined under any circumstances to yield, then the British Government were in no position to resort to arms against Ireland.

But even de Valera, though he did not like them, had accepted the Ulster terms of the Treaty and had embodied them in his own solution. The more fervent became the insistence on the Republic, the further receded the possibility of breaking down the new border.

As the Debate neared its end after a Christmas adjournment, Document No. 2 was noticed again. It had lain underneath the Debate like felt under a carpet with the edges protruding. A Deputy protested that de Valera's veto on publication prevented his putting the alternatives to his constituents. At once, de Valera offered to bring it into the open, on condition that he could put it as an amendment to the Treaty. He wanted the carpet thrown out and the underfelt used instead. Griffith insisted on a straight vote on the Treaty and de Valera maintained his veto on Document No. 2.

Then, on January 4th, de Valera gave notice that he intended to introduce his Document No. 2 as an amendment to Griffith's motion. He distributed copies and Griffith discovered that the underfelt had been trimmed. In the new version six clauses had been dropped. De Valera, who considered he had done no more than polish the original draft, protested that Griffith was quibbling. Incensed, Griffith gave copies of both versions to the Press. If he was acting against de Valera's expressed wishes, he did so because he felt that de Valera was using unfair tactics.

The next day was taken up by examination of the proposal by Collins that those against the Treaty abstain from voting and on January 6th de Valera offered his resignation. He proposed to stand for re-election and if he won he would form a new administration, jettison the Treaty and offer Document No. 2 to the British. "If there was not a gun in Ireland we would carry out that programme," he declared.

His biographers explain that he was "finding his position as President intolerable. The publication of Cabinet and other private documents as party propaganda showed him that the divisions had ended all semblance of united cabinet responsibility. When a pro-Treaty minister interfered in the work of other ministers, he had no means of controlling him."[28]

The fact remains that de Valera was suggesting a straight vote between Griffith and himself, winner take all. He, the man who had led Ireland through a difficult four years, whose inspiration had held together incompatible personalities and contending factions, dovetailed conflicting views into corporate aspiration and fired the determination of a whole people, was challenging a man who had always chosen to be second in command but who had also throughout the Treaty Debate demonstrated that he had the stature of a leader. Collins pointed out that de Valera could form a republican government within minutes if the Treaty were rejected, and Griffith protested against a vote on personalities at this stage. At this, de Valera denied any intention to produce a red herring and, having declared himself "sick and tired of politics—so sick that no matter what happens I would go back to private life", agreed to a straight vote on the Treaty if it came within forty-eight hours.

By the small majority of seven the Treaty was approved. The Debate ended on a quiet, almost conciliatory note except for a cry of "betrayal" from Miss Mary MacSwiney. De Valera declared that until the people voted the Dail must remain the supreme Government and supported Collins's insistence that public safety was their first duty. De Valera attempted to speak again but was frustrated by his own emotion. Deeply moved, the fervent Brugha quietly promised discipline in the army.

De Valera resigned his office as President and at once a great swell of sympathy washed over the Dail. "No one here in the assembly or in Ireland wants to be in the position of opposing President de Valera," said Michael Collins, meaning that he hoped he would not stand for re-election. Mrs Clarke proposed his re-election. Patrick Hogan put the proposal in perspective: "If you elect the President again on a policy of fighting the Treaty after the resolution that has been passed by this House, let us have no more talk of constitutionalism." But to many who had voted for the Treaty there was no paradox in re-electing de Valera as President.

De Valera snapped, "Go and elect your President and all the rest of it. You have sixty-five. I do not want office at all." Griffith saw no reason for de Valera's resignation if Dail Eireann were to

continue until the election. He suspected yet another manœuvre
to nullify the vote on the Treaty. The Dail voted and only two
votes precluded de Valera's re-election. Griffith spoke generously
of him and de Valera answered in the same strain. He promised,
"We will not interfere with you, except when we find that you are
going to do something that will definitely injure the Irish Nation."
Griffith was elected after de Valera and his supporters had left the
assembly. He had reiterated that he would "keep the Republic in
being until such time as the establishment of the Free State is put
to the people to decide for or against".

7

THE PROVISIONAL Government was elected by the pro-Treaty Deputies meeting away from the Dail but still refusing to acknowledge that they were the Southern House of Commons provided for by the 1920 Act. Griffith, as President of the Dail, did not join the Provisional Government, of which Collins was elected Chairman. For the next few months the two administrations worked virtually as one, though nominally at least sovereignty belonged to the Dail. De Valera was determined that the new Dail Government should not weaken the Dail's position. It was still the elected Parliament of the people, the Parliament of the Republic. It should remain so until the people could state their views. This gave him time to try to convince the people that they should keep their Republic in being.

De Valera was afraid that the Provisional Government, which was not responsible to any elected Parliament, was beginning to usurp the authority of the Dail, that the Ministers, most of them members of both administrations, were running their departments in the name of the Provisional Government. It was difficult for Griffith and Collins to concentrate the work in the Dail departments because Britain was financing the transition to the Irish Free State, but to de Valera it meant that Griffith was not honouring to the full his promise to keep the Republic intact.

Interrupting a tour of the country during which large crowds heard him denounce the Treaty, de Valera presided at the Sinn Fein Ard Fheis of February 21st, and he and Collins agreed that there should be no election for three months. This precluded another demonstration of disunity for, like every other national

organisation, Sinn Fein had been split. On both sides there were
dissenters from the agreement. Griffith was anxious for an election
as soon as possible, anti-Treaty members were confident that a
vote at the Ard Fheis would have gone their way. Collins, on the
other hand, as he was to show in the next months, was ready to go
to great lengths to try to heal the split and was as glad to avoid an
anti-Treaty vote as de Valera was to defer the verdict of the
country. The two men had had an uneasy relationship since de
Valera's return from America and each was a little suspicious of the
other's personal ambitions. In reality, both were doing what they
thought best for the country but their minds, their methods and
their temperaments were far apart. The Dail set its seal of approval
on the agreement.

The opponents of the Treaty now grouped themselves formally
as *Cumann na Poblachta*, the League of the Republic, the formation
of which was announced on March 15th 1922. It seemed to promise
a constitutional flavour. De Valera was angered when what he
claimed were simply prophecies that blood would one day be shed
over the Treaty were represented as incitement to civil war. Lord
Longford, both in the biography of which he is joint author and in
Peace By Ordeal, vehemently defends de Valera. True, the language
of some of his speeches was tortuous and could perhaps have been
misinterpreted. But at Dungarvon on March 16th he said, "If you
don't fight today, you will have to fight tomorrow; and I say,
when you are in a good fighting position, then fight on." It is
difficult to find that ambiguous. He may have meant to fight on
constitutionally, not with arms, but he was addressing crowds
which included many IRA men, some of them armed, whose
Convention had just been proscribed by the Dail Cabinet. At
best, de Valera did not choose his words wisely.

It was the army which now made de Valera's dilemma almost
intolerable. They re-established as their controlling authority the
Army Executive and, in de Valera's eyes, their repudiation of
parliamentary control was at best premature. The Dail was still
the parliament of the Republic. He himself had claimed in a statement to the Press that "there are rights which a minority may justly
uphold, even by arms, against a majority". Nevertheless, the

recalcitrance of the IRA, its pre-emption of authority, did not promise well for any government of the future.

De Valera himself now had no control over the army and he was dismayed when the Four Courts and other buildings were seized by extremists under Rory O'Connor. These were men who despaired of politicians altogether and saw no virtue in Document No. 2. They had fought for a republic and were prepared to go on fighting. They wanted no links of Empire, however tenuous. With other, more moderate, anti-Treaty officers both de Valera and Collins kept in close touch. All believed that somehow there was a way of restoring unity in the army and elsewhere but sporadic incidents all over the country were ominous.

The Archbishop of Dublin brought Griffith, Collins, de Valera and Brugha together, "with the object of a peaceful election", Griffith told the Dail which reassembled on April 26th after an eight-week recess. Nothing came of these meetings but a few days later, on May 1st, prominent army officers from both sides produced the "Army Document" and gave the first hint of hope. It offered no solution but it did recognise that "if the present drift is maintained a conflict of comrades is inevitable". Ireland would be "broken for generations". It recognised that the majority of the people accepted the Treaty and suggested an *agreed* election with a view to forming a government of the whole country. This was the basis of the Collins–de Valera Pact of May 20th, an agreement which gave de Valera the first real hope that disaster could be avoided, and chagrined the British Government—not so much because an agreed election was hardly democratic, but because a cabinet which included de Valera and his friends could not be expected to operate the Treaty. They could not even take office without rupturing Article 17—unless they were willing to subscribe to it in writing. Only the acceptance by the British Government of the draft Constitution would have enabled the Pact to work and that was a non-starter.

After the election de Valera and his colleagues received no call to office, nor is it conceivable that they would have accepted office under the Constitution published on election day, but without the Pact the elections would have been a shambles, if they had been possible at all. The people's vote went for the Treaty but twenty-nine panel nominees, twenty-two of them anti-Treaty, lost to Farmers, Labour and Independent candidates. Forty per cent of the votes went to non-panel candidates, an indication that, not only were the people in favour of the Treaty and peace, but that they looked towards men who talked about factories and farms and the construction of a new life.

De Valera could see no lasting peace that was not built on justice. He saw no justice in the settlement England had foisted on the plenipotentiaries and now it seemed to him that Irish, not British, troops would act as Ireland's gaolers. The Ulster compromise he accepted for the moment because it pushed a solution no further than the horizon, but he did not admit to England's right to impose any solution, either to establish a border or to take it away. The people of Ireland, of all its four provinces, should be left to work out the problem for themselves.

If de Valera still nourished any hope of a call to establish a coalition government, the attack on the Four Courts extinguished it. The new Dail was to have assembled on July 1st but the tide of civil war came rushing in.

Until then, de Valera had frowned on Rory O'Connor's occupation of the Four Courts and O'Connor had made it clear that he would brook no interference from the former President. Aghast at the use of arms by Irishmen against Irishmen, for which he held pressure by the British Government responsible, still convinced that the Pact "would have given us an opportunity of working for internal peace and of taking steps which would make the Nation strong against the only enemy it has to fear, the enemy from outside", he hailed the Four Courts garrison as "the men who have refused to forswear their allegiance to the Republic, who have refused to sacrifice honour for expediency and sell their country to a foreign King". Challengingly he exhorted, "Irish citizens! Give them support! Irish soldiers! Bring them aid!"[29] His own position now was difficult but he saw no alternative to taking up arms himself. The political situation bristled with anomalies.

Griffith had promised to keep the Republic in being until the people had either accepted or rejected the Treaty, but only until then. As leader of the majority party, he considered he now had a mandate to set up the machinery of the Free State Government, although the Free State would not come into being officially until twelve months from the signing of the Treaty. But now the dichotomy would end. When the new Dail assembled, as indisputably the elected Parliament of the people, there would be but one administration, presumably led by Griffith.

The de Valera group did not concede an electoral victory to the pro-Treaty party. They held that the people had voted for the Panel candidates and a coalition government, that although they had voted in favour of the Treaty they had done so, most of them, without having seen the proposed Constitution of the Irish Free State. One thing was plain to de Valera: with the attack on the Four Courts, the political arena was sealed off.

He signed on as a private soldier under the command of the Executive and joined the troops who had taken over the buildings in O'Connell Street. At once he became involved in attempts to arrange an armistice, but, having taken the decision to remove the Executive forces from public buildings they had occupied, the Provisional Government would accept no terms which did not include the surrender of arms.

The Four Courts fell, the garrison of the Gresham and Hammam Hotels and the rest of the O'Connell Street stronghold were driven out by flames. Cathal Brugha was killed. Liam Lynch, who had been at odds with the Four Courts garrison until the evening before the assault by Provisional Government troops, left Dublin and, resuming his position as Chief of Staff, set up his headquarters at Clonmel, where de Valera joined him. The moderate Lynch was to become the most stubborn and fanatical opponent of the Provisional Government and to prolong the war long past the point where de Valera thought it mete to cease resistance. As military leader of the republican movement, he seemed for a time to be seeking complete control, brushing de Valera cursorily aside.

Once again, at a time of crisis, de Valera had stepped back. Neither on this nor any other occasion did he seek to side-step responsibility, but, just as he had embarked on the America mission in 1919 and stayed at home during the Treaty negotiations, now he chose a rôle in which he was unable to make the big decisions. This time the choice was far from clear-cut. He was a political leader but the struggle for the Republic had moved to military ground and, although he had proved himself an inspiring military leader in 1916 when all were novices, he naturally deferred to those who had become experienced warriors in the Black and Tan days. Months later, when the reins had all but slipped from his hands, he set up a Republican "government in exile", hoping perhaps to achieve what the Dail Government had achieved in its underground days. This is a step he might profitably have taken immediately the Four Courts was attacked. The Executive forces vaunted their allegiance to the Republic, and if he had set up a political framework, he could at least have insisted on the army's responsibility to civil authority. But those were days of turmoil and there was no reason to think then that the struggle would drag on into 1923. Moreover, de Valera was not yet sure that the Republic was to be immediately disestablished as a result of the election.

Each passing day seemed to bring its own tragedy. His great friend—and Collins's—Harry Boland, was killed. Then came Griffith's death and, within a fortnight, the fatal ambush of Michael Collins at Beal na mBlah. Everywhere Provisional Government troops were gaining the upper hand. Possession of coastal shipping enabled them to land men at points along the coast. The big guns which had blasted the Four Courts and O'Connell Street now appeared at Limerick, Waterford and elsewhere. Fighting was sporadic. Sean McEoin conducted a soldierly campaign in the West; in the Dublin Hills there was a planned encirclement of anti-Treaty strongholds; in the south the Limerick-Waterford "line" was systematically breached and the segments eliminated. But there was no real overall strategy on either side.

The Executive forces, having first occupied barracks and other buildings in the towns, found themselves in the same kind of defensive rôle that the men of the Easter Rising had adopted and that the British had been forced to take up in 1919 and 1920. Soon they began to abandon and burn their defensive posts and resume the guerrilla tactics which were so much more familiar to them.

But now their adversaries knew this kind of warfare as well as they did and were equally familiar with the hills and the hidden glens. The anti-Treaty troops seemed to have no heart for the fight. They had never believed that their resistance to the Treaty would have been carried to the extreme of civil war. Prepared to fire bullets in the name of the Republic, they preferred that they did not hit their old friends. And, in spite of their unshakeable conviction that they were right, the fact that the majority of the people did not share it disheartened them. Somehow, they believed, Michael Collins would find a formula which would enable them all to put away their guns—or turn them again on the British. Collins, himself, was eager for reconciliation. He put his faith in old friendships, old loyalties, especially those of the Irish Republican Brotherhood, but he was not prepared to make any concessions. With his death these hopes disappeared. A tragic bitterness crept in and with it the pitilessness which characterises civil war.

Though sick at heart, de Valera was ready to fight on if there was a chance that the cause of the Republic would prevail. Desperately he desired peace and he still believed that it could be achieved if only the Provisional Government would make a further attempt to persuade Great Britain to modify the Treaty. To this end, by arrangement he met General Mulcahy, the Provisional Government's Minister of Defence and Collins's successor as Commander-in-Chief. Although he had consulted some of his Cabinet colleagues informally, Mulcahy's attempt to come to terms with the former President was upon his own responsibility. Like Collins, Mulcahy would not compromise. He knew there could be no compromise acceptable to the British. The Treaty had been signed in good faith, the Dail had approved it and so had the electorate. There could be no going back.

On September 9th the Dail assembled at last. W. T. Cosgrave was elected President, having first stated that he intended if elected to "implement the Treaty, enact the Constitution, support and assist the National Army and ask Parliament if necessary for any powers thought necessary to restore order, to expedite a return to normal conditions and to speed reconstruction and reparation". Asked by Gavan Duffy whether "the present system of govern-

ment would be unified", Cosgrave answered that it would. He
nominated his Ministers. There would be only one Cabinet now.
The Dail was no longer the Parliament of the Republic but the
future Parliament of the Irish Free State.

Thomas Johnson, the impressive Labour leader and, in the
absence of the anti-Treaty Deputies, most of whom were on the run,
virtually Leader of the Opposition, pointed out that the country
had never been told why the Collins–de Valera Pact had come
to nought, that they only knew they were caught up in a civil
war. The present situation, as he saw it, arose from "a different
interpretation of the promises, the undertakings, the pledges that
men gave, and of the temperaments of those men". It should be
made clear that the country was accepting "something very definitely short of its rightful demands" and he urged that the new
Government should not set out to crush absolutely those who were
in arms against them.

The certainty that the Pact with Collins was a dead letter came to
de Valera only with Cosgrave's statement of intent. It confirmed
his worst fears. He did not dispute that the vote of the people had
been in favour of the Treaty but he did not accept that it had
given a mandate to disestablish the Republic. In his view, by voting
in the majority for Panel candidates, the people had returned a
coalition. Instead, the pro-Treaty party had interpreted the defeat
of so many Republican candidates on the Panel, which had completely upset the agreed proportions, as a signal to implement the
Treaty and set up the government of the Free State, so disestablish-
ing the Republic. Had the British accepted the Constitution origi-
nally submitted to them, there would have been no problem, or at
least a much less pressing one. Once that was rejected, de Valera's
only hope was that the dual system would be retained and that,
back in the Cabinet himself with some of his supporters, he might
be able to persuade his pro-Treaty colleagues to throw out the
Treaty after all. The fact that Robert Barton, one of the Treaty
signatories, had already swung back to his side was in itself
encouragement.

In December the Parliament of the Free State would come into
being as the result of an Act passed in the British Parliament. In the

meantime, the new Dail would function as a provisional Parliament. This to de Valera was unlawful. The Parliament of the Republic of Ireland could not be obliterated by the Parliament at Westminster. It had been maintained by the pro-Treaty party until the election. Now that the stronger party were opting out it was up to the Opposition to take over. It was now that he began to think of a Republican "government in exile", not so much because he believed it could govern, even in the manner in which the First Dail had functioned, but so that what he passionately held was the legal government of Ireland was preserved.

Cosgrave, in his turn, maintained that the enemies of the Treaty could have continued in opposition on constitutional lines. Instead, they had tried to secure unity by provoking the common enemy to return.

"There must not, and will not, be an armed body in the community without the sanction of Parliament," he declared. De Valera would not have disagreed with Cosgrave's principle, only with the assumption that Cosgrave's Parliament had right or authority.

The Constitution Bill was introduced by the rising Kevin O'Higgins was often critical of the National Army, but he never as Minister of Local Government in de Valera's Cabinet. Intent upon ending the armed opposition which was sapping the authority of the Government and would reduce the country to anarchy, O'Higgins was often critical of the National Army, but he never really understood its difficulties. Mulcahy, Chief of Staff and Minister of Defence, asked for special powers. After much heart-searching, the Cabinet agreed to the proposals and the Dail confirmed their decision. On October 10th, following an amnesty offer, the granting of Special Emergency Powers to the army was promulgated. From October 15th, military courts were to be set up with power to inflict the death sentence on men in unauthorised possession of firearms, or who took part in the destruction of private or public property or in attacks on Provisional Government troops.

It was in the atmosphere generated by this decree that the IRA Executive met on October 17th. De Valera had sought a meeting for some time but Liam Lynch had been offhanded about it. A proclamation was issued:

"We, on behalf of the soldiers of the Republic in concert with such faithful members of Dail Eireann as are at liberty, acting in the spirit of our oath as the final custodians of the Republic, have called upon the former President, Eamon de Valera, to resume the Presidency and to form a government which shall preserve inviolate the sacred trust of National Sovereignty and Independence."

Even now, there was a reluctance on the part of the Executive to relinquish authority to political leaders and de Valera had some difficulty in composing an acceptable Cabinet. Liam Mellows, taken prisoner at the Four Courts, was named as Minister of Defence and Lynch and de Valera both were to sign documents in his name. The Executive also insisted upon the right to veto any peace proposal.

In November, the first executions under the new powers took place. Four young men were executed while Erskine Childers, arrested on November 10th, was still on trial. Childers, detested by pro-Treaty leaders, had been technically armed and the execution of the four seemed to be setting the stage for a bigger scene. Erskine Childers, who had been no more than the publicity officer of the Executive forces, died with characteristic courage, absolving the unhappy firing squad of responsibility for their deed. De Valera, who had done all he could to save him, was deeply grieved. Childers had been close to him, and he had leaned heavily on his counsel. In some ways they were very alike, austere men who seemed to some doctrinaire in their stubborn adherence to the republican ideal and pernicketty in their preoccupation with minutiae. Curiously, Michael Collins, the antithesis of these men, admired them both.

The shooting of Childers and the four young soldiers engendered a cold anger in Liam Lynch, who gave retaliatory orders for the execution of members of the Provisional Government. Until now, Lynch had striven to avoid reprisals: he remembered the Black and Tan days, the deadly tit-for-tat campaign of both sides which had threatened to get out of control. De Valera neither approved nor disapproved the decision, against which in any case he was powerless to act, but he did insist on due warning. On November 27th, in a letter to the Speaker, Lynch gave warning. Three more executions followed almost at once and Lynch's men acted. Two Deputies were fired at in Dublin. One, Sean Hales, whose brother Tom was a senior officer in the Executive forces, died; the other was wounded.

The Government acted swiftly, mercilessly but effectively, to deter any further attacks on Dail Deputies. Applying the emergency powers retrospectively, they summarily executed Rory O'Connor, Liam Mellows, Joseph McKelvey and Richard Barrett, all of whom had been taken at the Four Courts. That unique generation of Irishmen who had carried through a revolution, who exemplified all that was best in the heroes of the past and brought to their task qualities which their forbears had never owned, now seemed bent on decimating itself. Kevin O'Higgins told the Dail that the Government was based on force and that force must be met with greater force if it were to survive.

There were no more assassinations of Dail Deputies and Senators. The second House had come into existence with the passing of the new Constitution. Among the Senators were many Southern Unionists who had accepted the new order of things and no longer linked their fortunes with the Unionists of the North. They came for the most part from the land-owning Ascendancy and were a different breed from the commerce-orientated Northern Unionists.

Eamon de Valera was not against burning the offices of Free State officials but drew the line at attacks on homes and families. "I am against such methods on principle," he wrote to his Minister for Home Affairs, "and believe we will never win this war unless we attach the people to our Government by contrast with theirs."[30] And he told Liam Lynch, "The recent burnings were, in my opinion, puerile and futile from a military point of view."[31]

Lynch justified his actions on military grounds and, as the Free State Government relentlessly continued its policy of executions, claiming as the British had done that they were dealing with a rebellion, not fighting a war, the Republican Chief of Staff lengthened the list of those against whom reprisals were to be taken.

Caught between military and political considerations, de Valera temporised. He had not agreed to Lynch's order, "merely indicated that I regarded it as possible that we would be forced to adopt as defensive measures some of the drastic proposals . . . on the understanding that the execution of the orders would be kept strictly under the control of GHQ . . ."[32]

As early as December 15th de Valera wrote to P. J. Ruttledge[33] that there was "little prospect of that type of victory which would enable us to dictate terms . . ." He did not want surrender but he wanted the awful struggle brought to an end. But he could do little without the cooperation of the Executive and Lynch remained polite but uncooperative, even uninformative. It was dawning on de Valera that for the moment the cause of the Republic was lost. He would have to wait for another opportunity. The Free State Government was unlikely to be shaken from its plinth of power. Not only were they winning the Civil War, they were already building up the new State, establishing a civil service, organising local government, setting up a police force, legislating for the future well-being of the country.

If he found Lynch uncooperative, Lynch must have wondered in his turn what course de Valera was trying to follow. When Lynch wanted to take the war into England, which he regarded as the real enemy, de Valera agreed and urged a powerful blow. One day he wrote to Lynch that to abandon the Republic now "would be a greater blow to our ideals and to the prestige of the nation than even the abandonment on December 6th 1921. In taking upon ourselves to be champions of this cause we have incurred obligations which we must fulfil even to the death."[34] But a few days later he was telling Lynch, "We can best serve the nation at this moment by trying to get the constitutional way adopted." He recognised the key to the situation: "In this matter it is all a question of what the Army is prepared to do."[35]

Lynch went his own way and an anxious de Valera heard little from him until he was invited to attend a meeting of the Executive on March 23rd 1923. A resolution put by Tom Barry, that the Executive should recognise that continued resistance would not further the cause of independence, was narrowly defeated. After three days there was an adjournment until April 10th but Liam Lynch, the most unyielding of them all, was fatally shot in the Knockmealdown Mountains on his way to the second meeting.

Ten days later the Executive met, with Frank Aiken succeeding Lynch as Chief of Staff, and resolved to call on de Valera to arrange peace terms with the Free State Government. Following a meeting of de Valera's Republican Government and the Army Council— Aiken, Barry, and Pilkington—on April 26th, de Valera announced readiness to negotiate and Aiken suspended the operations of the Executive forces from April 30th.

Through Senators Douglas and Jameson the Government's conditions were put to de Valera who at once put counter proposals. He wanted Republican arms to be stored and guarded by Republicans, not surrendered, and he insisted that no citizen should be debarred by "political oath, test or other device" from taking his seat in Parliament. Cosgrave, now styled President of the Council, had promised freedom of political action provided it was constitutional. He was not prepared to start another argument about the Oath. Discussions went no further. The war ended, as bizarrely as it had begun. The Republicans simply dumped their arms. Further sacrifices on their part "would now be in vain and continuance of the struggle in arms unwise in the national interest", de Valera announced. No principle was conceded but "military victory must be allowed to rest for the moment with those who have destroyed the Republic". De Valera's adherence to an ideal was to be admired but it sometimes led him close to sophistry. He was naturally low in spirit at this time but was ready to transfer the struggle to the political field where he felt it should have been pursued all along. Now that military operations were at an end, he was again the acknowledged leader.

8

A GENERAL election was held in August, 1923. Courageously de Valera addressed a meeting in Clare, knowing that his freedom and perhaps his life were at risk. He was arrested and taken to Arbour Hill. Thousands of Republican soldiers were already in captivity. Democracy had not had much of a chance, he was to say later, but then he had not given democracy much of a chance either.

Cosgrave was returned to power with 63 of 153 seats. Including de Valera, who won easily, 44 Republicans were elected under the old name of Sinn Fein. Most were in prison and the remainder were not allowed to take their seats. De Valera half expected a State trial and half hoped for one, intending to make it a trial not just of himself "but of the whole system which brought the Free State into existence". There was no trial, but in October 1923 he was transferred to Kilmainham Gaol and put in solitary confinement.

The Free State Government was treating its prisoners with scant consideration, but as 1924 wore on there was some relaxation of conditions and men began to be released. By that time the Government had an army crisis on its own hands. Resentment built up as the size of the army was scaled down and thousands of men were put out on to jobless streets. But the main factor in what came to be called the "Army Mutiny" was realisation that the Republic was not just around the corner. Many men had followed Collins because "what is good enough for Mick is good enough for us" and had accepted his idea of "stepping stones to the Republic". But Collins was probably thinking in terms of years; they wanted to achieve their goal within months. The crisis began in March and dragged on until October, when O'Higgins brought the situation

under control and established at last that the army was responsible
to the people through their elected Parliament.

Eamon de Valera was released on July 10th 1924 and at once
embroiled himself in party politics. He found in the Republican
movement differences of opinion as difficult as those which plagued
his opponents. Unlike some of the extremists, he acknowledged
that the Cosgrave Government derived its power from the people,
but he regarded the elected Parliament as illegal because the second
Dail had never been dissolved. It existed still and he was determined
to keep it in being as a base for further operations. He appointed
a cabinet. His, he claimed, was the rightful, if impotent,
government.

In various speeches de Valera listed the three conditions he
would fight to alter. Two of these, the Constitution and financial
arrangements between Ireland and Great Britain, he succeeded
eventually in overturning, but the third, the isolation of the Six
Counties, remains. The Six Counties Government prohibited his
entry into their territory, though he was still an elected representative of County Down. In November 1924, defiantly he crossed the
border, was arrested and served a month's imprisonment.

The IRA still saw itself as politically orientated and the relationship with what de Valera called his "Emergency Government"
was uncomfortable. Frank Aiken found his dual rôle as Minister
for Defence and Chief of Staff incompatible and resigned the
Cabinet post. On November 14th 1925 the IRA decided to sever
its connection with the political wing of the Republican movement.
Let de Valera try to eliminate the border by political means, the
IRA would blow it off the map. The break coincided with Press
forecasts of the Boundary Commission's findings.

The agreement which Cosgrave's Government signed on
December 3rd 1925 drew bitter protests from de Valera. That any
Irish Government should recognise the dismemberment of
Ireland was to him a gross betrayal. He was longing to discard his
self-imposed rôle of political outlaw and to return to the legislative
assembly of his country. He could accept now that the Second Dail
was no more than a ghost but could not bring himself to take the
Oath which would open the doors of the new Dail to him and his

followers. But not all his followers were willing to lay the ghost of the Second Dail, and at the Sinn Fein Ard Fheis of March 1926 he resigned as President and shortly afterwards founded his own party, Fianna Fail. The greatly weakened Sinn Fein was soon moribund.

Fianna Fail won forty-four seats at the election of June 1927, only three less than Cumann na nGaedheal, Cosgrave's party. The successful Fianna Fail candidates attempted to take their seats but, refusing to take the Oath in accordance with Article 17 of the Constitution, were not admitted. Backed by legal opinion, de Valera proposed to use another Article of the Constitution to secure abolition of the Oath by constitutional amendment, a process which would have required a referendum.

William T. Cosgrave saw no stable political future for Ireland if the properly elected members of the Opposition excluded themselves from the legislative chamber. He was a conscientious man, conservative in outlook, modest and easy to get on with. Except for the huge Shannon electricity scheme and Patrick Hogan's Land Act of 1923, the Cosgrave Administration was responsible for few innovations, but it did end the chaos of the Civil War and create an orderly State in which the army became the responsible defence force, an unarmed and respected police force was constituted, and religious tolerance overcame prejudice. It was a State sturdily founded on democratic principles and it was for the sake of those principles, the danger to which was underlined by the murder of Kevin O'Higgins on July 10th, that Cosgrave introduced, in August 1927, the Electoral Amendment Bill. This required election candidates to sign an affidavit undertaking that upon election they would take both their seat and the Oath. The Bill also abolished Article 48 of the Constitution by which de Valera had hoped to secure amendment by referendum.

Cosgrave's intention was to ensure that all candidates who were elected to the Dail took their seats, to end a situation where close on half the people were not represented in their Parliament. The challenge put de Valera on the rack of his conscience but he found a way out of the difficulty and Cosgrave's Bill then lapsed. De Valera read to the Clerk of the Dail a statement in Irish declaring that he was proposing to sign the book as a formality and not as

any indication that he had taken the Oath. Removing the Bible
and covering up the text of the Oath, he signed the book. It was a
pity he had not thought up this bit of pantomime earlier. At all
events, from August 10th Cosgrave had his Opposition and he was
not unduly perturbed by the possibility that his Government might
be ousted. De Valera's biographers write that "De Valera's
performance, however one interprets and assesses it, made it
certain that parliamentary democracy would in fact prevail."[36]
One may be forgiven for suggesting that Cosgrave's contribution
to democracy was even more valuable.

Within a few days of his entering the Dail, de Valera almost
succeeded in becoming head of a coalition government. Cosgrave
just held on but his position was so precarious that he called another
election in September. Cumann na nGaedheal and Fianna Fail
both increased their holding of seats at the expense of small parties.
With sixty-two seats and support from the Farmers' Party,
Cosgrave had a safe majority over Fianna Fail, which had won
fifty-seven seats. De Valera strongly refuted allegations that his
party had entered the Free State Parliament with the intention of
destroying it. Instead, he said, they wanted to broaden and widen it
"so as to free it from all foreign control or interference". There was,
in fact, neither control nor interference by Great Britain but the
tie was anathema to him. He still maintained that the Cosgrave
Government had gained power by *coup d'état* in 1922 and that the
Constitution was illegal, but he accepted that they were all elected
representatives of the people and that the Dail at Leinster House was
the only going concern in which they could operate.

From 1929 until October 1931, when a Public Safety Act of
great severity brought in by the Cosgrave Government came into
force, the IRA became increasingly active and the law of the gun
had too many adherents. A rapidly deteriorating economic situation as the great Depression hit Ireland caused further unrest and
the popularity of the Cosgrave Government waned. The violence
of IRA activity, which included murder, was an embarrassment
for de Valera who took up an ambivalent attitude, deploring
violence but claiming that, because the people were not permitted
to remedy their grievances peacefully, it was to be expected that

they would resort to force. Repressive measures were no answer.

De Valera never let up on his campaign against the Oath. Again he sought to use Article 48 of the Constitution and again Cosgrave frustrated him. There were many who professed themselves satisfied with the Irish Free State as a British dominion and their view was usually reflected in the national Press. De Valera had long tried to build up funds to establish a Republican newspaper and in September 1931 his dream was realised with the launching of the *Irish Press*. He spent much of his time working for the paper but soon had to give his attention to electioneering. The next election was set for February 16th 1932.

9

It was with some trepidation that the British Cabinet contemplated the possibility of de Valera's winning the election. "A difficult situation would be produced," J. H. Thomas, Secretary of State for Dominion Affairs, told his Cabinet colleagues.[37] The British Government expected trouble on two counts, the Oath of allegiance and the payment of land annuities. By an agreement of 1926 the Irish Free State were handing to Britain payments from farmers who were buying their land under the Land Purchase Acts of the late nineteenth and early twentieth centuries, in particular those of 1903 and 1909, which had enabled land tenants to become proprietors. The British Government had bought out the landlords and so claimed the annuities as their due. But under the 1920 Government of Ireland Act provision had been made for these revenues to be retained by the two Irish Governments. The Northern Government did retain them, but as the Act did not apply to the Irish Free State a different arrangement had been come to. De Valera's claim was that the Treaty did not invalidate the 1920 arrangement. With other payments the Irish Free State was contributing to the British Exchequer about £5 million each year. That was approximately 20 per cent of the national revenue.

On February 24th, Thomas reminded the British Cabinet that before he could abolish the Oath, de Valera would first have to take it. Otherwise he could not become President of the Council, or Prime Minister.[38] He was nominated by Michael Kilroy and Oscar Traynor, both leaders of the Executive forces during the Civil War, and was elected. The Governor-General, James MacNeill, spared de Valera's feelings by himself coming to Leinster House and confirming the appointment. Fianna Fail had won 72 seats, Cumann na nGaedheal 57, but 24 seats were held by other interests so de Valera did not have an absolute majority.

In a making-the-best-of-it memorandum,[39] J. H. Thomas claimed that time was on the side of the British Government. There was to be a Eucharistic Congress in Dublin during the summer and political controversy would be avoided. Furthermore, de Valera was able to command a majority only with the support of Labour members, who would probably vote in favour of abolishing the Oath but on the whole were committed to the Treaty. Again, Cosgrave's supporters had an overwhelming majority in the Senate and could hold up legislation on the Oath—but not on annuities—for something like eighteen months, unless de Valera dissolved the Dail and had a new election in which case the Senate could not reject an abolition bill.

The first move should come from de Valera, and in the meantime he should not be provoked. But the Oath was an integral part of the Treaty, and in Britain's own interests, and in loyalty to Kevin O'Higgins and others who had given their lives for the Treaty and Cosgrave who was risking his, the British Government "should stand by the sanctity of the Treaty". Britain's claim to the annuities was valid but arbitration before a Commonwealth Tribunal would be considered.

A Cabinet Committee comprising Thomas, Neville Chamberlain, Sir Herbert Samuel, Viscount Hailsham, Walter Runciman and Viscount Snowden was appointed to consider the annuities situation.

Thomas wrote to de Valera on both contentious issues and received a very lengthy answer.[40] It began: "Whether the Oath was or was not 'an integral part of the Treaty made ten years ago' is not now the issue. The real issue is that the Oath is an intolerable burden to the people of this State and that they have declared in the most formal manner that they desire its instant removal." The Irish President of the Council took exception to the suggestion that the course he proposed was dishonourable. "The pages of the history of the relations between Great Britain and Ireland are indeed stained by many breaches of faith, but I must remind you that the guilty party has not been Ireland," he wrote. He went on to slate the 1921 Treaty which, he said, was "directly opposed to the will of the Irish people and was submitted to by them only under the threat of immediate and terrible war". For Ireland the Agreement had meant "the consummation of the outrage of Partition, and the alienation of the most sacred part of our national territory . . ." Protesting that British maintenance parties were still in occupation of Irish ports—"even in the area of the Free State"—de Valera went on that, in time of war or of strained relations with a foreign power, Britain claimed the right to make demands which would make Ireland's right to neutrality a mockery.

As a consequence of the Treaty, which had set brother's hand against brother and given Ireland ten years of blood and tears, a financial tribute had been extracted from Ireland "which, relatively to population, puts a greater burden on the people of the Irish Free State than the burden of the war reparation payments on the people of Germany and, relatively to taxable capacity, a burden ten times as heavy as the burden on the people of Britain of their debt repayments to the United States of America."

As for the Oath, he maintained that its elimination was "a matter of purely domestic concern", a measure required "for the peace, order and good government of the State". He claimed that the competence of his Government to pass such a measure was not open to question.

De Valera was quite right, for the Statute of Westminster of 1931, to which Ireland, and especially Kevin O'Higgins, had contributed much, conferred upon dominions the right to repeal or amend legislation passed by the United Kingdom which also was embodied in the law of the dominion concerned. Churchill himself had warned that the Statute gave the Irish Free State the right to abrogate the Treaty and rescind or revise the Constitution.

The answer on annuities was curious. De Valera asked what was the "formal and explicit undertaking to continue to pay the Land Annuities to the National Debt Commissioners" to which the British despatch had referred. His Government was "not aware of any such undertaking, but the British Government can rest assured that any just and lawful claims of Great Britain, or of any creditor of the Irish Free State will be scrupulously honoured by its Government".

The Cabinet noted when publication of the letter was considered that it was "a political manifesto addressed to Irishmen all over the world more than a reply to the Secretary of State". This is doubtful. De Valera's letter concluded with the reminder that friendly relations between the two countries could have been established on "a solid foundation of mutual respect and common interest" had not England tried to dominate her smaller neighbours. He wanted to drive it home that Ireland had been split asunder by Britain's maintenance of a dominating attitude, that he believed Britain was still trying to dominate Ireland and that he was determined to end that state of affairs.

He was beginning to realise that Britain herself had conferred powers he could use to dismantle the Treaty and he set about doing this systematically. Throughout almost a decade his struggle with Britain went on and always he seemed to have the upper hand. In Ireland he won a tremendous following. Often riding black-cloaked on a white horse, his aquiline head held imperiously, an aloof, electric figure, he seemed the embodiment of piety and authority. British Ministers found him an implacable adversary and more than once gave way to him in the forlorn hope that he might unbend.

De Valera went ahead with his Bill to abolish the Oath and it became law in May 1933. In the meantime, the British Government decided that it did not disqualify the Irish Free State from the Commonwealth but that it was in breach of the Treaty.[41] (It is a grim fact that only ten years earlier the British Government could have prevented the Civil War by taking the attitude it did now.) In the Dail the Opposition fought the Bill largely on the grounds that it was in breach of the Treaty and, therefore, that the Irish Free State was demonstrating that international agreements were of no importance to her. Not surprisingly, the British Cabinet shared that view and considered it would be impossible to enter into any fresh engagements with her.

Once he had seen his Bill to abolish the Oath through the Dail, de Valera re-opened the question of land annuities. He now knew that the explicit undertaking referred to by Thomas had been signed by Cosgrave in 1923 but never put to the Dail. J. H. Thomas and Lord Hailsham visited Dublin from June 6th to 8th, 1932, and two days later de Valera travelled to London accompanied by Sean T. O'Kelly, Vice-President of the Executive Council, to continue the discussions. He was not to be moved on the elimination of the Oath but was willing that the annuities dispute should go to arbitration. The difficulty now was the British Government's insistence that, in accordance with the unanimous decision taken at the Imperial Conference of 1930, any tribunal set up to arbitrate in disputes between members of the Commonwealth should comprise representatives from other Commonwealth countries. Refusing to admit for a moment that Ireland *was* a member of the Commonwealth, considering only that she was tied to it by an unwanted leash, de Valera demanded the jury be drawn from outside the Commonwealth as well as from within it. For one heady moment the British feared that he might ask for an Indian extremist to sit.[42]

The British Cabinet had now to consider what action to take if the Irish defaulted on the annuities payment due. "It would be necessary carefully to examine the implications involved in a possible tariff war between the United Kingdom and the Irish Free State and the reactions on Ulster of the policy in contemplation."[43] Ministers were afraid that once the Eucharistic Congress was out of the way the internal situation in the Free State might deteriorate. They were apprehensive of the IRA. An attack on the Six Counties was thought unlikely but any serious organised attack on British coastal defences could not be resisted, nor did the British Cabinet believe the IRA could be held by official Irish custodians of law and order.

De Valera did not share their pessimism. Honouring a pre-election pledge, he had released IRA prisoners held under Cosgrave's Public Safety Act and the measure itself was revoked. The IRA was a constant irritant but de Valera chose to deal with it in a way which was both less provocative and less likely to alienate his own more extreme Republican supporters. Only when their activities hazarded the well-being of the community were the IRA hounded down and punished.

Implacably hostile to Cosgrave's Cumann na nGaedheal which derived from the pro-Treaty party of the Civil War, the IRA continually harassed their election meetings and the police were powerless to curb their violence. Inevitably, Cosgrave's supporters took matters into their own hands and the Army Comrades Association, which was to evolve into the Blueshirt movement, was formed in August 1932.

General Eoin O'Duffy, recently dismissed by de Valera from his post of Commissioner of Police, took command of the new organisation between whom and the IRA a non-stop running battle commenced. By August 1934 de Valera's Government was compelled to bring back Cosgrave's unpopular Public Safety Act and a year or so later the two hostile groups showed signs of breaking up, O'Duffy leading the staunchest Blueshirts into the Spanish Civil War. The struggle between the right-wing Blueshirts and the socialist-republican IRA, permeated by old animosities, also, as Timothy Patrick Coogan points out in *Ireland Since the Rising*, reflected the ideological conflicts of the 'thirties in Europe. Both movements interested themselves in the land annuities problem, the IRA supporting de Valera's stand and the Blueshirts intervening when the Government took action against farmers who defaulted on payment.

Unlike the Free State Government, the British Cabinet could not bring in bailiffs and resorted to the imposition of special duties on Irish goods. J. H. Thomas asseverated in a memorandum to the Cabinet,[44] and repeated in the House of Commons, that "the question of Land Annuities should be kept distinct from the question of the Oath of Allegiance", but the Irish were convinced the British were being vindictive because of the Oath's abolition.

A rather curious reason for the imposition of special duties was urged in the British Cabinet. Cosgrave had been warning the electorate of the likely consequences of de Valera's policy and if it appeared that he had been "crying wolf", he might lose support at the next election—which, it was believed, would be called shortly. In the event, de Valera dissolved the Dail in January

1933 and in the same month was returned with an enhanced majority.

In initiating legislation to impose the duties the British Government insisted that they did not want a tariff war but were simply recouping their losses resulting from breach of contract. They realised, however, that the Free State would retaliate and that, on balance, there might be losses. In spite of Thomas's contention that the allegiance question was separate, in the same memorandum he put it that the annuities issue really involved the whole question of sovereignty and warned the Cabinet that the measures might stimulate nationalist feeling.

The Bill went through both Houses of Parliament early in July 1932, but the Cabinet were ready to suspend the Order if de Valera agreed to arbitration on Commonwealth conditions or if there was a likelihood of negotiation proving successful. But they required the outstanding money, which the Free State Government was holding in a suspense account, to be paid over to a "neutral" bank such as the Bank of Montreal. A last minute conference between de Valera and Ramsay MacDonald, the British Prime Minister, failed and the Order was put into effect. Almost at once the Dail countered with protective duties.

In August, a Miss Ellis made a private visit to Dublin and put a "truce" proposal to de Valera who accepted it, but the British Government saw little virtue in the proposals she brought back and insisted that the basis of any discussion would remain the Treaty and continuance of the Irish Free State as a member of the Commonwealth.

Another conference was arranged for October 10th when de Valera was scheduled to pass through London. The British delegates were briefed to try to convince the difficult Irish leader that the financial bargain made with Cosgrave was "far from unfavourable to the Irish Free State". If they succeeded they were to raise the question of the Treaty and advise him to drop his Bill to abolish the Oath, then held up in the Free State Senate. The Irish were to revoke their Import Duties Act, since the situation would have changed, but Britain's Import Duties Act would, in the absence of other arrangements, come into operation automatically on November 15th as a sanction for the breach of the Treaty involved in the elimination of the Oath.[45]

In other words, if there were a successful outcome to financial negotiations, the Irish would have no cause to implement their retaliatory legislation, but the British would retain their special duties as a punitive measure for something which they themselves had declared to be an entirely separate issue. Little wonder that the fish ignored so blatant a hook.

The British Government were becoming apprehensive of de Valera's further attempts to cut the Commonwealth strings. Free State delegates had attended the Imperial Conference in Ottawa during the summer, but only as observers. Stanley Baldwin, Lord President of the Council, reported with incredible optimism that the Irishmen had "learned a lot about the position of a dominion within the British Commonwealth". He believed they felt "a genuine regret at their inability to play any effective part, and that they had gone home with a desire to do so in the future, though this depended on the difficult personality of Mr de Valera".[46]

The position of the Governor-General became the next point of contention. James MacNeill, tactful holder of that office, was often embarrassed or slighted. If, for instance, he appeared at an official function any members of de Valera's Government present departed ostentatiously. They did not object to the man but to the symbol. Finally, the King was requested to remove him which, after some hesitation, he did. MacNeill's successor, Domhnall Ua Buachalla, a man of no pretensions, simply signed essential documents and stripped the office of all other trappings. Within a year, de Valera had introduced legislation to reduce the already thin powers of the Governor-General and to end the procedure of appeal from the Irish courts to the Privy Council.

The Free State Constitution had now become a thing of shreds and patches. Worse, fundamentally it still derived from British authority. In the end, though it rankled, de Valera had taken the Oath with his eyes closed so that he could once again play an effective part in the political life of his country. Once in power, he had turned the Constitution against itself. Then, in 1935, he set about drafting an entirely new Constitution which would embody the concept of an externally associated republic which the Irish plenipotentiaries had advocated in the Treaty negotiations of 1921.

The trade war with Britain dragged on and, although the Irish Free State was hit badly at a time when the foundations of the world's economic structure had crumbled, the dispute had compelled her people to build up their own resources, to make changes in agriculture and to move towards greater self-sufficiency. From the beginning, de Valera's policy had been protectionist and the British sanctions pushed him further and faster, but in the direction that he wanted to go.

In May 1936 he gave notice to the Dail of his intention to introduce the new Constitution and in June informed King Edward VIII that the office of Governor-General would be abolished and his functions would belong to an elected President. The new Constitution would apply to the internal affairs of Saorstat Eireann and would leave "unaffected the consitutional usages relating to external affairs".

10

THE KING was facing a constitutional crisis of his own making and de Valera was informed of it at the end of November. When he learned early in December that the King's abdication was imminent, he was disconcerted. Abdication would mean special legislation and it came at an awkward time when he was preparing under the new Constitution to exclude the King altogether from the internal affairs of the Irish Free State. He had planned further legislation to define the King's functions in external affairs.

It was Sean MacEntee, his Minister for Finance, who gave him the solution. This was to make one further amendment of the existing Constitution, deleting all references to the King and the Governor-General except in Article 51 where, the British Cabinet noted sorrowfully, the King was referred to as an "organ" for certain purposes connected with external relations. The certain purposes were described in an External Relations Bill such as de Valera had intended to put through after the new Constitution had been dealt with. There was no question of any hold-up of legislation in the Senate—de Valera had abolished it earlier in the year—and there was practically no opposition in the Dail. De Valera might well have cut the British connection entirely but it was complicated and the abdication crisis had forced speedy action. Moreover, he knew that he ought to preserve some link with Britain if ever the Six Counties were to be reunited with the Twenty-six.

Malcolm MacDonald, Secretary of State for Dominion Affairs, met de Valera in London on January 14th 1937 and the Cabinet discussed the situation on January 25th.[47] They considered the position of the Crown was "very inadequately and unsatisfactorily expressed in the new Irish Free State Legislation" but it seemed to them that de Valera agreed Ireland was still a full member of the Commonwealth and the King was King of Ireland. Lord Halifax was surprised that de Valera had been able to persuade his supporters to go so far in accepting the Crown but the Marquis of Zetland was disconsolate about the likely effect on nationalist opinion in India. That India would take inspiration from the independence movement in Ireland had been the bugbear of British Cabinets for decades.

The Prime Minister, Stanley Baldwin, wondered whether de Valera "intended to remain permanently within the Commonwealth on the basis of his new legislation or whether it was his object to use his new position as a lever to secure even more far-reaching concessions hereafter". He thought, and the Cabinet were agreed, that they would be "justified in stretching a point to keep the Irish Free State within the Commonwealth".

Their verdict was to be taken as that of one member of the Commonwealth only; the Dominions would have to be consulted.

The new Constitution was accepted by the Dail on June 14th but de Valera wanted to leave no lingering question marks. In July, a referendum was carried by 685,105 votes to 526,945, but 30 per cent of the voters abstained. Though it could not be said that the country's approval was wholehearted, de Valera had gone to endless trouble to produce an enduring Constitution which acknowledged the authority of the people and the right of every section of them to tolerance and justice. Though it recognised the special position of the Catholic Church as "guardian of the faith professed by the great majority of the citizens", it did not overlook the rights of other denominations.

What concerned the British Cabinet was the reaction to be expected in Northern Ireland. Article 2 of the new Constitution laid down that the national territory consisted of the whole island of Ireland, its islands and the territorial seas; Article 3 states that, pending the reintegration of the national territory, and without prejudice to the right of the Parliament and Government established by this Constitution to exercise jurisdiction over all the whole of that territory, legislation should apply only to the area of the Irish Free State; Article 4 declared the name of the State to be Eire, or, in the English language, Ireland.

All three articles offended the Unionists of Northern Ireland who acknowledged no right whatever of the Twenty-six Counties area to claim jurisdiction over the whole of Ireland. Strangely, it was the name of the State which most engaged the attention of the British Government. Malcolm MacDonald explained that while the title "Irish Free State" would suit Britain best, de Valera felt strongly that it had been imposed on his country by the Treaty. "He is capable of refusing to receive communications addressed to the Government of the Irish Free State even though his own country might be the principal sufferer from such obstinacy," said MacDonald. He thought America would probably not oppose de Valera's wishes, while Germany and Italy "might regard this as a convenient occasion for ingratiating themselves with the new State".[48] He recommended that "Eire" be used always and "Ireland" reserved as a geographical expression denoting the whole island.

The Cabinet agreed "to take note of the new name but make a declaration to the effect that we cannot recognise that the adoption of this name involves any right to territory or jurisdiction over territory forming part of the United Kingdom of Great Britain and Northern Ireland and that the use of the name in this connection is regarded as relating only to that area which has hitherto been known as the Irish Free State".[49]

The new Constitution was to become operative on December 29th 1937 and MacDonald was to communicate the terms of the statement to the Press twenty-four hours beforehand. The statement had been rephrased on representations made by Craig on the telephone before the Cabinet met. MacDonald warned that the amendments were "likely to ruffle the feelings of Mr de Valera" but recognised the difficulties of the Government of Northern Ireland.

In communicating the statement to the Press MacDonald was also to comment on the position of the Irish Free State as a member of the Commonwealth ". . . in a manner which makes our attitude clear but reduces to a minimum the opportunity for further hairsplitting by Mr de Valera".

When he succeeded J. H. Thomas at the Dominions Office towards the end of 1935, the thirty-four year old Malcolm MacDonald set himself the task of ending the ruinous economic conflict which had continued since de Valera's advent to power. From March 1936 he met de Valera on a number of occasions, usually when the Irish leader was passing through London on his way to Geneva. The meetings were informal and unpublicised, but MacDonald had the backing of both the Prime Minister, Stanley Baldwin, and the Chancellor of the Exchequer, Neville Chamberlain. The two men got on well and within a few months the Irish High Commissioner, John W. Dulanty, was exploring the ground with British officials. The British Government were extremely anxious to come to a settlement on trade, finance and defence, but de Valera was determined to find rock bottom before building up a structure of agreements. Rock bottom was the elimination of the detested border.

Apart from Partition, the most contentious issue was Britain's continued occupation of the Treaty ports. De Valera demanded their return. Dulanty was more optimistic than MacDonald that a formula could be devised to allow Britain use of the ports when the interests of both countries were vitally involved. He was also encouraging on finance but, MacDonald commented, "Mr Dulanty is not always a reliable guide on his master's mind . . ."

On November 24th 1937 de Valera sent a dispatch[50] to Malcolm MacDonald. "For some time past the Government of Saorstát Eireann have been considering how best to protect the people of this country from the dangers to which they will be exposed in the event of an outbreak of another European war," wrote de Valera and went on that any measures "must depend fundamentally on the relations that will exist between our two countries at the time . . ." A meeting between the two Governments was therefore essential.

MacDonald thought the dispatch might indicate that de Valera was "in a more yielding mood" but the Irish leader was also facing domestic difficulties, partly political, partly economic, and MacDonald was "rather sceptical about so rigid a mind".

What really concerned de Valera was the need to ensure Ireland's neutrality in the event of war. If Britain were not prised from Irish ports then, willy nilly, Eire would be dragged into a conflict which she felt was no business of hers.

Talks began on January 17th 1938. The Irish delegation—de Valera himself, Sean Lemass (Minister for Industry and Commerce), Sean MacEntee (Finance) and Dr James Ryan (Agriculture)—were given "a boisterous welcome at Euston", MacDonald reported to the Cabinet. The British team was also a strong one, comprising the Prime Minister, Neville Chamberlain, the Chancellor of the Exchequer, Sir John Simon, the Home Secretary, Sir Samuel Hoare, and MacDonald himself.

Reporting the Conference,[51] MacDonald explained that de Valera insisted the Partition question was fundamental. "While it lasted there could be no complete friendship and co-operation between the people of Eire and the people of this country." De Valera had in mind "something in the nature of a Joint Council to consider certain matters of common interest". It was his old scheme of a Northern Parliament with existing powers but subordinate to Dublin, the whole of Ireland being outside the Commonwealth but associated with it in certain matters of external affairs. Emphasising Northern Ireland's dependence on the United Kingdom Government, de Valera suggested that "from the point of view of a wider Imperial outlook it was their business to use their influence with the Northern Ireland Government in the direction of a united Ireland".

The answer from the British Prime Minister also echoed the words of an earlier Government: Ulster was not to be coerced. It was a matter primarily between Eire and Northern Ireland. If the latter changed her views and moved towards a united Ireland there would be no obstacle from the United Kingdom. But present information suggested the Northerners were still strongly against unity. "Mr de Valera must therefore get out of his head any ideas that anything could be done at present. The best way in which Mr de Valera and his Government could promote their aims was to conduct their policy so as to remove the suspicion that they were drifting away from the Empire and, by entering on an agreement with ourselves to show their desire for better relations."

De Valera had appeared to appreciate the position but had "made it clear that he could not reach an optimum agreement on such matters as defence, finance and trade without some advance in the question of Partition". His line now was that at least Eire should have absolute control of her ports.

The British Government considered vacating the ports, with the proviso that they were made available in time of war; but that would have denied Ireland's right to maintain neutrality. They consulted the Chiefs of Staff of the armed services, who took the realistic line that to attempt to use the ports in face of the hostility of the Irish people would be futile. This view the Government decided to accept, provided the proposed defence agreement was worked out satisfactorily. From the Irish point of view any defence agreement had some danger as it would imply that the two countries were military allies.

At the end of three days, MacDonald continued, the draft of a tentative defence agreement had been taken back to Dublin. De Valera, admitting that the maintenance of Ireland's freedom was no longer threatened by Great Britain, had talked instead of a "common peril". Although anxious for cooperation on defence he could not promise use of the Irish ports in time of war. He had hinted that if Partition were ended he might be able to consider it. In the meantime Britain should base her plans "on alternative hypotheses according as the ports were or were not available ..."

On finance the two sides were a long way apart. The capital equivalent of the annual payments claimed from Ireland was reckoned at £100 million. Special import duties were yielding £4 million and the problem put by the Chancellor of the Exchequer was to find a compromise which would compensate reasonably for the loss of income. Mr de Valera had been "very stiff" on this and would not agree to pay a penny of Land Annuities or anything in substitution for them. He had offered a lump sum of £2 million but stepped up his offer, first to £8 million, and then to £10 million. Ireland would be involved in heavy defence expenditure if a defence agreement were arrived at, he pointed out. The British Ministers had expressed willingness to drop Land Annuities if Eire assumed liability for other payments, capitalised at £26 million.

An agreement on trade hinged on success on the financial front but, in general terms, the two sides were disposed to drop the trade war impositions.

Taking all the negotiations to date, the Cabinet were hopeful of an agreement unless some practical move on Partition were demanded. Chamberlain was perturbed that de Valera might be having difficulty in Dublin but said hopefully, "He is a persuasive person and might succeed in carrying his own Cabinet."

Sir Samuel Hoare, Home Secretary, surmised that the attitude of Northern Ireland would be governed by commercial concessions. 'His information was that a few years ago there had been a movement in Northern Ireland in the direction of getting rid of Partition, but, mainly owing to the higher taxation in Eire, it now had no support."

On February 23rd de Valera returned to the conference table, even more insistent that without the end of Partition a defence agreement was impossible, but the British Ministers remained as adamant as he. The meeting produced no result.

The Conference was resumed on March 2nd. Earlier that day, Malcolm MacDonald explained the situation for his Cabinet colleagues.[52] On defence the position was difficult, the Eire Cabinet having rejected the draft agreement "on the grounds that we were unable to do anything on the subject of Partition". Two courses were open:

"1. To agree to hand the ports back to Eire and trust that they would bring their defences up to date and allow us to use them in time of war.

"2. To remain in the ports—which would not necessarily prevent an agreement on finance and trade, but would not conduce to good relations between the two countries."

MacDonald favoured the first, which he admitted was a gamble.

He believed de Valera would base his policy on the draft defence agreement. Sir Thomas Inskip commented that, whichever country had the ports, it would take years to bring them up to date. If Eire were hostile in war it was better not to have them, but as she was dependent on overseas trade, he was convinced she would come in on the British side.

The Home Secretary was anxious that the ports should not be surrendered as part of a bargain, but politically "it was important to obtain a trade agreement so satisfactory that Northern Ireland would not stir up agitation in Parliament against handing back the ports".

Chamberlain said there was no question of a bargain and that de Valera did not expect the ports in return for a trade agreement. Goodwill was vital—"to continue the occupation of the ports would be represented as an affront to the people of Eire and would keep open the old sore".

The trade conversations now turned on the free entry of Northern Ireland goods to Eire. De Valera had envisaged no more than a system of reciprocal preference. MacDonald told the Cabinet on March 9th[53] that at this point the Prime Minister had "addressed some well-chosen words" to the Eire Ministers. He had told them the ports would not be handed back, and probably there would be no agreement on trade and finance, unless something were done for Northern Ireland. Chamberlain, who had had private discussion with de Valera, thought an agreement with him was worth more than one with anyone else "as he alone had influence with the parties of the Left". He was convinced that de Valera wanted an agreement and wanted to help break down differences between North and South but was "apprehensive as to its effect on his own political position". In Sir Samuel Hoare's opinion, the people of Northern Ireland saw the Special Duties as a lever which could be used to relieve their brittle economic position. There was a good deal of politics mixed up with the attitude of Northern Ireland, Chamberlain remarked tersely.

Before their return to Ireland on March 12th, the Eire Ministers were handed proposals under four heads.[54] These were amplified in a document subsequently handed to J. P. Walshe who had stayed for further talks. The Treaty ports were to be returned and Land Annuities and other annual payments commuted to a lump sum of £10 million. Special Duties on Eire produce were to be abolished and retaliatory duties were to be withdrawn.

But on two points the proposed agreement was not acceptable to Eire. Special treatment was to be given to goods from Northern Ireland; an immediate reduction was to be made on specified items and after four years there was to be free entry for another list of items. Again, Partition was the snag. The Eire Ministers had asked the British Government for a clear statement that Partition would be ended. They claimed that Britain had legal authority to do this. Instead, they were offered a declaration that no change would be made without the consent of the Government of Northern Ireland but that if there were a desire for closer relations the British Government would actively help. On this basis Eire was not willing to offer special trade concessions to the obdurately separated North.

MacDonald recognised that it would be politically difficult for de Valera to get approval of the proposals and anticipated counter proposals "including concessions to Northern Ireland wrapped up in the form of concessions to the United Kingdom".

Ironically, it was Lord Craigavon who opened the way to a settlement. Reluctant to upset the prospect of agreement, he intimated to the Irish Situation Committee that he would accept a case he could defend in Parliament. He was concerned most with unemployment in Northern Ireland and the Chancellor of the Exchequer promised certain subsidies, pointing also to the possibility that munitions manufacture would alleviate unemployment.

The Agreement was signed in an atmosphere of cordiality at 10 Downing Street on April 25th 1938. Eire got her ports back, promising nothing in return. She was to pay a lump sum of £10 million to settle for all time the annual payments which Britain had capitalised at ten times that figure. There was to be free entry of Eire produce, subject to quantitative regulations, and some concessions in return.

When the British Cabinet discussed the terms on April 13th,[55] MacDonald observed that it was not a good agreement on paper but would "open a new chapter in Anglo-Irish relations" and the Prime Minister remarked that "in this kind of agreement what was not included was sometimes more important than what was". The Ambassador of the United States "had spoken strongly to him of the valuable effect on opinion in America of an agreement with Eire". The last word was uttered by Chamberlain in Cabinet on April 25th. A *quid pro quo* had proved impossible—"the negotiators had felt it necessary to content themselves with the best they could get". Though de Valera had not succeeded in shifting the border by a single inch there was no doubt as to whose was the victory. But to Eamon de Valera there was no thought that by his skilful bargaining he had wrung concessions from the British Government: he had simply stood out for his country's rights.

Eire's vulnerability to attack remained an anxiety to the British Government. De Valera himself was anxious for an immediate improvement of the country's defences, including the Treaty ports, and put his predicament to the British Government in November 1938. He had thought to ask for a British officer to advise his Government but this was repugnant to too many Irish politicians. Nor was an officer from any of the Dominions acceptable. He proposed instead to engage a French general but the British Chiefs of Staff objected "as it appeared to involve the disclosure to a French officer of secret information on defence matters". Finally, the British Government agreed to the Frenchman but decided to withhold certain information until he had gone his way. Secret information was given to the Dominions as a matter of course and Eire was to be dealt with on the same footing, but there was some doubt as to the extent to which defence secrets should be entrusted to a country likely to embrace neutrality in the event of war.

De Valera pushed on with his programme of severing the tie with the Commonwealth and, in March 1939, the British Government learned that a new passport, omitting the King's name and any reference to the Commonwealth, was to be introduced. Sir Thomas Inskip, now Secretary of State for Dominion Affairs, proposed to reply expressing regret and pointing out that the step would "widen the separation which Mr de Valera deplored between Eire and Northern Ireland".[56] MacDonald rejoined that the Northern Ireland Government, who were adopting a very difficult attitude at this time, took the view that the gulf between them was immeasurable.

De Valera continued to press for the abolition of the border. In a newpaper interview he repeated that the Northern Ireland Government could keep its present powers, though he did not consider they were entitled to them, provided they guaranteed fair play for the minority and transferred to an all-Ireland Parliament the powers reserved to Westminster. At one time he would have reduced the Six Counties to four, now he was prepared to let the border stand, but only as a local boundary.

The IRA now took a hand, threatening reprisals if British troops were not withdrawn from Northern Ireland. A bombing campaign began in England, culminating in the horrifying incident at Coventry when five people died. Sir Thomas Inskip discussed the IRA campaign with Dulanty on February 16th and was told that de Valera was willing that the Eire police should try to prevent such outrages but not that they should obtain evidence in Ireland to assist the conviction of IRA men arrested in England. Again, de Valera was bowing to political considerations. In June, to protect the State's own authority, he was compelled to declare the IRA an illegal organisation.

Eire's cause was now viewed with scant sympathy by the British public and strain appeared in the relationship between the two Governments. De Valera became very agitated when the old bugbear of conscription reappeared. Chamberlain, announcing the British Government's decision to introduce conscription, had no intention of applying it in Northern Ireland although Craigavon pressed him to do so. Later, when Churchill bad become Prime Minister, Craigavon again urged conscription for Northern Ireland but Churchill would not listen. De Valera was afraid that if Nationalists in the North were drafted into the British forces the IRA would step up its campaign, but he was much more concerned with what he considered a violation of Ireland's freedom. Neither Chamberlain nor Churchill was willing to risk the alienation of even the sad remnants of Irish support.

That support, de Valera maintained as war made its inexorable approach, would be immeasurably stronger if an individual Ireland were free to make its own decisions, but so long as Britain insisted upon isolating unnaturally one part of Ireland from another she could expect only resentment from Eire. Too optimistically, the British counted on self-preservation driving Eire into a military alliance.

I I

IN A telegram despatched on August 31st 1939, de Valera informed Chamberlain that the German Minister in Dublin had told him Germany was anxious to respect Eire's neutrality. He had replied that his Government's policy was to maintain neutrality but that German activities, including propaganda, would not be tolerated.[57] Somewhat ruefully, Inskip remarked that "it had been contemplated that we should ask Eire at the least to break off diplomatic relations with Germany if we became involved in war". More cheerfully, he reported that Dulanty believed attacks on shipping would induce Eire's entry into the war within a week.

This was probably wishful thinking on Inskip's part, rather than indiscretion on Dulanty's. De Valera sent his Secretary to the Department of External Affairs, the invaluable J. P. Walshe, to explain to Anthony Eden, now Secretary of State for Dominion Affairs, his attitude of friendly neutrality. He also asked for a British representative in Dublin and Sir John Maffey, a man of great wisdom and infinite tact, was appointed. The title settled upon was United Kingdom Representative to Eire.

Within the first weeks of the war the Royal Navy found their inability to use the Treaty ports frustrating and a plea went to the Irish Government for facilities at Berehaven in Bantry Bay. Maffey reported, with not a little sympathy for de Valera's position, the fruitless meeting he had with him on October 21st. No Government in Ireland could exist for twenty-four hours if it departed from the principle of neutrality, was the gist of his message. "The question of the ports was at the very nerve centre of public interest in that matter . . ." Pressed by Maffey to discuss the matter with Chamberlain, de Valera declined. The answer could not be different and de Valera valued his friendship with the British Premier too much to wish to argue with him. Maffey was emphatic in his report that even pro-British sections of the community, including the one-time "loyalist" families, were determined against Eire's becoming involved in the European conflict. Churchill, who had been vehemently critical of the handing over of the Treaty ports in the first place, now, as First Lord of the Admiralty, would not allow that Eire's neutrality was valid, and wanted to take the harbours. He had no support from his colleagues. Despite de Valera's pleas for official recognition of neutrality as a way to winning the hearts of the Irish people, the British Government never did accord that recognition.

Warily de Valera made his way along a very prickly political path. There were still diehards who, despite the new Constitution and the gradual severance of ties with the Commonwealth, still saw Dail Eireann as the bastard child of British imperialism. They were also intent upon burning the boundary off the map of Ireland and would have had de Valera look the other way while they used their own country as a base for their bombing campaign in England. De Valera not only despised their methods, though he understood the very grain of their motives, but feared they might lead to British intervention. He took special powers by legislation and there were a number of arrests. Again he appealed to the British Government to remove the dangerous irritant, Partition.

By January 1940 the British Government were worried about the "serious internal situation developing in Eire". If de Valera were to fall a new Government was likely to be more sympathetic to the IRA than he—"and still less amenable to our influence".[58] Eden told the Cabinet that they must consider the fate of the Coventry murderers under sentence of death. If they were hanged they would be proclaimed martyrs by the IRA and de Valera's position would be weakened.

Largely on these grounds, de Valera interceded for the two condemned men, writing and telephoning Eden and Chamberlain. He neither condoned the murders nor underestimated the difficulties of the British Government, but he knew that many Irish people would think not of the deaths of innocent people but of young Irishmen dying for the cause they believed in. "The execution of these men will give rise to new and bitter antagonisms between us which countries who see their profit in them will not hesitate to exploit," he warned.

The men were executed on February 7th and Maffey telegraphed that there was tension in Eire. It was a bad sign that Eire radio, which previously had refrained from quoting from German radio, had repeated with approval an attack on Britain's attitude to small nations broadcast from Germany two hours earlier.

But, as Germany overwhelmed Europe efficiently and ruthlessly, Irish opinion swung against her and to some extent against the IRA which appeared to be intriguing with Germany against England, albeit warily on the German side.

After heroically facing a battering in the House of Commons, when even his friends deserted him, Chamberlain saw that a national Government was essential. He knew that he was not acceptable to the Opposition and, on May 10th 1940, he resigned, recommending Winston Churchill as his successor. And so the inspired bellicosity of Churchill came into its own, Chamberlain becoming his Lord President of the Council. The change seemed unlikely to improve Britain's relations with Eire.

Naval Intelligence reports and the British Ambassador in Lisbon suggested German "fifth column" activities in Ireland and the Cabinet feared German parachutists would land there. They were agreed that at all costs they must avoid swinging public opinion in Eire against Britain by infringement of her neutrality and thought the Germans might be spreading rumours to tempt them to such action. On May 27th the Cabinet agreed on an immediate approach to de Valera to bring home the danger facing Eire and the need for early and free co-operation. In particular they would ask again for the use of Berehaven for the navy. Significantly they proposed also to invite Craigavon to take part in an all-Ireland Council during the emergency.

Three days later, even Chamberlain was talking of being ready to send forces to Southern Ireland. Referring to the "serious situation" there, he explained that the IRA forces were almost strong enough to overrun the Eire Government forces. Again, on June 1st, he wanted the troops in readiness to dislodge any German troops who landed in Eire. There were reports of a German expeditionary force at Cadiz which was to invade Ireland. The Cabinet noted that it was impossible to evaluate such reports but that it would be unwise to ignore them.

On June 16th 1940 the British Cabinet had before them a telegram from General Smuts, de Valera's old friend and theirs, suggesting that "the Irish Atlantic ports should be seized at once, even in the face of Irish opposition, to prevent them suffering the same fate as the Norwegian ports".[59] Chamberlain presented "a very alarming picture of German preparation in Southern Ireland and made it clear that a body of some 2,000 German troops could probably capture the whole country". He had invited de Valera to London to discuss the position, pointing out that the security of the whole of Ireland was at stake. For this reason, he proposed that Craigavon should join them. Chamberlain had asked Craigavon early in June for some conciliatory gesture from the people of the North of Ireland, having first pointed out to him "how difficult it would be to separate questions of defence from the burning question of Partition". Craigavon had not yet replied. De Valera did not see his way clear to leave Ireland and, instead, Chamberlain had sent Malcolm MacDonald to see him in Dublin. "It is most important," said Chamberlain, "that Mr de Valera should be told frankly of the arrangements that the Germans had made. He must realise that it would be too late to do anything after the invasion had started, when bridges would be blown up to impede troop movements, and Mr de Valera himself probably shot."

Chamberlain wished de Valera would throw neutrality aside and invite British troops to the rescue, but he knew this was too much to hope for. However, MacDonald should insist on the rounding up of the IRA and the internment of Germans. "If this precipitated a rebellion, as it well might, so much the better. The Eire army would then be fighting the IRA and upsetting the German arrangements."

De Valera was certain to bring up Partition and MacDonald had been brief to suggest a Council for the defence of all Ireland which would also "form a bridge for eventual discussion on Partition".

The Prime Minister summed up the discussion. He welcomed the MacDonald project and agreed that "although as a last resort we should not hesitate to secure the ports by force, it would be unwise at this moment to take any action that might compromise our position with the United States of America, in view of the present delicate developments".

MacDonald and de Valera met for over three hours on June 17th. As cogently as he could, MacDonald put Britain's case that Ireland was next on Hitler's list and could be overrun in a matter of hours. On neutrality de Valera would not budge. Nor would he countenance the use by the Royal Navy of Irish ports or troops to guard strategic points. This might well provoke the Germans to invade Ireland. The position might have been different if there had been a united Ireland. The idea of a Defence Council de Valera also rejected as a breach of neutrality. He had rounded up as many IRA leaders as he could lay hands on and there was no evidence of any un-neutral act on Germany's part. In the War Cabinet Chamberlain remarked that MacDonald "had evidently succeeded in instilling some sense of reality into Mr de Valera".[60]

Chamberlain referred to the opinion of the Chiefs of Staff that without the British armed services taking up station in Ireland both Ireland and the United Kingdom were vulnerable. The question of taking the Irish ports by force would have to be considered but, because reaction in America was likely to be unfavourable, he proposed that MacDonald return to Dublin with the same requests as before but this time offering a declaration that the Government were, in principle, in favour of a united Ireland. Craigavon "would have to be told that the interests of Northern Ireland could not be allowed to stand against the vital interests of the British Empire". A united Ireland would be part of the Empire, of course, but "full Dominion status carried with it the right to secede from the Commonwealth".

To borrow the Irish ports for the duration Chamberlain was acknowledging that de Valera could have everything he had ever asked for—a united Ireland which could secede from the Commonwealth. Churchill did not agree that the loyal province of Ulster should be urged to join in such an arrangement. He was not convinced that the military picture was as black as Chamberlain painted it, and he preferred to let the Germans make the first move.

MacDonald saw de Valera again on June 26th and presented proposals which the British Government regarded as tentative but which they acknowledged would be interpreted as an offer. Chamberlain therefore wrote to tell Craigavon what was going on.

The proposals, which were to be taken together as a whole, were:

"1. A declaration to be issued by the United Kingdom Government forthwith accepting the principle of a united Ireland.

"2. A joint body including representatives of the Government of Eire and the Government of Northern Ireland to be set up at once to work out the constitutional and other practical details of the Union of Ireland. The United Kingdom Government to give such assistance towards the work of this body as might be desired.

"3. A joint Defence Council representative of Eire and Northern Ireland to be set up immediately.

"4. Eire to enter the war on the side of the United Kingdom and her allies forthwith, and for the purposes of the Defence of Eire, the Government of Eire to invite British naval vessels to have the use of ports in Eire and British troops and aeroplanes to co-operate with the Eire forces and to be stationed in such positions as may be agreed between the two Governments.

"5. The Government of Eire to intern all German and Italian aliens in the country and to take any further steps necessary to suppress Fifth Column activities.

"6. The United Kingdom Government to provide military equipment at once to the Government of Eire [in accordance with the particulars given in the annex]."[61]

MacDonald reported that he had discussed the document with de Valera, Sean Lemass and Frank Aiken on the afternoon of June 27th.[62] Aiken did most of the talking and "was even more persistent than de Valera himself has been in urging that the proper solution is a united Ireland which is neutral". Lemass he found more reasonable. The Dail Cabinet regarded the plan as unacceptable because they did not believe a united Ireland would emerge from it. MacDonald felt "their attitude would be different if they had not the impression that we are going to lose the war, and that it would be a mistake for them now to throw in their lot with us".

Although not optimistic, MacDonald urged amendment of the document and a fresh note was handed to de Valera on June 29th.[63] The declaration clause was strengthened. It was to "take the form of a solemn undertaking that the Union is to become at an early date an accomplished fact from which there shall be no turning back". As Chamberlain made clear that the assent of Northern Ireland was essential and no guarantee of that could be given, the amendment did not advance Britain's proposal very far.

Clause 2 also was extended, de Valera having indicated that a joint Defence Council was not enough to demonstrate to the people the genuineness of the change towards the Union of Ireland. The purpose of the work of the joint body was "to establish at as early a date as possible the whole machinery of Government of the union".

Clause 4 was vitally overhauled. A declaration of war would not be necessary if Britain were given facilities to guard, in conjunction with Eire's forces, against a sudden attack such as had overcome neutral Norway, Holland, Belgium, Denmark and Luxembourg.

A long reply, dated July 4th and addressed to Chamberlain, was considered by the Cabinet the following day. De Valera wrote: "We are unable to accept the plan outlined, which we note is purely tentative and has not been submitted to Lord Craigavon and his colleagues." His Government were aware of the dangers of neutrality but regarded the dangers of departing from it greater still. He reiterated that the only way unity could be secured was "by the immediate establishment of a single sovereign all-Ireland Parliament, free to decide all matters of national policy internal and external . . ." He had suggested to MacDonald "creating such a Parliament by the entry into the Parliament here of the present representatives in the Parliament at Belfast".

Given unity, de Valera would still maintain neutrality. The ability to mobilise the whole manpower for national defence offered, he thought, "the surest guarantee against any part of our territory being used as a base for operations against Britain".

Britain's whole attempt to protect her vulnerable and dyspeptic underbelly had failed. De Valera was adamantine as ever and Craigavon had been filled with suspicion and indignation. Even the link with de Valera which Chamberlain's friendship with him provided was soon to be lost. In October, ill-health forced his resignation and, on November 9th, he died.

Apprehension in the British Cabinet in these suspenseful days as the Germans piled up their armour on the French coast is understandable. The Cabinet were already alarmed by reports that the Germans were buying Irish land, removing hedges and filling ditches in preparation for parachute landings. In Eire the attitude towards Britain had soured and on July 17th Sir John Maffey was called by de Valera to discuss the deteriorating relations. He was anxious to remedy the situation. Reporting home,[64] Maffey gave de Valera's opinion of the causes under four headings. One cause, he thought, was inherent in the war and no one was to blame. It was a grim struggle becoming grimmer and de Valera feared that a desperate Britain would attempt to seize the ports. Another was British Press propaganda against Eire's neutrality which seemed to be Government-inspired. Other more subtle causes gave the impression that Britain was almost eager for the Germans to invade Ireland as an excuse to move in herself. Talk of a military pact had done harm. Finally, after the MacDonald conversation, it was thought that Britain was resentful.

De Valera said frankly that a British attack rather than a German one was expected. He referred to Major Byass, a British officer from the North arrested for espionage. Maffey was able to produce a telegram from London which explained Byass's activities and de Valera was relieved. Sir John worked hard to ease the tension. He was able to reassure de Valera that Britain's reluctance to supply arms and equipment was because of her own desperate need. De Valera took the point that arms carried by British troops, had they been allowed entry into Ireland, remained in Britain's reserve. Nevertheless, he begged Britain to consider arms to Eire as insurance for herself.

"Why will you not trust us?" he asked. "If you think we might attack the North, I say with all emphasis we will never do that. No solution there can come by force. There we must now wait and let the solution come with time and patience."

It had gone hard with him to turn down the scheme for unity, the dream of his life. But it would have meant civil war. His regret was genuine and he asked that Chamberlain be told that.

In Cabinet Lord Caldecote suggested a public declaration that Britain had no intention of sending forces to Ireland uninvited but the Cabinet felt this would be "lacking in frankness, since circumstances might arise which would compel us to do so".

It was essential to restore good relations, if only because Eire was turning a blind eye to British infringements of her territorial waters and air space. But it was even more important not to jeopardise the secret understanding that "in the event of a serious invasion they will resist the enemy and call upon us for aid".[65] The British Cabinet thought that if they provided arms there would be a risk of their capture if Germany invaded Ireland and a further risk that they might be used by the Irish, presumably the IRA, against Britain. Furthermore, the withholding of arms "might well be the most effective way of bringing to the Eire Government a greater realisation of their dangers". By the end of July the Cabinet had decided to take the risk and a list of equipment for despatch to Ireland was approved, but no material was actually sent for a considerable time.

In the meantime, the Eire and British Governments were negotiating a trade agreement. There was some disagreement on prices and it appeared that a concealed subsidy of £500,000 per annum to Irish farmers would be involved. Churchill grumbled that he saw strong objection to subsidising a disloyal dominion. It was admitted that Eire was a near source of supply but she could send little. But if no agreement were concluded, "a policy of increasing industrialisation might be adopted to our disadvantage".

Even in the heart of war the future of British trade had to be safeguarded. A real advantage of the agreement was the provision for transhipment of goods from large ships to small in Eire ports. Despite Churchill's grumbles, he agreed that negotiations should go ahead, but they continued to hang fire.

As the U-boat campaign took a heavier and heavier toll, Churchill again began to cast longing eyes on the Treaty ports. He referred in the House of Commons on November 5th to the "most heavy and grievous burden" which inability to use Irish facilities placed on Britain's shoulders, and two days later told the Cabinet that air attacks on convoys emphasised the need for the protection of fighter aircraft working from the Irish coast. On November 8th he said that shipping losses on the present scale could not be tolerated. In five weeks, to November 3rd, Britain had lost 420,300 tons of shipping.

In the Dail de Valera reiterated that, so long as Ireland remained neutral, there was no question of conceding use of the ports on any condition whatsoever. Churchill decided to try another tack. He proposed to telegraph Roosevelt on the following lines:[66] "It will be at least two years before America can give us any effective help since she is only now laying out her armament factories. The question is whether Great Britain can hold out for so long without the Treaty ports. Anything which can be done to get for us the use of the Treaty ports would thus be in defence of American interests."

Maffey advised from Dublin that de Valera was in a "very agitated and bitter mood". His attitude was that Irish sentiment towards the United Kingdom had been steadily improving until the issue of the ports had been suddenly raised.

Public opinion in Britain also was becoming inflamed and the Cabinet were finding it difficult to restrain angry MPs from putting down Questions in the House. Churchill's line of reply to them was that Britain was "prepared to go to the limit of suffering" before any move was taken against the ports.[67] Every political expedient should be tried to influence de Valera and the navy should try to find some way of overcoming the threat to British shipping without the use of the Eire ports.

To the Secretary of State for the Dominions (Viscount Cranborne) Churchill wrote on November 22nd that de Valera should be left to stew in his own juice for a while.[68] Rather dryly, he added, "Sir John Maffey should be made aware of the rising anger in England and Scotland, and especially among the merchant seamen, and he should not be encouraged to think that his only task is to mollify de Valera and make everything, including our ruin, pass off pleasantly."

On November 28th it was reported to the Cabinet that the American Minister in Dublin, Mr David Gray, had pressed de Valera strongly to allow Britain to use Eire's ports but de Valera had been entirely unreceptive. Maffey was to be instructed to leave the matter be. Churchill remarked that if Eire had been willing to come into the war public opinion might well have brought about a united Ireland. As it was, the people would be strongly opposed to any pressure on Northern Ireland.

In December the Cabinet considered withdrawing from Eire shipping facilities urgently needed for Britain's own use. It was important that the measures proposed should be presented as an economic necessity arising from shipping difficulties, which was true so far as it went, but the primary object was "to bring home to the people of Eire their dependence on shipping".[69] The result might well be "a state of sullen animosity or general hostility on the part of the people of Eire", but the Chiefs of Staff considered the risk worth taking if it led to the ports being made available. Before taking action, it was thought mete to refer the matter to President Roosevelt who, in response to a letter from Churchill, would be putting to Congress proposals about the financing of munitions contracts. Britain could not afford to lose the sympathy of Congress.[70]

"We are so hard-pressed at sea that we cannot undertake to carry any longer the 400,000 tons of feeding stuffs and fertilisers which we have hitherto convoyed to Eire through all the attacks of the enemy," wrote Churchill.[71] De Valera would have plenty of food for his people "but they will not have the prosperous trading they are making now". Churchill also advised Roosevelt that the British Government could no longer continue the subsidies hitherto paid to Irish agricultural producers.

In a memorandum dated January 17th 1941, Churchill stated that lack of the Irish bases was a "grievous injury" but not "vital to our survival". He personally did not recognise Irish neutrality as a legal act, nor Eire as a sovereign state, and he was not prepared to give a guarantee that under no circumstances would her

II

neutrality be violated. If it became a matter of self-preservation for Britain, or if Germany invaded Ireland, he reserved the right to send troops.[72]

No declaration of Britain's new shipping policy was made, but the effects were soon felt in Ireland. Some rationing was shortly introduced but the efforts to raise agricultural production during the economic war of the thirties were intensified and during the "emergency" of 1939–45 the area of land under the plough was doubled. Frank Aiken was sent to America to try to obtain ships, arms, supplies and sympathy, but Roosevelt was strongly pro-British and Gray in Dublin was furnishing critical reports on de Valera. Aiken himself was extremely able but his views on Britain were notably hostile and an offer of two ships was made, over his head, direct to de Valera. He declined the offer because of the snub to his Minister, but eventually the two ships were received and formed the nucleus of a small fleet.

In May 1941, at the behest of the Government of Northern Ireland, the question of conscription in the Six Counties came up again. De Valera made vehement protest and this time Gray took his side. Churchill's Government took the matter no further, though Churchill was made exceedingly irate by what he considered an intrusion by de Valera into British affairs. But Churchill could not conceive of de Valera's extreme repugnance to compulsory service, not only of the Nationalist minority in the North but of anyone who lived in Irish national territory.

Britain had no complaint about the availability of Irish manpower. The response from the Six Counties was spontaneous and generous but about 50,000 volunteers from Eire also were serving in Britain's armed forces. Thousands more were working in war industries. The present author knows a Kerry man who was imprisoned in Eire for IRA activities and upon his release joined the RAF and became a rear-gunner.

When Belfast was bombed in May 1941 de Valera scarcely hesitated before sending every available fire engine to help. On May 30th Dublin was bombed in error, much to the alarm of the German Minister who had worked very hard not to antagonise the Irish and had, indeed, urged that Belfast be spared further assault because of the hostility it aroused in Eire. An explanation of the Dublin error was given to the author when he was stationed at an Operational Training Unit at the time. An instructor related how one of the German radio beams which intersected over Belfast had been detected and "bent" by superimposing another signal.

Hitler's attack on Russia in June 1941 relaxed invasion nerves both in Britain and in Ireland. Then, on December 7th, the assault on Pearl Harbour brought America into the war. Churchill was naturally elated and having initiated various necessary moves in consequence, he "turned at once to what has always lain near my heart".[73] He telegraphed de Valera: "Now is your chance. Now or never! A nation once again! I will meet you wherever you wish." (Longford and O'Neill point out that the message received by de Valera differed slightly from Churchill's version, the last sentence reading, "Am very ready to meet you at any time.")

The two leaders did not meet but, at de Valera's suggestion, Lord Cranborne visited him secretly on December 17th. Neutrality and Partition were both discussed, as usual to no avail. Shortly afterwards, when American troops were landed in the Six Counties, de Valera took the line that, although he did not wish to offend America and could not prevent the occupation of the Six Counties by belligerent forces, they were on part of Ireland's national territory.

The Americans themselves became involved in the issue of bases in Eire. Though less significant than they were when invasion seemed imminent, they would still have had immeasurable value to the Allies in the Battle of the Atlantic. American proposals, apparently initiated by Gray, had little support in the British Cabinet, apart from Churchill who was always pleased to jump on his old war-horse. An American demand for the expulsion of Nazi and Japanese diplomats did have British support; it also had the hint of an ultimatum about it. Throughout the war de Valera had taken every possibly step to ensure that the representatives of the enemies of Great Britain and America indulged in no activities inimical to those powers. Furthermore, although their presence attracted vituperative criticism in the British and American Press, he had maintained a secret military liaison with Britain, co-operating with British Intelligence in a way he did not dare divulge.

His fears now that the Allies might yet invade Ireland were smoothed and de Valera replied diplomatically. Somehow the exchange of notes was published and there was a violent public reaction in all three countries.

Prior to the Normandy landing of June 1944 the British Government took measures to restrict all trade with Ireland to prevent the leakage of information concerning the great build-up of forces in England. Writing to Roosevelt in March,[74] Churchill stated that he did not propose to stop necessary trade between Britain and Ireland or to prevent anything going in to Ireland, but he did propose to stop ships going from Ireland to Spain and Portugal and other foreign ports until "Overlord" was launched. He made it clear that Britain was not motivated by spite but sought only to protect British and American lives. Nevertheless, he said also, "It seems to me that far from allaying alarm in de Valera's circles we should let fear work its healthy process. Thereby we shall get behind the scenes a continued stiffening up of the Irish measures to prevent leakages, which even now are not so bad."

But, when Churchill announced the measures in the Commons, he made them appear as sanctions against a country too accommodating to enemy diplomats. This was as short-sighted as it was unjust; an appeal for cooperation might have been even more efficacious, and good will need not have been lost.

The confidence of the Irish people in de Valera, which seemed to have slipped a little in 1943 when at a general election Fianna Fail failed to gain an overall majority, was pledged anew in mid-1944. To the end of the war he maintained Ireland's neutrality, supported absolutely by the Irish people and by all political parties. His policy even brought him into communication with Cosgrave after nearly two decades of silence between them. Eire remained friendly to the Allies, despite the pressures they exerted upon her, and de Valera dealt firmly but courteously and correctly with German and Japanese diplomats.

When Roosevelt died in April 1945, de Valera paid him a warm tribute, but he aroused great indignation in Britain and America when, with unexampled correctitude, he called on the German Minister to offer consolation when Hitler died in his Berlin bunker on April 30th. Partly he intended to assuage the humiliation of Edouard Hempel who had conducted himself honourably in difficult circumstances throughout the long, tension-packed struggle, but one would have thought the discovery of Belsen and Buchenwald, and even the uncertainty of Hitler's fate, absolved him of the need to offer sympathy for the death of the German Head of State. He could have contented himself with a personal tribute to Hempel.

But that was de Valera's way. His feelings did not enter into it. His actions, as always, were governed by what he believed to be right, however impracticable, tactless or plain pig-headed they might seem to other people. This implacability was at once his weakness and his strength.

In his victory broadcast on May 13th 1945, Churchill could not resist an arrow at de Valera. "Owing to the action of the Dublin Government, so much at variance with the temper and instinct of thousands of Southern Irishmen who hastened to the battle-front to prove their ancient valour, the approaches which the Southern Irish ports and airfields could so easily have guarded were closed by the hostile aircraft and U-boats . . . If it had not been for the loyalty and friendship of Northern Ireland we should have been forced to come to close quarters or perish for ever from the earth."

That was factual. The sting had yet to come. Commending his own Government's restraint, he went on, "We left the Dublin Government to frolic with the German and later with the Japanese representatives to their heart's content." The accusation was bitter and unjust but de Valera replied, also on the radio, with generosity and restraint, though he took the opportunity, once more, to nail Partition as the villain of the piece.

12

De Valera made one more attempt to solve the problem of Partition. Ireland's exact status had become the subject of controversy. It was, in truth, somewhat vague, both the British Government and de Valera having refrained, following the introduction of the new Constitution in 1937, from using the word "republic", although both recognised that that was what Eire had become. Pressed in the Dail, de Valera stated that by every test that could be applied to that Constitution the State was a republic. The ambiguity lay, not in the Constitution, but in the External Relations Act which preserved one last link with the British Commonwealth.

De Valera informed Lord Rugby, formerly Sir John Maffey, to his discomfiture, that he intended to repeal the External Relations Act. He might be persuaded to drop the legislation if the nearly forgotten Council of Ireland proposed in the 1920 Government of Ireland Act were resuscitated by the British Government. But, so soon after the war, the British were hardly likely to show their gratitude by putting unwanted pressure on Stormont.

Early in 1948, de Valera called a general election. Fianna Fail retained only 68 of 147 seats. It was still the largest party, but the vote reflected a yearning for change after sixteen years. Young voters were tired of the old heads whose ears still seemed cocked for the echoes of gunfire and ancient arguments; diehard Republicans remembered resentfully the executions and gaolings of IRA members during the war and the benevolent grain of de Valera's neutrality. The post-war economic situation was difficult. Recently higher taxes had been introduced. Inflation and unemployment engendered strikes and emigration. Militancy even stole into the hearts of housewives.

There might have been a chance for the Labour Party but they were hopelessly split. Clann na Talmhan, a Farmers' party which had enjoyed some success during wartime elections had faded, but a new party had emerged. This was Clann na Poblachta, led by Sean MacBride, son of the executed 1916 leader and of Maude Gonne. It was this party which attracted votes from the traditional Republican Party, Fianna Fail.

In February 1940 a new Taoiseach, John A. Costello, took office, leading a precariously scratched together coalition. It was this Government which put through the Republic of Ireland Act, so severing the link with the Commonwealth provided by the External Relations Act. Many Fianna Fail Deputies argued against the measure on the grounds that it put the end of Partition even further out of reach, but they voted for it in the end. De Valera welcomed the step, though rather wryly pointing to the *volte face* of Fine Gael which had always seemed in favour of the Commonwealth connection. His absence from the inaugural ceremony on Easter Monday, 1949, was widely interpreted as a sign of displeasure, although Longford and O'Neill put it down to reluctance to celebrate "any political or constitutional event short of the final reunification of the whole island as a Republic".

The Attlee Government brought in a Bill which was seen as retaliatory but which was necessary to knot the end of the broken Commonwealth link. Not only did the measure recognise that the Republic of Ireland was no longer a dominion, but it laid down that, without the consent of its Parliament, Northern Ireland would not cease to be part of the United Kingdom.

Such reassurance was more than ever necessary to the Six Counties, but it drew bitter protest in the Dail where de Valera, charging Britain with responsibility for Partition in the first instance, deplored her continued recognition of the minority in the North and urged her to accede no longer to their claim for privilege. Britain, according to de Valera, should say, "We are not going to permit this small minority of the two peoples to continue to set the two peoples by the ears and to stir up and continue the old antagonisms between them."

In 1951 de Valera returned to power, the unwieldy coalition

having collapsed over a controversial Health Scheme which had led the Government into conflict with the views of the Catholic hierarchy. The Taoiseach was now sixty-nine and full of vigour, though his eyesight was failing. He, too, had a brush with the Church over a Health Bill, which included much of the earlier scheme, but he was able to smooth over the situation. Three years later he lost office again but seesawed back in 1957, this time with a clear majority.

Through the fifties, Ireland was in sad decline economically and only the safety valve of emigration prevented an explosion. But it was not a palliative which de Valera would have wished to encourage. Then a brilliant Treasury official, Thomas Kenneth Whitaker, worked out a plan for salvation. In May 1958 the Government published *Economic Development* as a white paper and, unusually, Whitaker's name was authorised to appear on it. As a result of Whitaker's work a long-term plan, followed in 1963 by a second programme, was adopted and Ireland was put on her feet.

The ageing, but still zestful, de Valera announced to an almost disbelieving Fianna Fail Party in January 1959 that he intended to make way for a younger man. That man was the enlightened and dynamic Sean Lemass who, in February 1965, was to have historic talks with Captain Terence O'Neill, then Premier of Northern Ireland. Those talks came not three years after a five-year campaign begun by the IRA in 1957 had fizzled out along the blood-stained border. Even today, when bloodshed and tragedy are the daily round in Belfast, the meeting of those reasonable men shines still like a lighthouse through a storm. When that storm blows itself out, it remains to be seen whether the lighthouse will still be within range or whether it has been lost over a horizon of hatred.

On June 25th 1959 Eamon de Valera became, once more, President of the Republic of Ireland, not the head of the Executive as he was in 1921 but the symbol of the Republic. He has seen Ireland become a nation in its own unquestioned right, respected at the Council tables of the world. That Ireland is a force in international politics is due in no small measure to the work of Eamon de Valera as President of the League of Nations Assembly in the 1930s and to the achievements of his Ministers in the United Nations. To de Valera, more than to any other man or group of men, Ireland owes what she is today. But his great dream of a united Ireland, the threat to which first drew him into the revolutionary movement and for which he campaigned unrelentingly through his marathon political career, has not been fulfilled. It is unlikely that Partition will end in his lifetime. And the irony of it is that had the Republic meant less to him the reunion of his country might have been more attainable. But the more strenuously he worked to dismantle the Treaty of 1921, the nearer he brought Ireland to her destiny as a free and independent republic, the more deeply embedded the Border became.

Notes

Arthur Griffith

1. Jules Abels, *The Parnell Tragedy*, p. 231.
2. Padraic Colum, *Arthur Griffith*, p. 80.
3. ibid., p. 19.
4. ibid., p. 239.
5. Cabinet conclusion 76 (21) App. III, Conference of Ministers, 21/9/21.
6. The Earl of Longford and Thomas P. O'Neill, *Eamon de Valera*, p. 149.
7. Colum, p. 278.
8. Piaras Beaslai, *Michael Collins and the Making of a New Ireland*, Vol. II, p. 280.
9. Cabinet record of Treaty Negotiations, CAB 43/4, Ref. 22N143, 18/10/21.
10. Colum, p. 302 (footnote).
11. Memoranda of 10/11/21, Cabinet papers SFB 21 and 22A.
12. Letter Arthur Griffith to Lloyd George, 8/12/21, Cabinet paper CP 3535.
13. Article 17, Articles of Agreement (The Treaty).
14. Cabinet conclusion 30 (22) 3, 30/5/22.
15. ibid.
16. ibid.
17. *Observations on the criticism of the British Government on the Draft Irish Constitution*, Cabinet record SF (b) 60 App. I.
18. Cabinet conclusion 32 (22) 1, 2/6/22.
19. Cabinet paper CP 4014 II, 2/6/22.

Michael Collins

1. War Cabinet minute 405 (14) of 6/5/18.
2. Quoted by Margery Forester in *Michael Collins—The Lost Leader*.

3. Rex Taylor, *Michael Collins* (Four Square Edition), p. 96.
4. Cabinet conclusion 77 (20) 6 of 24/12/20.
5. Letter of 21/2/22 quoted Taylor.
6. Cabinet paper CP 3644.
7. Cabinet conclusion 16 (22) 1 of 8/3/22.
8. ibid.
9. Cabinet paper CP 3932 of 4/4/22.
10. Cabinet paper CP 3933 of 1/4/22.
11. Cabinet conclusion 30 (22) 3 of 30/5/22.
12. Quoted Taylor.
13. Michael Collins, *The Path to Freedom*, pp. 15–19.
14. Thomas Jones, *Whitehall Diary*, Vol. 1, p. 198.
15. P. S. O'Hegarty, *The Victory of Sinn Fein*, p. 122.
16. Quoted Taylor.
17. Quoted Forester, p. 329.
18. Cabinet conclusion 43 (22) 7 of 3/8/22.
19. ibid.

James Craig

1. St John Ervine, *Craigavon, Ulsterman*, p. 113.
2. Letter from Carson to Craig, 29/7/11, quoted Ervine, p. 185.
3. Harold Nicolson, *King George the Fifth*, p. 226.
4. Asquith to George V, CAB 41 (35) 6 of 5/3/14.
5. ibid.
6. Asquith to George V, CAB 41 (35) 7 of 12/3/14.
7. Asquith to George V, CAB 41 (35) 8 of 18/3/14.
8. Asquith to George V, CAB 41 (35) 12 of 2/5/14.
9. Quoted Nicolson, p. 242.
10. Ian Colvin, *The Life of Lord Carson*, Vol. 3, p. 33.
11. Asquith to George V, CAB 41 (35) 43.
12. Asquith to George V, CAB 41 (37) 27 of 19/7/16.
13. Asquith to George V, CAB 41 (37) 28 of 27/7/16.
14. Asquith to George V, CAB 41 (37) 34 of 6/10/16.
15. Cabinet conclusion 5 (19) 2 of 11/11/19.
16. Cabinet conclusion 8 (19) App. II of 20/11/19.
17. Cabinet conclusion 16 (19) 9 of 19/12/19.
18. Cabinet conclusion 10 (19) 2 of 3/12/19.
13. ibid.
20. Cabinet conclusion 12 (19) 10 of 10/12/19.

21. Cabinet conclusion 14 (19) 2 of 15/12/19.
22. ibid.
23. Cabinet conclusion 16 (19) 6 of 19/12/19.
24. Cabinet conclusion 16 (19) 5 of 19/12/19.
25. Cabinet conclusion 8 (19) App. IV re Conference of Ministers 11/11/19.
26. Lord Longford and Thomas P. O'Neill, *Eamon de Valera*.
27. Memorandum by Lady Craigavon, P.R.O. of Northern Ireland, Ref. D1415/B32.
28. Cabinet paper CP 3331 (XVIII).
29. Record of Treaty negotiations, CAB 43/4, 22N143.
30. Lord Riddell's *Intimate Diary of the Peace Conference and After*.
31. CAB 43/4 SFB 22.
32. CAB 43/4 SFB 24.
33. CAB 43/4 SFB 27.
34. CAB 43/4 SFB 26.
35. CAB 43/4 SFB 29.
36. CAB 43/4 SFB 21.
37. Margery Forester, *Michael Collins—The Lost Leader*.
38. Cabinet conclusion 16 (22) 1 of 8/3/22.
39. Thomas Jones, *Whitehall Diary*, Vol. I, p. 277.
40. Cabinet paper CP 403 (24).
41. Cabinet paper CP 426 (24).
42. Harold Nicolson, *King George the Fifth*, p. 397.
43. Quoted Ervine.
44. Cabinet paper CP 300 (32) App. IV, Annex iii.

Eamon de Valera

1. E. de Valera to S. Donnelly, Easter 1917, quoted by Lord Longford and Thomas P. O'Neill in *Eamon de Valera*, p. 55.
2. Ibid. 23/4/17, p. 57.
3. War Cabinet minute 354 of 26/2/18.
4. War Cabinet minute 406 of 7/5/18.
5. War Cabinet minute 375 (2) of 27/3/18.
6. Cabinet paper GT 4189, telegram of 10/4/18.
7. War Cabinet minute 392 (12) of 16/4/18.
8. War Cabinet minute 398 (9) of 24/4/18.
9. War Cabinet minute 407 (5) of 8/5/18.
10. War Cabinet minute 417 (1) of 24/5/18.

11. Piaras Beaslai, *Michael Collins and the Making of a New Ireland*, Vol. 2, p. 15.

12. Quoted Longford and O'Neill, p. 115.

13. Cabinet conclusion 74 (20) 1 of 20/12/20.

14. Beaslai, Vol. 2, p. 146.

15. Press statement of 30/3/21.

16. Quoted by Basil Williams in *Erskine Childers 1870–1922*.

17. Longford and O'Neill, p. 119.

18. Thomas Jones, *Whitehall Diary*, Vol. 1, p. 130.

19. Cabinet conclusion 41 (21) 3 of 24/5/21.

20. Cabinet conclusion 47 (21) 2 of 2/6/21.

21. J. C. Smuts, *Jan Christian Smuts*.

22. Cabinet conclusion 60 (21) 6 of 20/7/21.

23. Cabinet paper CP 3219 of 9/8/21.

24. Cabinet paper CP 3261 of 25/8/21.

25. Cabinet conclusion 76 (21) App. III of 21/9/21.

26. De Valera to Joe McGarrity, 27/12/21, quoted Longford and O'Neill.

27. ibid.

28. Longford and O'Neill, p. 177.

29. Poblacht na h-Eireann (War News) No. 2, 29/6/22.

30. De Valera to P. J. Ruttledge, 15/12/22, quoted Longford and O'Neill.

31. De Valera to Liam Lynch, 12/12/22, quoted Longford and O'Neill.

32. De Valera to Maurice Twomey, 14/3/23, quoted Longford and O'Neill.

33. De Valera to P. J. Ruttledge, 15/12/22, quoted Longford and O'Neill.

34. De Valera to Liam Lynch, 2/2/23, quoted Longford and O'Neill.

35. ibid., 7/2/23.

36. Longford and O'Neill, p. 258.

37. Cabinet conclusion 14 (32) 10 of 17/2/32.

38. Cabinet conclusion 15 (32) 3 of 24/2/32.

39. Cabinet paper CP 36 (32) para. 21.

40. Cabinet conclusion 20 (32) 3 App. II of 6/4/32.

41. Cabinet paper CP 156 (32).

42. Cabinet paper CP 248 (32) App. I.

43. Cabinet conclusion 37 (32) 2 of 22/6/32.

44. Cabinet conclusion 38 (32) 3 of 24/6/32.

45. Cabinet conclusion 50 (32) 11 of 11/10/32.

46. Cabinet conclusion 46 (32) 1 of 27/8/32.
47. Cabinet conclusion 3 (37) 1 of 25/1/37.
48. Cabinet paper CP 300, App. I.
49. Cabinet conclusion 48 (37) 8 of 22/12/37.
50. Cabinet conclusion 45 (37) 6 of 1/12/37. (Irish Department of External Affairs Despatch No. 126.)
51. Cabinet conclusion 2 (38) 4 of 26/1/38.
52. Cabinet conclusion 10 (38) 6 of 2/3/38.
53. Cabinet conclusion 11 (38) 8 of 9/3/38.
54. Cabinet conclusion 14 (38) 7 of 16/3/38.
55. Cabinet conclusion 19 (38) 6 of 13/4/38.
56. Cabinet conclusion 10 (39) 6 of 8/3/39.
57. Cabinet conclusion 47 (39) 3 of 1/9/39.
58. War Cabinet conclusion WM 4 (40) 8 of 5/1/40.
59. War Cabinet conclusion WM 168 (40) 5 of 16/6/40.
60. War Cabinet conclusion WM 173 (40) 9 of 20/6/40.
61. Cabinet paper WP (40) 233, Annex I.
62. ibid., Annex II.
63. ibid., Annex III.
64. Cabinet paper WP (40) 274, Annex I.
65. ibid., Annex II.
66. War Cabinet conclusion WM 285 (40) 2 of 8/11/40.
67. War Cabinet conclusion WM 293 (40) 5 of 21/11/40.
68. Winston S. Churchill, *The Second World War*, Vol. 2, p. 614.
69. War Cabinet conclusion 301 (40) 8 of 6/12/40.
70. War Cabinet conclusion 310 (40) 6 of 27/12/40.
71. Churchill, Vol. 2, p. 536.
72. ibid., Vol. 3, p. 641.
73. ibid., Vol. 5, p. 614.
74. ibid.

Notes on official documents

British Cabinet Documents at Public Record Office, London:
  CAB 41 Royal archives.
  CAB 23 War Cabinet minutes and Cabinet minutes and conclusions.
  CAB 24 Cabinet papers and memoranda, GT and CP series.
  CAB 65 War Cabinet (Second World War) conclusions.
  CAB 66 Cabinet papers and memoranda WP series.
  CAB 2   Minutes of Committee of Imperial Defence.
  CAB 43 Conferences on Ireland including record of Treaty negotiations (22N143) and documents (SF series).
  CAB 27 Record of committees concerned with Provisional Government of the Irish Free State and legislation relating to Irish affairs.
Craigavon papers at Public Record Office of Northern Ireland, Belfast. Reference D. 1415/B.
Dail Eireann official reports.

Author's Acknowledgments

I am indebted to the Public Record Office, London, for material taken from British Cabinet records and to the Public Record Office of Northern Ireland for the use of Lord Craigavon's papers. The friendly help of staff in both offices was very much appreciated.

Mr James McGarry and Mr Larry Slattery gave me valuable advice and encouragement, as did also many friends made during my researches for *Ireland's Civil War* some years ago. I am especially grateful to Mr A. R. Mills whose help in the preparation of the manuscript has been generously given as always.

Finally, I wish to thank Mrs Margaret Mahon, Miss Sylvia Mann and my wife, Dee, who with never-failing patience between them typed the manuscript.

Bibliography

Abels, Jules: *The Parnell Tragedy*, The Bodley Head, 1966.

Beaslai, Piaras: *Michael Collins and the Making of a New Ireland*, Phoenix Publishing Co. (Dublin), 1926.

Beaverbrook, Lord: *The Decline and Fall of Lloyd George*, Collins, 1963.

Birkenhead, Frederick, 2nd Earl of: *F. E. Smith, first Earl of Birkenhead*, Eyre & Spottiswoode, 1959.

Brennan, Nial: *Dr Mannix*, Angus & Robertson (Sydney), 1965.

Bromage, Mary C.: *De Valera and the March of a Nation*, Hutchinson, 1956.

Caulfield, Max: *The Easter Rebellion*, Muller, 1964.

Churchill, Winston S.: *The Second World War*, 6 vols, Cassell, 1948–54.

Clark, Wallace: *Guns in Ulster*, Constabulary Gazette (Belfast), 1967.

Collier, Basil: *Brasshat: A Biography of Field Marshal Sir Henry Wilson 1864–1922*, Secker & Warburg, 1961.

Collins, Michael: *The Path to Freedom*, Talbot Press (Dublin), 1922.

Colum, Padraic: *Arthur Griffith*, Browne & Nolan, 1959.

Colvin, Ian: *The Life of Lord Carson* (3 vols, the first by Edward Marjoribanks), Gollancz, 1934.

Coogan, Timothy Patrick: *Ireland since the Rising*, Pall Mall, 1966.

Coogan, Timothy Patrick: *The IRA*, Pall Mall, 1970.

De Paor, Liam: *Divided Ulster*, Penguin Books, 1970.

Ervine, St John: *Craigavon, Ulsterman*, Allen & Unwin, 1949.

Fergusson, Sir James: *The Curragh Incident*, Faber, 1964.

Forester, Margery: *Michael Collins, The Lost Leader*, Sidgwick & Jackson (London), 1971.

Gallagher, Frank: *The Anglo-Irish Treaty*, Hutchinson, 1965.

Griffith, Arthur: *The Resurrection of Hungary, A Parallel for Ireland*, Pamphlet, 1904.

Gwynn, Denis: *The History of Partition (1912–1925)*, Browne & Nolan (Dublin), 1950.

Hammond, J. L.: *C. P. Scott of the Manchester Guardian*, Bell, 1934.

Hastings, Max: *Ulster, 1969: The Fight for Civil Rights in Northern Ireland*, Gollancz, 1970.

Hobson, Bulmer: *Ireland Yesterday and Tomorrow*, Anvil Books, 1968.

Jones, Thomas: *Whitehall Diary, Vol. I 1916–25*, (Ed.) Keith Middlemas, Oxford University Press, 1969.

King, Clifford: *The Orange and the Green*, MacDonald, 1965.

Lloyd George, David: *War Memoirs*, Odhams, 1933–6.

Lloyd George, Richard: *Lloyd George*, Muller, 1960.

Longford, Lord and O'Neill, Thomas P.: *Eamon de Valera*, Hutchinson.

Lyons, F. S. L.: *The Irish Parliamentary Party 1890–1910*, Faber & Faber, 1951.

Macardle, Dorothy: *The Irish Republic*, Irish Press (Dublin), 1951.

Macardle, Dorothy: *Tragedies of Kerry*, Irish Book Bureau.

Macready, General Sir Nevil: *Annals of an Active Life*, Hutchinson, 1942.

Neeson, Eoin: *The Life and Death of Michael Collins*, The Mercier Press, 1968.

Nicolson, Harold: *King George the Fifth*, Constable, 1952.

O'Brien, William and Ryan, Desmond: *Devoy's Postbag, 1871–1928*, G. J. Fallon (Dublin), 1953.

O'Connor, Frank: *The Big Fellow, Michael Collins and the Irish Revolution*, Clonmore & Reynolds (Dublin), Revised edition, 1965.

O'Donoghue, Florence: *No Other Law*, Irish Press (Dublin), 1954,

O'Hegarty, P. S.: *The Victory of Sinn Feinn*, Talbot Press (Dublin). 1924.

O'Neill, Terence: *Ulster at the Crossroads*, Faber & Faber, 1969.

O'Sullivan, Donal: *The Irish Free State and Its Senate*, Faber, 1940.

Owen, Frank: *Tempestuous Journey: Lloyd George, his life and Times*, Hutchinson, 1954.

Pakenham, Frank (Lord Longford): *Peace by Ordeal*, Geoffrey Chapman, 1962 (First published Cape, 1935).

Phillips, W. Alison: *The Revolution in Ireland 1906–23*, Longmans Green, 1923.

Riddell, Lord: *Intimate Diary of the Peace Conference and After*, Gollancz, 1933.

Shakespeare, Sir Geoffrey: *Let Candles be Brought In*, MacDonald, 1949.

Smuts, J. C. *Jan Christian Smuts*, Cassell, 1952.

Stewart, A. T. Q.: *The Ulster Crisis*, Faber & Faber, 1967.

Taylor, Rex: *Michael Collins*, Hutchinson, 1958.

Taylor, Rex: *Assassination*, Hutchinson, 1961.

White, Terence de Vere: *Kevin O'Higgins*, Methuen, 1948.

Williams, Basil: *Erskine Childers*, Private printing, 1926.

Wilson, Trevor (Ed.): *The Political Diaries of C. P. Scott 1911–1928*, Collins, 1970.

Younger, Calton: *Ireland's Civil War*, Muller, 1968.

Index